Cost-Benefit Analysis and the Environment

Nick Hanley and Clive L. Spash

Department of Economics
University of Stirling
Scotland

Edward Elgar

Published by
Edward Elgar Publishing Limited
Gower House
Croft Road
Aldershot
Hants GU11 3HR
England

Edward Elgar Publishing Company
Old Post Road
Brookfield
Vermont 05036
USA

Reprinted 1994

British Library Cataloguing in Publication Data
Hanley, Nick
  Cost-benefit Analysis and the Environment
  I. Title II. Spash, Clive L.
  333.7

Library of Congress Cataloguing in Publication Data
Hanley, Nick.
    Cost-benefit analysis and the environment/Nick Hanley and Clive L. Spash.
      p.   cm.
    Includes bibliographical references and index.
    1. Environmental policy—Cost effectiveness. 2. Environmental
  protection—Cost effectiveness. I. Spash, Clive L. II. Title.
  HC79.E5H329 1993
  338.4'33637—dc20

93–18898
CIP

ISBN 1 85278 455 5
     1 85278 947 6 (paperback)

Printed and bound in Great Britain by
Hartnolls Limited, Bodmin, Cornwall

Contents

PART II: CASE STUDIES

Acknowledgements

We thank Butterworth-Heinemann for permission to reproduce Tables 10.1 and 10.3, from J S Jacobson, "Ozone and the growth and productivity of agricultural crops" in M H Unsworth and D P Ormrod (eds) *Effects of Gaseous Air Pollution in Agriculture and Horticulture*; Elsevier Science Publishers for permission to use Figure 11.1, which comes from I-M Andreasson, "Cost of reducing farmers' use of nitrogen in Gotland, Sweden", *Ecological Economics*, 2, 287-300; Kluwer Academic Publishers for permission to use Figure 13.3, which first appeared in R Ayres and J Walter, "The greenhouse effect: damages, costs and abatement", *Environmental and Resource Economics*, 3, 237-270; Academic Press to use Figures 9.1 and 6.1 which appeared respectively in R Porter "The new approach to wilderness appraisal through benefit-cost analysis", *Journal of Environmental Economics and Management*, 1982, 59-80, and T Bartik, "Evaluating the benefits of non-marginal reductions in pollution using information on defensive expenditures", *Journal of Environmental Economics and Management*, 1988, 111-127; and the Journal of Agricultural Economics for permission to use part of a table which first appeared in K Wilis and G Garrod, "An individual travel cost method of evaluating forest recreation", *Journal of Agricultural Economics*, 42, 33-42, and which appears here in Table 5.1.

Preface

This book is an introductory guide to the theory and practice of Cost Benefit Analysis (CBA) as applied to environmental management. It derives principally from two sources: the courses which we have both taught in the M.Sc. in Environmental Management here at Stirling and our own research. We had in mind when writing the book an audience of graduate students on multi-disciplinary courses in environmental economics and management; undergraduates on second and third year courses in environmental economics; and professionals working in the area. We have assumed a knowledge of basic microeconomics on the part of the reader, which will certainly be needed if the first section is to be fully understood. The level of technical difficulty increases gradually as the reader moves through Part I: the material in Part II assumes that the substance of its predecessor has been read and understood. We have sought to avoid any heavy use of econometrics or mathematics. Where possible, arguments have been made in words and pictures, whilst in the case studies (Part II), all econometric results are explained in full. A complete set of references is provided at the end of each chapter.

This book is *not* intended as a complete text in CBA. We give very little attention to issues such as income distribution, risk and investment financing. We would refer interested readers to Gramlich (1990), Bohm (1987) and Johansson (1991) for more information on these points. We have also concentrated almost entirely on applications in developed countries, so this book is not a "green" version of Squire and van der Tak (1975) or Brent (1990).

We would like to say "thank you" to a large number of people. We both thank Alistair Munro for his contribution to Chapter 12, and his permission to use other bits of joint work elsewhere in the book. Both of us also thank Robin Faichney for helping sort out errors in the final manuscript.

Nick Hanley thanks the following for helpful and illuminating discussions in the past on many of the issues raised in this book: John Hartwick, Jay Shogren, Jim Shortle, Jack Knetsch, Ian Hodge, Jeremy Peat, John Jones and Peter Hopkinson. The Economics Department at Queens University, Kingston (Canada) provided research facilities to Hanley during much of the writing of his part of the book, and he is very grateful to the Department, especially to Julie McCarthy, for her labours. Nick Hanley would also like to thank his family for putting up with him retreating to the basement at the slightest provocation in order to write during the year at Queens.

Clive Spash thanks Andrew Brennan, Tony Clayton, Ken Fah and Ian Simpson for numerous stimulating discussions on the roles and uses of evaluation techniques. He also acknowledges an intellectual debt to members of the Economics Department at the University of Wyoming during the late 1980s, especially Tom Crocker and Ralph d'Arge, who provided the encouragement and stimulation required to nurture growing ideas. Clive also thanks his family, and most especially Patricia and David Spash, for their love and support over the years.

Finally, we both thank Mick Common, who must take full responsibility for introducing the authors to environmental economics in their formative years.

REFERENCES

Bohm, P (1987) *Social Efficiency* Basingstoke: Macmillan Educational.

Brent, R J (1990) *Project Appraisal for Developing Countries* New York: New York University Press.

Gramlich, E M (1990) *A Guide to Benefit-Cost Analysis* London: Prentice-Hall.

Johansson, P O (1991) *An Introduction to Modern Welfare Economics* Cambridge: Cambridge University Press.

Squire, L and van der Tak, H (1975) *Economic Analysis of Projects* Baltimore: Johns Hopkins University Press.

PART I

Theory and Methods

1 INTRODUCTION

1.1 ABOUT THIS BOOK

This book is intended as an introduction to Cost-Benefit Analysis (CBA) for people interested in its application to environmental management. The emphasis is very much on application, in that Part II of the book is devoted to cases where CBA has actually been applied to environmental problems. However, the application of a few rules and methods with no understanding of the underlying theoretical background would be dangerous and give a false impression of the robustness of the results. The theory behind CBA must be understood along with the assumptions it makes before presenting the case studies. As with every part of economic theory, there are disagreements concerning the correct approach. We have tried to represent most sides of the arguments over contentious issues, including, over the use of discounting and the choice of discount rate. Yet, to merely present all aspects of an argument without coming down in favour of a particular approach might leave the reader confused and our consciences unclear. We have therefore also felt the need to express our views as to the most useful way in which to proceed.

Although there are many techniques for appraising policies and projects which impact on the environment, this book concentrates rather single-mindedly on CBA and the closely related technique of Cost-Effectiveness Analysis (CEA). The reader should be fully aware that there are many methods of expressing such impacts that an environmental manager can and should consider singly or jointly. Other methods include environmental impact assessment, scenario analysis, and risk-effectiveness analysis; see Walthern (1988); MacAllister (1980). Indeed, in all the case studies considered, physical information about environmental impacts is shown to be an essential prerequisite to CBA/CEA. In addition, the concluding chapter of the book asks how useful CBA/CEA is for environmental management given: (a) the problems encountered in applying either technique; *and* (b) the availability of other methods of analysis. We conclude that both CBA and CEA are useful contributions to the decision-making process; but that neither is sufficient as a "stand alone" criterion.

In the rest of this chapter, we first of all take a brief look at the history of CBA. Next, the basic structure of a CBA is outlined. Finally, we summarize the major difficulties facing CBA analysts in considering environmental problems.

1.2 A SHORT HISTORY OF COST-BENEFIT ANALYSIS

The United States (U.S.) federal water agencies, principally the Bureau of Land Reclamation and the U.S. Army Corps of Engineers, were among the first to make use of cost-benefit analysis. As early as 1808 Albert Gallatin, U.S. Secretary of the Treasury, was recommending the comparison of costs and benefits in water-related projects. This precedes the, often cited, cost-benefit writings of the Frenchman, Jules Dupuit, by some 35 years. A chronology of important CBA-related events in the U.S. is shown in Table 1.1.

In the Federal Government, water resource development alone received formal attention with regard to the return on public spending. The Flood Control Act (1936) required the U.S. Army Corps of Engineers to evaluate the benefits and costs of all water resource projects, "to whomsoever they accrue". Early analytic efforts in the water resources area, while unsophisticated, served to stimulate research into the use of economics to aid budget allocation decisions in other areas.

Under the auspices of the Federal Interagency River Basin Committee a guide to CBA was produced, nicknamed the Green Book. This provided a practical guide for conducting CBA. Shortly after the Green Book a similar document was produced with the aim of replacing it, Budget Circular A-47. Besides providing practical guidance, these publications encouraged academic interest.

Eckstein (1958) related the CBA techniques being employed to welfare economic foundations. His book *Water Resource Development* critically investigates the techniques for benefit estimation using market information. Systems analysis was soon being applied to water resource management with the aim of exposing the interdependencies of river systems. A prime example of such research is Krutilla and Eckstein's (1958) *Multiple Purpose River Development*. Computer-aided systems analysis was also carried out at Harvard resulting in the publication of Arthur Maass and associates (1962) *Design of Water-Resource Systems*. During this era water quantity was the primary concern, but as the rate of dam construction slowed, attention began to turn to other issues. The 1960s saw growing concern over the

Table 1.1   *Development of CBA in the United States*

1808   A Gallatin Report on Transportation.

1902   Federal Reclamation Act: Created Bureau of Land Management and required economic analysis of irrigation projects.

1936   Flood Control Act: Benefits must exceed costs for flood control projects.

1946   Federal Interagency River Basin Committee, Subcommittee on Benefits and Costs set up.

1950   Proposed Practices for Economic Analysis of River Basin Projects (the "Green Book"), a report by the Subcommittee on Benefits and Costs.

1952   Bureau of the Budget, Budget Circular A-47.

1955   Harvard University Water Programme set up.

1958   *Otto Eckstein. Water Resource Development: The Economics of Project Evaluation.*

1960   Resources for the Future, Water Resources Programme. Start of water quality research.

1962   Arthur Maass and Associates. *Design of Water-Resource Systems.*

1964   Allen V Kneese. *The Economics of Regional Water Quality Management.*

1966   Marion Clawson and Jack L Knetsch. *Economics of Outdoor Recreation.* Movement towards evaluation of water-based recreation benefits.

1967   John Krutilla. "Conservation Reconsidered". Stressed the importance of use and nonuse values for preservation and of option value.

1981   Presidential Executive Order 12291.

---

quality of the environment ; this is evident in the work of the Water Quality Program at the independent research body, Resources for the Future, in Washington, D.C. Alternative policy instruments and institutions for controlling water quality were investigated, and methods for economic modelling of water quality developed. Still the main focus was upon supply-side efficiency and the supply of private goods from public projects; for example, efficiently meeting externally fixed ambient water quality standards, and maintaining the efficiency of a river system while introducing a new dam. However, some researchers began to focus upon the benefits of both water quantity and quality. The evaluation of the recreation-based benefits of new reservoirs raised interesting problems for CBA. Notable among this early benefits research is Clawson and Knetsch (1966), which includes the early development of the travel cost method. The emphasis here was on the methods and data required for measuring the benefits of environmental improvement in relation to outdoor recreation.

Interest expanded from water-based recreation into public goods such as wildlife, air quality, human health, and aesthetics. Techniques for the measurement of intangible benefits from environmental improvement have increased to include hedonics, the travel cost method and contingent valuation. Another new aspect of the research of the 1970s and 1980s was the recognition of the importance of nonuse values.

During this same period CBA has received increasing attention in relation to environmental aspects of U.S. government policy-making (for a comprehensive survey see Froehlich et al., 1991). Formal CBA techniques have been required to support environmental regulations since the early 1970s. The early requirements for the inclusion of environmental damages concerned physical measures and environmental impact assessment (EIA), similar to current legislation in the EC. A process of development occurred with the move from the National Environmental Policy Act (NEPA) of 1969 requiring EIAs, to Presidential Executive Order 12291 of 1981 explicitly requiring the application of CBA to new regulations. In the case of environmental legislation, the Executive Order enforces the need for the assessment of the environmental benefits of proposed legislation. CBA can also be required for particular environmental problems, for example the disposal of mine wastes and discharge of hazardous substances into public water systems. In addition, legislation such as the Comprehensive Environmental Response, Compensation and Liability Act (CERCLA) 1980 has brought the issue of environmental damage assessment before U.S. courts.

CBA in relation to the environment faces many challenges not least in relation to the treatment of long-term effects, irreversibilities, risk and uncertainty. A strong research community has been built up in the U.S., particularly around the Rocky Mountain region including the Universities of Colorado, New Mexico, and Wyoming. Meanwhile in Europe, development of both research and practice has been relatively slow. In the United Kingdom (UK), CBA applications have been largely transportation based, starting in 1960 with the M1 motorway project and including since then the closure of rail routes, the 1970s Channel Tunnel proposals, the Third London Airport, and road bridges over the river Tay and Severn. The Department of Transport provides a Manual of Environmental Appraisal (UK Department of Transport, 1983) which gives guidance on the inclusion of environmental impacts. COBA is the Department of Transport procedure for CBA for trunk road schemes. CBA was first applied to trunk road investment in the l960s and COBA was introduced in the early 1970s. The existing procedure computes a net present value which includes a monetary valuation of time and accident savings but excludes all environmental effects. The Standing Advisory Committee on Trunk Road Assessment (SACTRA) has reviewed environmental assessment procedures but has yet to recommend the use of CBA. There is a persistent belief that environmental considerations cannot be included in a monetary assessment like COBA. Such a position has been criticized as, at best, misleading (see Nash, 1990). The application of CBA to road schemes is discussed at length in Chapter 12.

In the 1970s other types of development projects besides transportation were subject to CBA, such as the New Covent Garden Market, while in the 1980s the Sizewell B Inquiry, pushing the methodology to limits, attempted to apply CBA techniques to the choice of sources for electrical energy generation. In general, the Treasury influences the extent to which a government needs to make monetary evaluations of environmental impacts. The Green Booklet (UK Treasury, 1984) is the guide provided by the Treasury for the appraisal of investments by government departments.

Expenditure plans are subject to an appraisal procedure which includes a CBA component. However, the monetary evaluation of environmental impacts has been limited. Currently, under the European Community Directive on Environmental Assessment, certain types of projects must under-go non-monetary assessment of environmental impacts (see Department of the Environment, 1989). As far as environmental-related CBA in the UK is concerned the lack of an Environmental Protection Agency may be an important factor hindering both practice and research.

The UK government began revising its cost-benefit analysis procedures with regard to the environment in 1990. This process can be traced to the publication of the Pearce Report, commissioned by the Secretary of State for the Environment (Pearce et al, 1989). Government and public reaction combined to produce a new White Paper in response, *This Common Inheritance* (HMSO, 1990). This recommended that environment impacts be brought into formal appraisal procedures wherever possible. The means to do this are currently being realized on two separate fronts, namely policy appraisal and project appraisal. Guidelines on incorporating environmental impacts in policy appraisal were issued in September 1991 and recommended use of the valuation methods described in this book. As the guidelines state (DOE, 1991, p.1):

> A governments' policies can affect the environment from street corner to stratosphere. Yet environmental costs and benefits have not always been well integrated into government policy assessments, and sometimes they have been forgotten entirely. Proper consideration of these effects will improve the quality of policy making.

1.3 THE STRUCTURE OF A COST-BENEFIT ANALYSIS

In any CBA, several stages must be conducted. Whilst many will disagree on how these stages are identified, the following structure provides a guide to the essential steps: defining the project, identifying impacts which are economically relevant, physically quantifying impacts, calculating a monetary valuation, discounting, weighting, and sensitivity analysis. We now discuss each of these in turn.[1]

Stage One: Definition of Project
This definition will include (i) the reallocation of resources being proposed (for example the construction of a new road bridge connecting an island previously only served by a ferry service to the mainland); and (ii) the population of gainers and losers to be considered. The reason for defining (i) is that a project cannot be appraised unless what is to be appraised is known. This definitional step may also be used to determine the boundaries of the analysis. For example, in the enquiry into the construction of a new nuclear power station at Sizewell in England, the analysis spread over into an appraisal of UK energy policy. In the subsequent enquiry at Hinkley Point, the public inspector was told to restrict admissible evidence to the power station, so excluding UK energy policy.

The motive for (ii) is to determine the population over which costs and benefits are to be aggregated. Sometimes, this population will be determined by law. More frequently, however, some discretion is permitted. In the bridge example mentioned above, do we count only those people in the immediate vicinity of the bridge (say, at the district level), or affected persons at the regional, national or supra-national level? This last category of potential beneficiaries and losers may seem unlikely, but further integration of, for example, environmental policies in the European Community (EC) is an example where supra-national interests may be the relevant ones.

Stage Two: Identification of Project Impacts

Once the project is defined, the next step is to identify all those impacts resulting from its implementation. For the bridge project, stage two would include a listing of all resources used in constructing the bridge (concrete, steel, labour hours); effects on local unemployment levels; impacts on traffic movements; effects on local property prices; and impacts on the quality of landscape in the area not "picked up" by changes in property values.

Two important concepts here are *additionality* and *displacement*. Additionality refers to the net impacts of the project. If a government were appraising the introduction of lower speed limits to reduce road fatalities, this benefit should be measured net of any reduction in fatalities that would have occurred without this policy change (due, for instance, to improvements in car design).

Displacement is often important when CBA is applied by development authorities at the regional level of government, when two possibilities arise. Consider a new car factory in Tayside in Scotland. Will this displace output from some existing plant in any other region of Scotland? If so, the extent of such "crowding out" needs consideration, as does whether the outputs of the two plants are truly homogeneous. This is unlikely, so that perfect (that is one-for-one) displacement is rarely encountered. Secondly, the Tayside plant may displace no Scottish output, but may displace output elsewhere in the UK; if the Scottish development agency is responsible to the UK national treasury, then this could be considered as another case of displacement. However, a weighting system of project costs and benefits can be used to discriminate in favour of increasing economic activity in depressed regions (see the discussion of shadow prices below).

Stage Three: Which Impacts are Economically Relevant?

Here we must run slightly ahead of the discussion in this book, since the question "what to count" is bound up in neo-classical welfare economics, in particular in the social welfare function which society is interested in maximizing. These points are discussed in the next chapter. For present purposes, however, assume that society is interested in maximizing the weighted sum of utilities across its members. These utilities depend upon, amongst other variables, consumption levels of marketed and non-marketed goods. The former include a range of items from bananas to theatre visits, while the latter include fine views and clean air. The aim of CBA is to select projects which add to the total of social utility, by increasing the value of consumables and nice views by more than any associated depletion in the levels of other utility-generating goods. CBA can in fact select the best (most efficient) projects from a list (portfolio) of alternatives.

Thus, what are counted as positive impacts, which from now on will be referred to as benefits, will either be increases in the quantity or quality of goods that generate positive utility[2] or a reduction in the price at which they are supplied. What we count as costs (that is negative impacts) will include any decreases in the quality or quantity of such goods, or increases in their price. These negative effects also include the using-up of resources (inputs to production) in a project, since if an hour of labour or a bag of cement is used up in constructing a bridge, it cannot be used simultaneously in constructing a dam. This is the concept of opportunity cost.

The crucial point here is that the environmental impacts of projects count so long as they either (i) cause at least one person in the relevant population to become more or less happy; and/or (ii) change the level or quality of output of some positively valued commodity. For example, the environmental impacts of the bridge could consist of a deterioration of landscape quality and of adverse effects on fish spawning grounds (due to hydrological factors). The former is relevant to the CBA if at least one person dislikes the landscape change; the latter is relevant if at least one fisherman finds he catches fewer fish per hour at sea (or alternatively must expend more resources to catch the same number of fish). The absence of a market for landscape quality is irrelevant; similarly, the absence of a market for air quality is irrelevant when we consider the impacts of a new coal-fired power station on acid rain.[3] In fact, many environmental effects will fail to be recorded by market price movements, since the stock of environmental quality frequently displays public good aspects (non-rivalness and non-excludability). All that matters is that an impact on production or utility can be recorded. Unpriced impacts are the most important feature of environmental CBA. These unpriced impacts are referred to as *externalities*, which may be either positive, in conferring benefits (my beautiful wood gives you enjoyment, yet you pay me nothing to enjoy it); or negative in exacting costs such as the acid rain example (where, since noone owns clean air, the power station pays nothing to use it up when polluting). A full discussion of externalities and public goods may be found, for example, in Baumol and Oates (1988). The central message of this book is that environmental impacts are very likely to be relevant both in carrying out a CBA and to the resulting decision on project choice.

One class of impacts that should be excluded from a CBA are transfer payments. Good examples are reductions of indirect tax revenue due to a project going ahead, or additional unemployment benefits becoming payable. Neither of these flows constitutes a using-up of real resources (such as labour hours), but are merely redistributions of money through (generally) the government. Less indirect taxes received (a loss) are cancelled out by less taxes paid (a gain). For this reason, most government guidelines on CBA (for example UK Treasury, 1984) recommend the exclusion of such transfer payment effects. There are, however, two exceptions: first, where a tax is designed to correct a market imperfection (for example, a pollution tax attempting to make polluters pay the social cost of their actions). Here, taxes are to be interpreted as shadow prices, as discussed below. However, this type of tax is rare, and even where set, is usually a bad guide to marginal external costs. The second exception is where the government decides to place unequal weight on gains and losses attached to different groups within society in any year. Here, gains and losses will not cancel out. However, such weighting is unusual in the OECD countries.

Stage Four: Physical Quantification of Relevant Impacts
This stage involves determining the physical amounts of cost and benefit flows for a project, and identifying when in time they will occur. In the bridge example, this would include: the number of vehicles a year crossing the bridge; the time savings accruing to those using the bridge instead of the existing ferry service; the number of years the bridge will last before major repairs are necessary; and the extent to which fish populations will be disrupted. For environmental impacts such as these, the use of Environmental Impact Analysis is clearly important.

All calculations made at this stage will be performed under varying levels of uncertainty. For example, the effect on fish populations may be very difficult to predict; whereas the amounts of concrete and steel needed to construct the bridge are relatively easy to predict. In some cases, it may be possible to attach probabilities to uncertain events and calculate an "expected value". For example, suppose that engineers know that there is a 30% probability that the bridge will last for 10 years, a 50% probability that it will last 15 years, and a 20% probability that it will last 20 years. The expected value for the bridge's lifetime is $[(.3*10)+(.5*15)+(.2*20)]$, or $[3+7.5+4]=14.5$ years (note that all probabilities must sum to one). This calculation of expected value can equally be applied to monetary flows.

Stage Five: Monetary Valuation of Relevant Effects
In order for physical measures of impacts to be co-measurable, they must be valued in common units. The common unit in CBA is money, whether dollars, pounds or yen. This is merely a device of convenience, rather than an implicit statement that money is all that matters.[4] Markets generate the relative values of all traded goods and services as relative prices: prices are therefore very useful in comparing tonnes of steel with working hours saved, since not only are both made co-measurable, but some indication of their current relative scarcity is provided. Prices carry valuable information. The remaining tasks for the CBA analyst are then to:

(i)   predict prices for value flows extending into the future;

(ii)   correct market prices where necessary; and,

(iii)   calculate prices (relative values in common units) where none exist.

When part of the output of a soil conservation project, for example, is an increase in crop outputs over a 30-year time period, knowledge of the prices of these crops over this time span is central to the estimation of project benefits. There is an important point here, since future prices may change in both real and nominal terms. If the former is occurring, then we need to know, for example, how the price of wheat will change relative to the price of corn (that is the rate of exchange between them). However, inflation can push up the prices of both without their relative values changing. The CBA should be carried out in real terms. Relative (real) price changes are of relevance, with discounting (see below) being done at the real discount rate[5]. Nominal historical values can be converted into real values using a price index: in this case, the most general measure of price changes available (such as the Retail Price Index) should be used, rather than a project-specific index, since the analyst is interested in the change in welfare at the broadest (economic) level.

Consider the following example. A new public transit system is expected to produce the earnings given in the second column of Table 1.2 over its first four years of operation. Year 0 is the first year of operation. If the inflation rate over this period is expected to remain constant at 5% per year, the real value of these returns is as shown in column three. For any year, the real value of benefits in year 0 currency is $B_t(1 + p)^{-t}$, where p is the inflation rate (so that $(1 + p) = 1.05$) and t is the number of years since year 0. The CBA analyst would use the second set of values in conjunction with the real rate of discount.

Tasks (ii) and (iii) consist of adjusting market prices. In a perfectly competitive market, under certain assumptions,[6] the equilibrium price indicates both the marginal social cost (MSC) and marginal social benefit (MSB) of the production of one more (or one less) unit of that good. This is because opportunity costs of production are given by the supply curve (given perfectly competitive input markets), whilst the demand curve is a schedule of marginal willingness to pay. Clearly there will be many cases,

Table 1.2 Nominal and Real Benefits

Year in which Benefit Occurs	Value of Benefit in Nominal Terms (£ millions)	Value of Benefit in Real Terms (£ millions)
0	400	400
1	440	419
2	750	680
3	825	713

however, when the market price is a bad indicator of both MSC and MSB. If this is the case, *shadow* prices can be used to reflect true resource scarcity. Three cases can be distinguished:

1. imperfect competition;
2. government intervention in the market; and
3. the absence of a market.

1. Imperfect Competition

If there is imperfect competition in a market, microeconomic theory shows that market price will not equal marginal cost in most cases. Consider Figure 1.1, which shows a monopolist facing a demand curve D. The monopolist maximizes profits by producing at X_m and charging a price P_m. Suppose that a project requires the output of this monopolist as an input: then, so long as consumers can buy all they effectively demand at P_m, the true cost to the economy of one more unit of X is not P_m but C_m, the monopolist's marginal cost. This will be true if only and only if all costs to society of producing X are also borne by the monopolist (that is, if no external costs of production are involved).

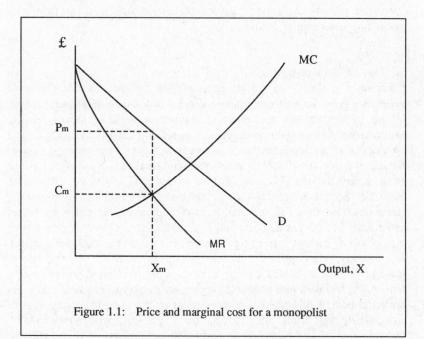

Figure 1.1:   Price and marginal cost for a monopolist

2. Government Intervention

Suppose the project in question will lead to an increase in agricultural output (say as a result of land drainage). How should one more unit of such output be valued? If more wheat is to be grown and sold, then surely the market price of wheat indicates the MSB? This will *not* be so if the government artificially holds up the price of wheat above world market levels. Most Western governments do indeed support their agricultural sectors, and most do it partially by holding up prices. This may be achieved by a mixture of import levies, intervention buying and deficiency payments. In Figure 1.2, the market for wheat in the EC is shown. Consumers could buy at a world price of P_w, but are prevented from doing so by import taxes which raise prices domestically to P_d. Farmers in the EC produce Q_s wheat in response to this latter price, and EC consumers buy Q_d, given their demand curve D_{ec}. This reduces the volume of imports to $(Q_d - Q_s)$, whilst the EC collects tariff revenues of $[(Q_d - Q_s)*(P_d - P_w)]$. Now P_d is the willingness to pay (WTP) of the marginal consumer for one more tonne of wheat; however, this consumer could have bought this extra tonne at the (lower) world market price of P_w. The consumer is in fact losing out as a result of the price support since the increase in price has reduced his or her consumers' surplus (see Chapter 2), although farmers in the EC and, in this instance, EC taxpayers have gained. Losses will in fact be bigger than gains, so that the MSB of the extra tonne of wheat is less than P_d.[7] With farm outputs, "producer subsidy equivalents" are calculated annually to adjust farm-gate prices into estimates of MSB.

3. The Absence of a Market

Commonly in CBA, the analyst is faced with the difficulty of placing a value on a good not traded in markets and for which no obvious price exists. In this case, there are a number of techniques available which seek to estimate the MSB of such goods. For example, if a CBA is being conducted on a new nuclear power station, one benefit is that less electricity is needed from alternative, fossil-fuel powered-generating stations. Fossil-fuel stations emit sulphur dioxide (SO_2) and nitrous oxides (NO_x), both contributors to acid rain. So one benefit of the nuclear station is lower acid-rain-causing emissions, and thus (on this measure) cleaner air. But clean air is not something that people buy and sell in markets, as we have already noted. No obvious market price thus exists to value this project impact. Equivalently, one cost of the nuclear power station is the possibility of a leakage, leading to deaths through cancer. But how should the value of a human life be taken into account? Again, we can try to estimate either the marginal benefit of keeping someone alive or the marginal social cost of someone dying. Whilst such calculations might seem repugnant to many, the valuation of life turns out to be crucial for projects as diverse as the

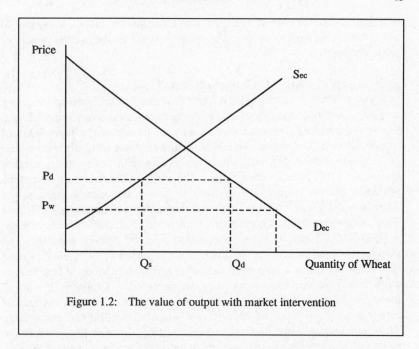

Figure 1.2:   The value of output with market intervention

construction of a new motorway or research into brain cancer. Some way will be found of dealing with this problem when society chooses between alternative uses of scarce resources for human life as well as for clean air, for wilderness areas and Beluga whales although the extent to which valuation is a reasonable or desirable course of action is hotly debated.

Much of Part I of this book is taken up with the methodologies now being developed to estimate MSB and MSC for such non-market resources. The techniques include contingent valuation, the travel cost method, hedonic pricing, avoided cost and dose-response approaches. Here the reader should simply note the existence of such techniques and that CBA offers a methodology which aims explicitly to take environmental values into account. As Randall (1986, p.193) has commented:

> No longer can it be claimed that there are overwhelming economic arguments for the development option, while the benefits of the preservation option are confined to sentiments and emotions existing only in the woolly heads of environmentalists.

Bringing environmental values into business and political calculations as an everyday input to decision-making is a major goal of environmental CBA. However, there are limits to CBA, as this book will make clear, whilst (as mentioned earlier) we are not recommending CBA as the sole decision criterion. Also, the role of sentiments and emotions is just as important to the future of humanity as the "objective" criteria in the woolly heads of some economists.

Stage Six: Discounting of Cost and Benefit Flows
Once all relevant cost and benefit flows that can be expressed in monetary amounts have been so expressed, it is necessary to convert them all into *present value* (PV) terms. This necessity arises out of the time value of money, or time preference. To take a simple example, an individual would differentiate, ceteris paribus, between receiving £100 today and receiving that same £100 in one years time. The more immediate sum might be preferred due to impatience (I want to spend the money right now). Alternatively, I may not want to spend the money for a year, but if I have it now I can invest it in a bank at an interest rate of say 10%, and have £100 x (1+i) = £110 in one years time, where i is the rate of interest. The motives for time preference are discussed in Chapter 8; here, all that need be recognized is that a sum of money, and indeed most kinds of benefit, are more highly valued the sooner they are received.[8] Similarly, a sum of money to be paid out, or any kind of cost, seems less onerous the further away in time we have to bear it. A bill of £1 million to re-package hazardous wastes seems preferable if received in 100 years time rather than in 10 years time. *This is true even if inflation is zero in every time period, so long as the time preference rate (discount rate) is positive.*
So how is this time effect taken into account, and how are cost and benefit flows made comparable regardless of when they occur? The answer is that all cost and benefit flows are discounted, using a discount rate which, for now, is assumed to be the (real) rate of interest, i. The present value of a cost or benefit (X) received in time t is calculated as follows:

$$PV\ (X_t) = X_t\ [(1 + i)^{-t}] \tag{1.1}$$
or
$$PV\ (X_t) = X_t\ [1/(1 + i)^t] \tag{1.2}$$

The expression in square brackets in equation (1.1) is known as a discount factor. Discount factors have the property that they always lie between +1 and 0. The further away in time a cost or benefit occurs (the higher the value of t), the lower the discount factor. The higher the discount rate i for a given t, the lower the discount factor since a higher discount rate means a greater preference for things now rather than later. Figure 1.3 shows this graphically, whilst Table A1.2 in Appendix 1.1 lists discount factors for a selection of values for t and i.
The rationale behind equations (1.1) and (1.2) is simple. Take £1 invested now at an interest rate of 10%. In one years time, this will have grown to £1*(1+10%) or £1*(1+0.1), which is £1.10, as noted above. This means that

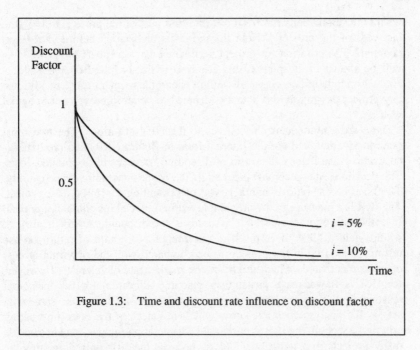

Figure 1.3: Time and discount rate influence on discount factor

£1.10 in one years time is worth the same as £1 now. In other words, the present value of £1.10 is £1. The process of accumulating interest through saving is called compounding; discounting is simply the procedure in reverse.

Discounting may be done in CBA in one of two ways: either by finding the net value of benefits minus costs for each time period (usually each year), and discounting each of these annual net benefit flows throughout the lifetime of the project; or by calculating discounted values for each element of a project, then summing the discounted elements. For example, adding up total discounted labour costs, total discounted material costs and total discounted travel benefits. Both approaches should give identical answers.

Stage Seven: Applying the Net Present Value Test
The main purpose of CBA is to help select projects and policies which are efficient in terms of their use of resources. The criterion applied is the Net Present Value (NPV) test. This simply asks whether the sum of discounted gains exceeds the sum of discounted losses. If so, the project can be said to represent an efficient shift in resource allocation, given the data used in the CBA. In other words, the NPV of a project is:

$$NPV = \Sigma B_t (1+i)^{-t} - \Sigma C_t (1+i)^{-t} \tag{1.3}$$

where the summations run from t=0 (the first year of the project) to t=T (the last year of the project). Note that no costs or benefits before year 0 are counted. The criterion for project acceptance is: accept iff NPV > 0. As will be shown in Chapter 2, this criterion is firmly based on the Kaldor-Hicks principle of neo-classical welfare economics; under these conditions, any project passing the NPV test is deemed to be an improvement in social welfare.

There are a number of alternatives to the NPV criterion. The two most commonly employed are the Internal Rate of Return (IRR) and the benefit-cost ratio. The latter is the ratio of discounted benefits to discounted costs. The decisions rule becomes: proceed iff the benefit-cost ratio exceeds unity. The benefit-cost ratio is another way of presenting the NPV of a project. The IRR is a measure frequently employed in financial investment appraisal. It is the rate of interest which, if used as the discount rate for a project, would yield a NPV of zero. It is interpreted as the rate of return on the resources used up in the project, to be compared with the opportunity cost of investment funds which might be the market rate of interest. However, the IRR is flawed as a measure of resource allocation for two principal reasons: first, many projects can generate multiple IRRs from the same data set, so the analyst does not know which to select as the decision-making criterion. Second, the IRR is unreliable when comparing performance across many projects in a portfolio. This is because the IRR only compares the return on one project relative to the opportunity cost of funds. For a detailed criticism of the IRR measure, the reader is referred to Lumby (1988). The recommendation here is to stick firmly to NPV as a measure of performance.

An optional part of the seventh stage involves changing the weights in the NPV function. As will become clear in Chapter 2, the NPV measure does assume implicitly that the existing distribution of income is, in some sense, acceptable. This is because benefits and costs are expressed partly in terms of WTP, which depends not just on preferences but also on ability to pay. For this reason, an optional stage which follows the NPV calculation is to examine the effects of different weighting schemes on NPV values. Suppose that the impacts of a motorway project can be divided up according to which group in society they affect, groups being defined on income grounds alone. This might give the results shown in Table 1.3.

The conventional NPV calculation implicitly puts an equal weight (equal to unity) on all these impacts, giving a NPV of +£1 million, so the project would be accepted. However, society might place more importance on each £1 of impact on poor groups than on rich groups. This could be reflected in a different weighting scheme. One possible set of weights would be $w = (Y^*/Y_i)$, where w is the weight to be attached to impacts on group i, Y^* is mean household income across all groups, and Y_i is mean income within group i. This gives a higher weight to poorer groups than to richer groups,

Table 1.3 Road Impacts by Income Group

Group Affected	Impact Discounted (- a loss, + a gain)
G1 Low income	-£2.4 million
G2 Mid income	+£1.1 million
G3 High income	+£2.3 million

and the NPV formula becomes:

$$NPV = w1\ B1 + w2\ B2 + ...\ wnBn \qquad (1.4)$$

where Bn are discounted net benefits to group n. This is a Bergson social welfare function.

This may seem like an attractive option, but there are severe problems here. First, what weights should be used? Income is only one grounds on which to differentiate between groups. Unless all weights sum to unity, NPV will be over-stated. How should these groups be defined, and how easy is it to work out how much each group will be affected? For these reasons, this unequal weighting procedure (sometimes known as "revisionism") is rarely practised at the public agency level (although weighting systems may be used informally). An exception would be projects undertaken by central government on regional development grounds.

Economists make a distinction between efficiency and equity, with CBA taking the existing distribution of income as given, and concentrating on efficiency tests. Changing the income distribution (and thus the effective demands of different groups in society) is left to separate policies, for example, taxation policy. However, at the developing country level, there is much more interest in unequal weighting systems; see Brent (1990). In any case, CBA is rarely if ever the sole input to a decision affecting different groups within society: income redistribution issues would be taken into account via the political process.

Stage Eight: Sensitivity Analysis
The NPV test described above tells us about the relative efficiency of a given project, given the data input to the calculations. If this data changes, then clearly the results of the NPV test will change too. But why should data be changed?

The main reason concerns uncertainty. In all ex ante cases of CBA, the analyst must make predictions concerning future physical flows (for example, traffic movements) and future relative values (for example, the price of fuel). None of these predictions is made with perfect foresight. Therefore, an essential final stage of any ex ante CBA is to conduct sensitivity analysis. This means recalculating NPV when the values of certain key parameters are changed. These parameters will include:

(i)   the discount rate,
(ii)   physical quantities and qualities of inputs,
(iii)   shadow prices of these inputs,
(iv)   physical quantities and qualities of outputs,
(v)   shadow prices of these outputs, and
(vi)   project life span.

The intention is to discover to which parameters the NPV outcome is most sensitive. For example, in appraising a new coal mine where the NPV has been calculated as positive, by how much in percentage terms does the world coal price have to fall before the NPV becomes negative? By how much do labour costs need to rise before NPV goes negative? By how much does our forecast of the lifetime of the pit need to fall before NPV goes negative? What is the impact of changing the discount rate? Once the most sensitive parameters have been identified, then (i) forecasting effort can be directed at these parameters to try to improve our best guess; and (ii) where possible, more effort can be made once the project is underway to manage these parameters carefully, although most will be outside the control of the decision-maker. The NPV decision will often depend crucially on the choice of discount rate: this will certainly be so for projects with long-term effects, such as woodland planting, toxic waste disposal and research and development of alternative energy sources.

This concludes the stage-by-stage description of the "bones" of a CBA. Readers who were previously unfamiliar with CBA should now turn to the example in Appendix 1.1 and follow through the calculations.

1.4 A PREVIEW OF MAJOR PROBLEM AREAS

The application of CBA to environmental management is fraught with problems. The intention of this book is to suggest ways around some of these, but also to indicate where substantial difficulties remain. In this way, the environmental limits of CBA can be identified. This short section flags the major problem areas which will be considered in much greater detail in the remainder of Part I, and in Part II. To begin with, consider three examples.

First, suppose we are conducting an appraisal of a policy to introduce a tax on nitrogen fertilizers to reduce nitrate pollution of drinking water supplies.

Here we must be able to predict (i) the response of farmers to the tax, and (ii) where these farmers are located. Point (ii) is important since the impact of a kilo of nitrogen fertilizer on water quality depends crucially on when and where that fertilizer is put on the land (as Chapter 11 shows). Once this difficulty has been resolved, we then need to be able to value the increase in water quality: how to value a reduction in the probability of getting stomach cancer?

Second, consider a project to flood a valley in order to generate hydro-electricity. The analyst knows that amongst the project costs will be labour and materials for construction. But wildlife will be destroyed as the valley is flooded; as we argued above, this is an economic cost which cannot be ignored. Yet some of the benefits of preserving, for instance, certain flora for medicinal purposes, might be unknown for several years. The dam might thus destroy a cure for cancer. Project benefits include cost-savings over generating electricity from the dam rather than by the next cheapest source. But how will these cost savings vary over the lifetime of the project? What will be the effect on the storage capacity of the dam as deforestation takes place further up the watershed? The dam will irreversibly change the valley it floods: are there special considerations in such cases? The NPV of the project will vary according to the discount rate. Which rate should be used? What is the value of wildlife?

As a last example, suppose a development authority plans to build a barrage across an estuary to increase property values and generate opportunities for marina developments. The barrage will harm waterfowl populations by flooding feeding grounds. The development authority is compelled to carry out a CBA of the project, but who will check that the benefit figures it uses are not over-optimistic, or that it has not excluded certain costs since they fall outside its jurisdiction? By bending the rules of the CBA procedure, the agency can maximize the likelihood that the project will go ahead.

In summary, the following problem areas arise in applying CBA to environmental issues:

(i)   The valuation of non-market goods, such as wildlife and landscape. How should this be done, and how much reliance should society place on estimates so generated? Are we acting immorally by placing money values on such things?

(ii)   Ecosystem complexity: how can society accurately predict the effects on an aquatic ecosystem of effluent inputs?

(iii)   Discounting and the discount rate: should society discount? If so, what rate should be used? Does discounting violate the rights of future generations?

(iv)   Institutional capture: is CBA a truly objective way of making decisions, or can institutions capture it for their own ends?

(v)   Uncertainty and irreversibility. How will these aspects be included in a CBA?

The rest of this book attempts to answer some of these questions and also throw light on the issues surrounding others.

APPENDIX 1.1 EXAMPLE OF A SIMPLE CBA

Consider a plan to plant trees on an area of land currently being farmed. Suppose that, for simplicity, unpriced non-market impacts of this scheme are ignored. The relevant costs will be all resource-using activities associated with the scheme. These costs might include the elements shown in the first column of Table A1.1, and occur as shown in the second column.

Table A1.1 Costs and Benefits per Hectare

		Year	Value
			(£ per hectare)
Cost			
	Land purchase	0	400
	Ploughing	0	30
	Fencing	0	650
	Planting	0	580
	Weeding	1,2,3	430
	Beating up	2	70
	Brashing	20	40
	Pruning	16,20,28	150
	Clear felling	45	250
Benefit			
	Value of crop	45	6500

The only benefit considered is the value of the timber crop in year 45. Further, assume that costs comprise capital, labour and raw materials (such as seedlings) and that market prices of all of these are thought to be reasonable indicators of marginal social cost. The only exception is land cost. Land prices represent the discounted sum of future rents that can be earned on land, plus some element of real appreciation in land prices (a speculative element). Land prices here will reflect expected rents from agriculture, which in turn depend upon profits to be made from farming. Suppose that 25% of farm profits on similar land are accounted for by payments from government. This 25% should be excluded from the market price since it represents a transfer payment. After this adjustment and after making some predictions concerning, for example, timber prices, the results shown in column three of Table A1.1 might be calculated.

Table A1.2 Discounting Costs and Benefits

Year	Net Cost (-) or Benefit (+)	Discount Factor	Discounted Values
0	-£1660.0	1.0000	-1660.00
1	-£30.0	0.9434	-28.30
2	-£100.0	0.8899	-89.00
3	-£30.0	0.8396	-25.20
4	-£30.0	0.7921	-23.80
16	-£150.0	0.3936	-59.00
20	-£190.0	0.3118	-59.20
28	-£150.0	0.1956	-29.20
45	+£6250.0	0.0726	453.75

The next step is to convert these cost and benefit items into annual net benefit flows. For year 0, then, land purchase, ploughing, fencing and planting costs are added together; and likewise for all other project years when an item occurs. This is shown in the first two columns of Table A1.2 In column 3, the discount factor for a discount rate of 6% is shown. Recall that this factor d is given by $\{(1+r)^{-t}\}$, where t is the time period during which the net benefit occurs, and r is the discount rate. For year 16, then, t=16, i=0.06, so that d=0.3936. The discounted net benefit flows are shown in column 4 (which is simply column 2 multiplied by column 3). Summing the values in column 4 shows that the Net Present Value (NPV) at a 6% discount rate is minus £1,5219.95. The project thus fails the cost-benefit test at this rate. The example shows clearly the impact of discounting. Year 0 costs count at their full value, yet the year 45 benefit, which is large in current value terms, becomes much reduced in present value terms. This result is of course sensitive to the discount rate: try to find out what happens to NPV as the rate is cut to (i) 4% and (ii) 2%. Note that land is not being resold at the end of year 45: this might be because the land is replanted, in which case returns over a perpetual rotation should be included.

REFERENCES

Baumol W and Oates W (1988) *The Theory of Environmental Policy*. Cambridge University Press.

Brent R J (1990) *Project Appraisal for Developing Countries*. New York University Press.

Clawson M and Knetsch J L (1966) *Economics of Outdoor Recreation*. Baltimore, Maryland: Johns Hopkins Press.

Department of the Environment (1991) *Policy Appraisal and the Environment*. London: HMSO.

Eckstein O (1958) *Water Resource Development: The Economics of Project Evaluation* Cambridge, MA: Harvard University Press.

Froehlich M, Hufford D C J and Hammett N H (1991) "The United States" in J Bardeand and D W Pearce (editors) *Valuing the Environment: Six Case Studies*. London: Earthscan.

HMSO (1990) *This Common Inheritance: Britain's Environmental Strategy*, London: HMSO.

Jungermann H and Fleischer F (1988) "As time goes by: psychological determinant of time preference" in G Kirsch (editor) *The Formulation of Time Preferences in a Multidisciplinary Perspective*. London: St. Martin's Press

Kneese A V (1964) *The Economics of Regional Water Quality Management*. Baltimore, Maryland: Johns Hopkins Press.

Krutilla J V (1967) "Conservation reconsidered" *American Economic Review*. September 57: 777-786.

Krutilla J V and Eckstein O (1958) *Multiple Purpose River Development: Studies in Applied Economic Analysis*. Baltimore, Maryland: Johns Hopkins Press.

Lumby S (1988) *Investment Appraisal* (3rd edition). Van Nostrand Reinhold.

Maass A and associates (1962) *Design of Water-Resource Systems*. Cambridge, MA: Harvard University Press.

MacAllister D M (1980) *Evaluation in Environmental Planning*. Cambridge, MA: MIT Press.

Nash C A (editor) (1990) Appraising the Environmental Effects of Road Schemes: A Response to the SACTRA Committee. University of Leeds: Institute for Transportation Studies, Working Paper 293.

Pearce D, Markandya A and Barbier E (1989) *Blueprint for a Green Economy*. London: Earthscan.

Randall A (1986) "Valuation in a policy context" in D W Bromley (editor) *Natural Resource Economics*. Boston: Kluwer-Nijhoff.

UK Treasury (1984) *Investment Appraisal: a Guide for Government Departments*. London: HMSO.

United Kingdom, Department of the Environment (1989) *Environmental Assessment: A Guide to the Procedures*. London: HMSO.

United Kingdom, Department of Transport (1983) *Manual of Environmental Appraisal*. London: HMSO.

Walthern P (editor) (1988) *Environmental Impact Assessment*. London: Unwin and Hyman.

ENDNOTES

1. We will use the terms "project" and "policy" synonymously here: what applies to the former will apply to the latter to a large extent.

2. The value that flows from services can be considered analogously.

3. Some elements of total environmental impacts will be picked up by markets in some cases: for example, the housing market might be depressed by the spoiling of the view. Indeed, such impacts are the foundation of the hedonic pricing, travel cost and avoided cost approaches to valuation as described later in the book. For the present, however, the simplification is useful.

4. The well-known jibe that economists know the price of everything but the value of nothing.

5. If the nominal rate of interest (sometimes referred to as the market rate) is i_n and the inflation rate is p, then the real rate of interest i_r is given as $i_r = [(1+i_n)/(1+p)] - 1$.

6. Principally that all agents are price-takers and that there are no externalities associated with production and consumption of goods.

7. To see this, note that farmers gain pure profits equal to area (Pd Pw d a). Taxpayers gain area (a d e c), but consumers lose area (P_d P_w d f). The net loss is [(a b c) + (d e f)].

8. For evidence on negative time preference rates, see Jungermann and Fleischer (1988).

2 THE WELFARE FOUNDATIONS OF CBA

2.1 CONSUMER WELFARE THEORY

2.1.1. The Consumer's Problem

Neo-classical consumer theory attempts to model the demand for goods given certain assumptions. The central assumptions appertain to the behavioural characteristics of the individual; that is, the consumer. The theory assumes that consumers, as an aggregate group, will act rationally. The rationality of the consumer can be used to determine how consumption decisions will be made. The goal of consumption is assumed to be utility maximization, which is restrained by certain constraints, principally income and prices. Given a rational, utility-maximizing consumer with a fixed income, faced by a certain price structure, a demand function can be specified.

A rational consumer will always choose the most preferred bundle of goods from a set of feasible alternatives. Furthermore, a consumer is assumed to be able to compare various bundles of goods and place them in an order of preference. (More formally, three conditions must hold: completeness, transitivity and reflexitivity.)[1] The main assumption for preference maximization is transitivity, the implications of which can be explained by a simple example. Take a consumer faced with three goods x, y and z. This consumer may prefer x to y and y to z. Then, by assumption of transitivity, x is preferred to z. On the addition of the assumption of continuity, a consumer's behaviour can be summarized in a utility function. An important consequence of continuity is that, if y is preferred to z and if x is a bundle close to y, then x must be preferred to z.

The consumer's problem is to choose from among the set of available goods the most preferred mix. This choice is assumed to be carried out so as to maximize the utility derived from the consumption of the chosen bundle of goods. However, the consumer is constrained by the prices of the goods and his/her income level. The ordinary or Marshallian demand curve

26

provides the solution to this problem. The Marshallian demand curve is given as:

$$x_i = x_i(P, M).$$

That is, the quantity of x_i demanded is a function of a vector of prices P and money income M. This is the solution to the utility maximization problem

maximize $U = U(X)$ subject to $\Sigma\ p_i x_i = M$

where X is the vector of quantities $(X = x_1, ..., x_i, ..., x_n)$.

Diagrammatically, a consumer's best choice is given where an indifference curve is tangent to the budget constraint. The budget constraint for a given good X_2 is defined as the line $X_2 = M/p_2 - p_1/p_2\ X_1$, where X_1 represents all other goods, and p_1, p_2 are prices. Indifference curves have a smooth shape and are convex to the origin if the utility function is continuous and strictly concave.

2.1.2 Dupuit Surplus

Dupuit (1844) described consumers' surplus as being the difference between the price actually paid when purchasing a commodity and the price the consumer would have been willing to pay. This willingness to pay diminishes as more units of the commodity are consumed. The reason for the diminishing WTP is that the extra satisfaction derived from a good declines the more of it an individual consumes. For example, the first cup of coffee in the day gives a high level of satisfaction but ten cups later, if offered another cup, there is little joy in the prospect and an individual may refuse the offer. Figure 2.1 shows the price a given consumer is prepared to pay for each successive unit of a commodity. For the first unit the consumer would be willing to pay p_1, for the second p_2, for the third p_3 and so on. If we assume the consumer can buy all the units from 1 through to q_0 at a constant price p_0, there will be a surplus of utility on every unit consumed up to, but not including, the last, q_0. Thus the Dupuit surplus from buying q_0 at p_0 is given by the sum of rectangular areas above the price and below the maximum willingness to pay for each unit. The net benefits of consuming q_0 are given by this area, while the gross benefits are given by the same area plus area $p_0 q_0$; that is, the net benefit plus the amount paid by the consumer.

Clearly, lowering (raising) the purchase price will increase (decrease) net benefits the Dupuit surplus. As Dupuit (1844, p.29) stated:

> Hence the saying which we shall often repeat because it is often forgotten: the only real utility is that which people are willing to

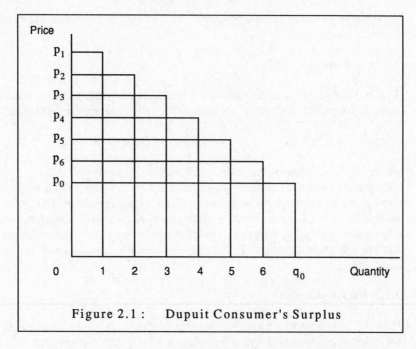

Figure 2.1 :   Dupuit Consumer's Surplus

pay for. We see that in general the relative or definitive utility of a product is expressed by the difference between the sacrifice which the purchaser would be willing to make in order to get it and the purchase price he has to pay in exchange. It follows that anything which raises the purchase price diminishes the utility to the same extent, and anything which depresses the price increases the utility in the same manner.

However, the underlying cause of the change in a price is important to welfare assessment. The producer can reap a similar surplus to the consumer (see section 2.2 below) by charging more for a commodity than it cost to produce. A price reduction which does not correspond to a reduction in production costs cannot increase the overall welfare of society. Such a price change merely reduces producers' welfare and increases consumers' welfare. As Dupuit (1844, p.41) remarked:

For an increase or decrease of utility to take place, there must be, provided there is no change in quality, a decrease or increase in the cost of production. When there is merely a change in the market price the consumer gains what the producer loses, or vice versa.

2.1.3 Consumer's Surplus

Marshall was concerned with finding the conditions under which a money measure of consumer welfare would equal the "true" utility surplus. He developed the association of consumer's surplus with the curvilinear triangle under the ordinary demand curve. In Figure 2.2 an individual's Marshallian demand curve, D, is shown. The Marshallian demand curve expresses the ideas of Dupuit for a consumer good which is perfectly divisible. This gives a continuous demand curve and allows the use of marginal analysis.[2] The area abc is the *net* benefit to the consumer of purchasing quantity od of the good. The difference between this and the gross benefit is the total cost of quantity od to the individual: area oacd for a price of a. Throughout this book, consumer's surplus will be taken to mean this triangular area, unless stated otherwise. Note that the equivalence of the triangle to the true surplus is not a definition; it is a theorem, true under certain restrictive assumptions, but only if these assumptions are granted. A detailed analysis of these assumptions can be found in the literature and only the main points are summarized here. (See Currie et al., 1971, and also Just et al., 1982.)

The use of a money measure of a utility change means uniqueness may not always be guaranteed. A money measure can vary depending upon the order

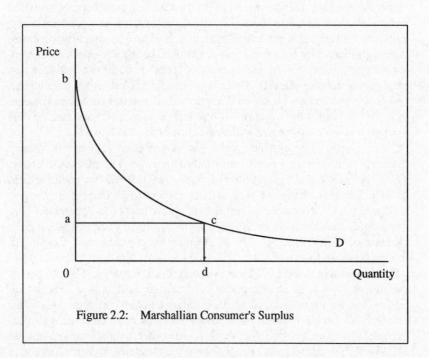

Figure 2.2: Marshallian Consumer's Surplus

in which certain changes are assumed to occur. In particular, this problem
arises where the utility change of interest involves a change in the price of
more than one commodity, or where income and price changes occur
simultaneously. In these situations the order in which the changes are
analysed can determine the size of the resulting money measure of welfare.
When the path of adjustment affects the outcome in this manner, there is
path dependence.

Certain conditions, when met; can ensure that the money measure is
unique; that is, path independent. For a simultaneous price and income
change, the consumer's surplus is unique if and only if the income effect (or
income elasticity) is zero. That is, the quantity consumed remains the same
when income changes. For a change in more than one price, the consumer's
surplus measure is unique if and only if all income elasticities of demand,
for the goods whose prices change, are equal. (If the prices of all goods are
changed, then the income elasticity of demand must equal one unity.) This
means that the consumer must adjust consumption of all goods whose prices
change, proportionally. For example, a ten percent increase in income
causes a five percent increase in the quantity of butter and petrol consumed
(if these are the only goods consumed, the ten percent increase in income
must cause a ten percent increase in the consumption of both goods).

These conditions restrict the scope of the analysis which can be performed
while maintaining unique results. This would not pose a problem if the
constraints were actually reflected by consumers' preferences. Unfortunately,
it seems unlikely that the conditions will hold in the majority of cases.
Although there may be some goods for which the income elasticity is zero,
for example salt, this is rarely true of most goods with consumption
changing with income levels. Perhaps even more unlikely is the requirement
that an income change causes consumption of all goods whose prices change
to alter in equal proportions. Empirical evidence argues against the
existence of such preference structures (Just et al., 1982, p.83).

Even if path independence were not a problem, changes in money
measures of consumer's surplus may fail to correspond to changes in utility.
This is because the marginal utility of money (MUM) may vary with respect
to all prices that change as well as with respect to income, if it changes.
Uniqueness of consumer's surplus is insufficient to guarantee any
meaningful interpretation of the change in consumer's surplus as a money
measure of utility changes. The MUM must be constant for a meaningful
money measure to exist.

Marshall assumed the MUM was constant for two reasons. First, to permit
the use of money as an acceptable cardinal index of utility. Second, to
ensure that, for movements along the ordinary demand curve, the area under
the demand curve measures total utility and that the consumer's surplus
triangle approximates the true surplus. In order to maintain a constant
MUM with respect to price changes, the price elasticity of demand needs to

be unity, and the marginal utilities of other goods should be unaffected (in fact Marshall went further and, as required by cardinal analysis, assumed independent marginal utilities).

In an in-depth review of consumer welfare theory, Just et al. (1982, p.82) conclude that the condition of constancy for the MUM is at least as restrictive as the implications of path independence. As they state:

> ... the economic implications of these conditions on the consumer indifference map are so restrictive as to prevent use of the "money measure of utility change" approach in an a priori sense for essentially all practical purposes. That is, one would have little basis for estimating money measures of utility change without first carrying out considerable empirical analysis to determine for example, whether or not all income elasticities of demand are consistent with the implications of path independence. Even then, constancy of marginal utility of income may not hold.

This is a strong attack upon the practicability of using the consumer surplus measure of utility. If this applied problem is combined with the underlying utilitarian background of cardinal analysis, the consumer's surplus measure as proposed by Marshall becomes totally unacceptable. However, cardinal analysis was replaced by ordinal analysis, and it was in this context that Hicks redefined consumer surplus. When Hicks (1941, pp.108-116) argued for the rehabilitation of consumer's surplus, he stated:

> If the marginal utility of money is constant, it implies that the consumer's demand schedules are unaffected by changes in his real income; all it need imply for this purpose is that the demand schedule *for this commodity* is unaffected (or substantially unaffected) by changes in real income which arise as a result of changes from one to another of various hypothetical situations which we may want to consider.

Hicks goes on to point out that the requirements for constant MUM can be realistic, and are equivalent to requiring that there be a small or negligible income effect:

> Whenever the commodity in question is one on which the consumer is likely to be spending a small proportion only of his total income, the assumption of 'constant marginal utility of money' can usually be granted; and it can still be granted, even if this condition is not fulfilled, provided the particular change under discussion does not involve a large *net* change in real incomes.

Thus, the practicability of the consumer's surplus measure will vary depending on the complexity of the analysis; for example, it might be argued that, for the case of a price change in one good which is a small part of total expenditure, no problems arise. The more commodities whose prices change, the less likely is a money measure of the change in consumer's surplus to match the change in the true surplus. Ordinal analysis, by concentrating on relative changes, allows money measures of consumer welfare to be developed which are independent of the unrealistic preference assumptions of Marshall. Consumer's surplus as a welfare measure in its own right implies unrealistic a priori assumptions and, if defined as a cardinal measure, departs from our understanding of people's preferences.

2.1.4 Compensation Measures of Consumer Welfare

Hicks refined four measures of consumer welfare change resulting from a price change. These are compensating variation, compensating surplus, equivalent variation and equivalent surplus. The compensating surplus and equivalent surplus measures require that the quantity consumed be held constant. Attention here is initially focused on the equivalent and compensating variation measures which allow the consumer freedom to choose the quantities purchased after a change in the economic situation. We then move on to the equivalent and compensating surplus measures which are relevant for many cases of public good supply.

In order to illustrate the meaning of these two measures, only one commodity is assumed to undergo a price change. The results of this analysis can be generalized to the many goods case and to more than one price change. The analysis assumes a rational, utility-maximizing consumer whose preferences correspond to certain basic axioms as mentioned in section 2.1.1.

In Figure 2.3 two goods X_1 and X_2 are shown along with the indifference mapping of an individual. Good X_2 can be regarded as a composite good with a price of unity; it acts as a numeraire. Good X_1 has an initial price of p_0; the initial equilibrium for the consumer is at point (X'_1, X'_2). Now, assume air pollution reductions cause the cost of producing X_1 to fall so that the price changes from p_0 to p_1. If income is held constant at m_0 the consumption of X_2 falls to X_2'', and the quantity of X_1 consumed increases to X_1''. This is the change shown by the Marshallian demand curve.

The welfare gained by the consumer from this change can be defined by the variation in income. The compensating variation of the price fall is the sum of money that, when taken away from the consumer, leaves him or her just as well off with the price change as if it had not occurred: that is, the change that holds the consumer at her or his initial level of utility, U_0.[3] In Figure 2.3 this is given by the distance m_0-m_1. This is the vertical distance between the new budget line $(m_0, m_0/p_1)$ and a parallel line which is

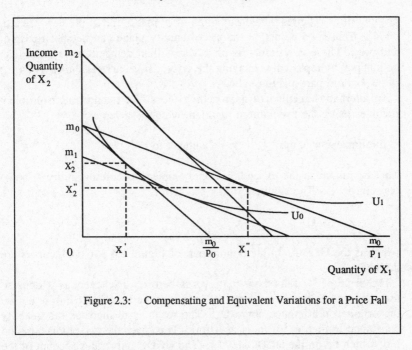

Figure 2.3: Compensating and Equivalent Variations for a Price Fall

tangential to the original indifference curve. Thus, removing a sum of money m_0-m_1 after the price change will return the consumer to the original utility level U_0.

The equivalent variation of a price fall is the sum of money that, when given to the consumer, leaves him or her just as well off without the price change as if it had occurred. Thus, the consumer is kept on his/her post-change utility level, U_1. In Figure 2.3 this is given by income m_2-m_0, or the vertical distance between the original budget line (m_0, m_0/p_0) and a parallel line tangential to the new indifference curve. The sum of money may differ from the compensating variation, because income is being increased here whereas the compensating variation reduces income. (This is the difference between willingness to pay and willingness to accept, to which we shall return, especially in Chapter 3).

In order to show the relationship between these two measures, deriving the Hicksian Compensated Demand Curve (HCDC) is helpful. This is done by expressing the changes just described in price/quantity space for X_1. The top part of Figure 2.4 is similar to Figure 2.3. There are two equilibrium price levels for X_1 (p_0 and p_1) and there are two utility levels, U_0 and U_1.

The Marshallian demand curve holds income constant and gives the quantity of a good demanded at different prices, while allowing utility to vary. In Figure 2.4 income is held constant at m_0 while the price of X_1 falls from p_0 to p_1. Maximizing utility subject to the budget constraint at the original price requires the consumption of q_1 of X_1, and at the new price q_2 of X_1. Thus, two points on the price/quantity plane can be specified p_0q_1 and p_1q_2. These two points lie on a Marshallian demand curve which can be mapped by repeatedly changing the price. This curve is shown as $D(m_0)$ in the bottom part of Figure 2.4.

An alternative method of approaching the utility maximization problem involves using the expenditure function, which is given as:

$$\text{minimize } E = \Sigma \, p_i.x_i \qquad\qquad \text{subject to } U(X) = \overline{U}$$

That is, minimize the expenditure on x_i subject to holding utility at some constant level. The solution to this problem is

$$x_i{'} = x_i{'} \, (p, U)$$

which is the HCDC. In the bottom part of Figure 2.4 two such curves are derived.

The price of X_1 falls from p_0 to p_1 as before. However, as it does so assume income is removed from the individual so as to leave him or her on the original indifference curve U_0. The result is to increase the quantity consumed from q_1 to q_3, not q_2 as before. This gives the two points p_0q_1 and p_1q_3 which lie on the HCDC, $H(U_0)$. The HCDC only takes account of the substitution effect, because the income effect is excluded by the reductions of income. As X_1 is a normal good, so the income effect is positive and the HCDC is less elastic than the Marshallian demand curve. The demand curve $H(U_0)$ relates to the compensating variation, which holds U_0 constant.

The equivalent variation for the price fall holds U_1 constant. The equivalent variation is the amount of income which, if given to the individual, would leave him or her just as well off without the price fall as with it. That is, the amount of income which shifts the original budget constraint to the right until it is tangential to the indifference curve which the individual would reach if the price had fallen. In the top part of Figure 2.4, after a fall in price to p_1 the individual would have consumed q_2. If instead, the price remains unchanged but income is increased until U_1 is reached, the quantity of X_1 demanded will be q_4. The two points which are plotted in the bottom part of the figure are p_1q_2; p_0q_4, both lie on the HCDC, $H(U_1)$.

The compensating variation associated with the price fall is m_0-m_1 in the top of the figure, and the area to the left of $H(U_0)$ and between the two price lines p_0 and p_1 in the bottom of the figure. The equivalent variation for the same price change is m_2-m_0 in the top of the figure, and the area to the left of $H(U_1)$ and between the two price lines in the bottom of the figure. In general, the area to the left of that HCDC which cuts through the original position defines the compensating variation, whereas the area to the left of

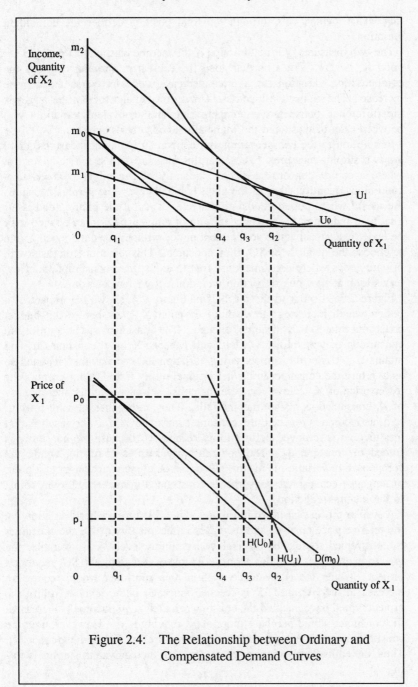

Figure 2.4: The Relationship between Ordinary and Compensated Demand Curves

that HCDC which cuts through the final position defines the equivalent variation.[4]

The two measures will be the same if the income elasticity of demand for good X_1 is zero. For a normal good the equivalent variation exceeds the compensating variation for a price decrease, and vice versa for a price increase. The higher the income elasticity of demand for X_1, the larger is the difference between the compensating and equivalent variation, and between each of these and the Marshallian consumer's surplus.

In addition to the compensating and equivalent variation measures, there are two surplus measures. These surplus measures are specifically for use where a choice concerns a discrete quantity of a good as opposed to a continuous quantity; that is, the good is indivisible. The surplus measures are useful where public goods are discrete. Thus, if the public good is air quality, a reduction in the concentration of ambient SO_2 in an airshed may be undertaken as an act of government policy without consumers being able to choose the quantity of SO_2 they consume. This situation contrasts with private goods where consumers are free to adjust their consumption. Now let us look at how this restriction would affect welfare measures.

Figure 2.5a, similar to the top half of Figure 2.4, shows the impact of a policy which increases the quantity of good X_1. As before the budget constraint rotates as X_1 becomes cheaper. The consumer was at equilibrium consuming q_1 with utility U_0, but with cheaper X_1 now consumes q_2 and attains U_1. Under the compensating variation income was then reduced so as to return the consumer to his/her original utility level U_0, but keeping the lower price of X_1. However, here the consumer cannot adjust the quantity of X_1 consumed as his/her income falls. Thus, rather than moving from q_2 to q_3 as income is reduced, the consumer must stay at q_2. The result is that less income is removed before utility reaches U_0 because the consumer is forced to consume q_2. The compensatory surplus is m_0-m_{cs}, while the compensating variation is m_0-m_1. Note, the outcome is no longer at a point of tangency because the consumer is constrained in his/her ability to adjust to the income reduction.

A similar process is shown in Figure 2.5b. This time, rather than allowing the relative price changes and increases in the quantity of X_1, the consumer is constrained to his/her original consumption level. For example, the government wishes to know the benefits lost of foregoing the SO_2 reduction project. Under the equivalent variation, this consumer would require an increase in income until U_1 is reached since U_1 is the level of utility the project would have enabled the consumer to attain. As income is increased, the consumer would purchase more of X_1 moving to q_4. However, now the consumer is restricted to q_1 and therefore requires more income to reach U_1. Thus, the equivalent variation was m_0-m_2, but the equivalent surplus is m_0-m_{es}.

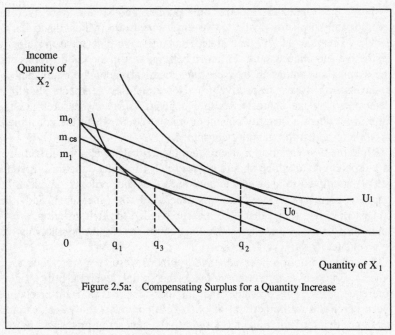

Figure 2.5a: Compensating Surplus for a Quantity Increase

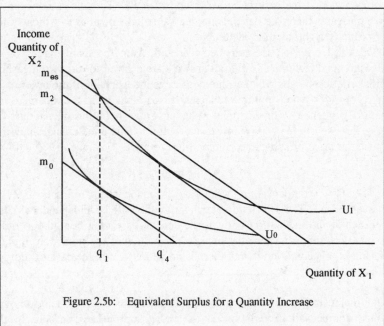

Figure 2.5b: Equivalent Surplus for a Quantity Increase

Many environmental goods are public goods and are therefore appropriately measured by these two surplus measures (Mitchell and Carson, 1989). Freeman (1979) has stated that these surplus measures are too restrictive and unnecessary. Freeman believes that in the public goods case, the surplus and variation measures are identical under the equivalent and compensating cases respectively. However, the approach should be determined by the characteristics of a good; surplus measures are then employed where a quantity change is imposed, and where the consumer is not free to adjust the quantity consumed.

While the two variation measures are theoretically well established, there is a problem as to which should be used in a particular situation. Freeman (1979) attempted to answer this question using four criteria: practicability, implied property rights, the uniqueness of the measures and their consistency. He found that both measures failed the first criterion. At the same time he noted that the Marshallian consumer surplus is relatively easy to calculate.

The second criterion does not favour either measure in preference to the other. Compensating variation takes the initial level of utility as the reference point. This presumes that the individual has no right or claim to make purchases at the new set of prices. In contrast; equivalent variation presumes that the individual has a right to the new set of prices and must be compensated if the new price set is not attained. The choice between the two measures therefore depends upon a value judgement as to which system of property rights is more equitable.

The third criterion is more decisive and, from the mathematics of the measurement technique, different answers are derived for the two measures. This criterion judges whether the measure is independent of the order of the price changes when multiple changes occur; that is, it is concerned with path dependence. For example, reducing ozone pollution may reduce the price of a sensitive crop by increasing output. This price change may then cause the price of substitute commodities to alter. Freeman (1979,p.45-46) states:

The CV (compensating variation) is independent of the order of evaluation. The EV (equivalent variation) will be independent of the order of the evaluation only in the special case of a homothetic utility function, that is, where the income elasticities of the goods are unitary. Unless this condition is met there is no unique EV in the case of multiple price changes.

The implausibility of unitary income elasticities has already been discussed. Thus, compensating variation is the more appropriate measure in this instance.

The final criterion involves the situation where more than one policy option is available. Where a comparison of two or more public goods is being made, the equivalent variation ranks the goods correctly while the compensating variation fails to do so (Johansson, 1987, pp.81-82). Thus, the compensating variation may provide a ranking of alternative policies that is inconsistent with individual preferences. The sole use of equivalence measures has been suggested by McKenzie (1983) and Morey (1984) on similar grounds. However, Mitchell and Carson (1989, pp.25-26) argue that the conditions under which the problem occurs are unlikely and the ranking errors so small as to be undetectable.

Thus, the choice between the two measures will depend upon the characteristics of the welfare change being analysed. For example, a price change which affects the prices of other goods but is the only policy option would favour the use of the compensating variation. However, while both measures are consistent with a theoretical definition of welfare, neither is readily observable from market data. The Marshallian consumer surplus is observable and lies between the two variation measures. This suggests the possibility of using consumer's surplus as an approximation to the more theoretically justified variation measures.

The bottom half of Figure 2.4 is redrawn as Figure 2.6. The compensating variation associated with a price fall is exactly equal to area x. The equivalent variation associated with a price fall is given by area x + z + w. The consumer's surplus is given by area x + z. Thus, for a commodity with a positive income effect, the change in consumer's surplus, due to a price fall from p_0 to p_1, is bounded from below by the compensating variation and from above by the equivalent variation; it differs from the former by area z and from the latter by area w.[5]

Robert Willig (1976) calculated the accuracy with which consumer's surplus could approximate the variation measures. Willig showed that under certain specific conditions area z and area w could be calculated as percentage confidence limits to the consumer's surplus estimate. In this way it could be shown that the areas z and w would be insignificant for most empirical studies. As Willig stated:

> ... observed consumer's surplus can be rigorously utilized to estimate unobservable compensating and equivalent variations - the correct theoretical measures of welfare impact changes in prices and income on an individual.

This can be achieved by deriving

> ... precise upper and lower bounds on the percentage errors of approximating the compensating and equivalent variations with consumer's surplus. These bounds can be explicitly calculated from

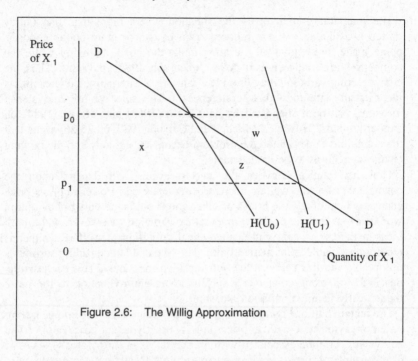

Figure 2.6:   The Willig Approximation

observed demand data, and it is clear that in most applications the error of approximation will be very small. In fact, the error will often be overshadowed by errors involved in estimating the demand curve.

Since Willig's initial work, alternative techniques for approximating or directly calculating compensating and equivalent variations have been put forward based upon the use of Marshallian demand data. Hausman (1981) suggested the use of a differential equations technique to avoid the need for approximation. The complexity of employing this method led Shonkwiler (1991) to suggest an alternative which is similar to Willig's approximation, but claims the advantages of avoiding differential equations and being more intuitive. Randall and Stoll (1980) extended the Willig results to the compensating and equivalent surplus measures, showing that the approximation is likely to hold for small quantity changes or small budget items. The interested reader is referred to the original sources.

2.2 PRODUCER WELFARE THEORY

Unlike consumer's welfare theory there has been relatively little controversy surrounding producer's welfare measures. Producer's welfare can be measured directly and is observable; that is, there need be no problems choosing the best method of approximating an unobservable concept such as utility. Despite this, there are several methods of measuring producer's welfare. These can be placed into two categories: input market measures and output market measures. The output market is where a firm sells its production. Two measures will be discussed in this context; namely, producer's surplus and quasi-rent. The input market is where factors of production (that is, land, labour and capital) are purchased by the firm. No measures are discussed in this context (as they are rarely used in empirical studies), but some of the theoretical advantages of this approach are mentioned.

Producer's surplus is the traditional approach to the measurement of producer's welfare and was developed by Marshall. Producer's surplus is defined as the area above the short-run supply curve and below the price line. The firm is assumed to operate in a perfectly competitive market, for both inputs and outputs. The supply curves for all variable inputs are perfectly elastic; that is, the firm is able to purchase all the variable inputs required at a fixed price. Also, the costs of fixed factors are assumed to be sunk during the short run. For example, a farmer pays rent for land at the beginning of the season and cannot recoup that sum of money.

The producer's surplus for a perfectly competitive firm is shown in Figure 2.7. The firm will supply nothing below the price p_1 because it cannot cover variable costs. As long as the price stays above the average variable cost (AVC) curve, the firm can make payments on fixed costs. Above the average total cost (ATC) curve, profits are made as all costs are covered. The short-run supply curve is Sb and equals the (short-run) marginal cost (MC) curve. If the price the firm receives for its output is p_0, then Marshall's producer's surplus is given by area p_0abp_1. The surplus accrues to the firm via the ownership of fixed factors. Factors can receive payments above their marginal costs because their supply is limited in the short run. In the long run these factors become variable and the surplus to the firm disappears as the factors can move from one firm to another and factor owners can gain the rent which previously went to the firm; that is, the rent becomes part of the factor cost.[6] This short-run economic rent is a quasi-rent to the firm, producer's surplus being one method of measuring it.

In the short run, the area above a competitive firm's supply curve and below the price line provides a measure of the excess of gross receipts over prime costs; that is, quasi-rent. Prime costs are the extra costs a firm incurs in order to produce a commodity and which are avoided if nothing is produced. Another measure of quasi-rent is total revenue (gross receipts) minus total variable costs (prime costs).[7] Figure 2.8 shows a similar situation to Figure 2.7. Total revenue is the quantity produced q_0 times the price p_0, and total variable cost is the quantity q_0 times the average variable cost AVC_0. Thus, quasi-rent is given by area x. Despite other possible

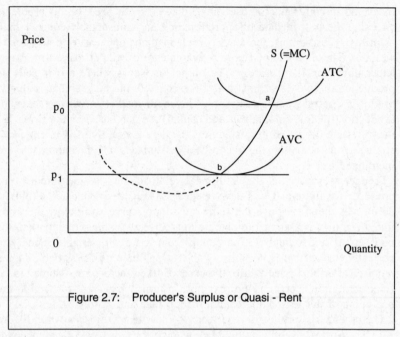

Figure 2.7:   Producer's Surplus or Quasi - Rent

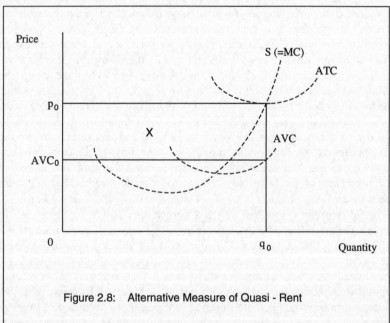

Figure 2.8:   Alternative Measure of Quasi - Rent

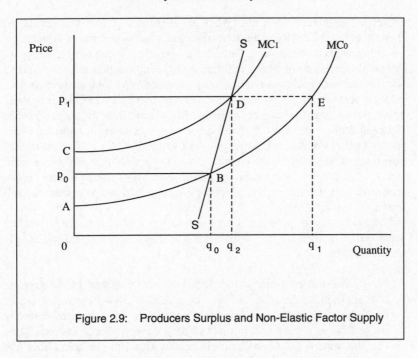

Figure 2.9:   Producers Surplus and Non-Elastic Factor Supply

measures of quasi-rent, the producer's surplus approach is the most commonly used in empirical and graphical theoretic work. The concept can also be applied to the industry. The industry supply curve is the sum of firms' marginal cost curves; the area above it and below the price line is the aggregate surplus accruing to the owners of the firms.

However, care is required when applying the producer's surplus measure. For example, relaxing the assumption of an infinite price elasticity of supply of variable inputs leads to the producer's surplus measure being unrelated to actual welfare. Producer's surplus will overstate actual welfare changes when the price of a necessary factor input increases as industry use of the factor expands. In Figure 2.9 the industry is in equilibrium at price p_0 and quantity q_0, the producer's surplus would thus be p_0BA (if supply equalled MC_0). If the price were to rise to p_1, the firms (expecting marginal cost to remain at MC_0), would supply q_1. Working on the presumption that marginal cost (that is, MC_0) equals the supply curve, the producer's surplus would be measured as p_1EA. However, as the demand for inputs increases so does their price, causing the marginal cost curve to shift to MC_1. The area of producer's welfare is p_1DC, with q_2 supplied (not q_1), at price p_1. The supply curve is SS and does not equal either aggregate marginal cost curve. The area above the supply curve and below the price line bears no relationship to the economic rent accruing to producers.

Certain other conditions must also be met; namely, that the income or welfare effect of a price change be zero, and that nonpecuniary advantages be unimportant to producers. A zero income effect is required to maintain economic rent as an objective measure which can be captured by producer's surplus without recourse to individual preferences. As long as the firms are explicit profit maximizers, they are unaffected by welfare effects since there is no utility function to affect the MUM. Thus, there is no divergence between money measures and welfare changes as there is with consumer theory (where compensating or equivalent variations, being different money measures of the same utility change, diverge when income effects are non-zero). Similarly, nonpecuniary goals must not conflict with profit maximizing behaviour or else producer's surplus will fail to capture the full extent of economic rent.

The conditions for producer's surplus to act as a good measure of welfare have been summed up by Mishan (1959). He concluded that the supply curve must be

> ... constructed for a period during which the output of the good in question can be increased only by adding to fixed-factors amounts of other factors that are imperfect substitutes for it but are perfectly elastic in supply with respect to their money prices. In such cases the rent of the fixed factor is exactly equal to the area above the supply curve under the conditions mentioned - zero welfare effect and complete indifference to nonpecuniary advantages. The further we move from these conditions, especially the latter condition, the greater the divergence between the true rent (either compensating or equivalent variation) and the area in question.

Mishan has contended that the term producer's surplus is misleading. The producer referred to is in fact the owner of the firm, while only via ownership of fixed factors does any surplus accrue to the firm. More accurately the term producer should be used in reference to the input factor of concern and therefore to the "owner" to whom the economic rent is directly attributable. Thus, the analyst should think in terms of rent to a short-run fixity of some factor of production: rent to land, rent to entrepreneurial ability, rent to market power and so on.

Mishan has thus argued in favour of input market measures. This approach is analogous to the consumer welfare measures of Hicks and involves individual preferences. The result is to work directly with the factors of production which create welfare. Mishan regards both consumer's surplus and economic rent as measures of the change in an individual's welfare when the price set changes or constraints are altered. Any distinction between the measures is then seen as one of convenience only with consumer's surplus having reference to demand prices and economic rent to supply prices.

The applied welfare economist then has a choice as to whether economic rent is to be measured in the input market or the output market. This choice may often be made for the analyst by the availability of data, with the area above the supply curve and below the price line often being the more practical measure. Divergences between the theoretical assumptions and actual market conditions can cause serious errors in measuring gains and losses using producer's surplus. Thus, the proximity of actual conditions to the theoretical must be assessed and corrections and qualifications made where necessary. If this is done and divergences are minor, the producer's surplus can be justified as a measure of economic rent.

2.3 AGGREGATION OF SUPPLY AND DEMAND

The preceding discussion of consumer and producer welfare theory has largely been in terms of the individual or firm. In practice analysis is rarely carried out at this level, even when this is desirable, because of the difficulty in obtaining data. Instead analysis is carried out at a more abstract level. Certain groups are normally identified and the economic units of interest are categorized; for example, consumers and producers are the aggregate groups of individuals and firms. This categorization procedure can cause problems.

An aggregate supply or demand curve can be viewed as the horizontal summation of individual curves. The supply curve is a summation of firm supply curves for a particular commodity and market, as in Figure 2.9. The aggregate demand curve is the summation of individual consumer's demand.[8] Representative aggregate supply and demand curves are given in Figure 2.10. Equilibrium is initially $p_0 q_0$. If the demand curve is taken to be Marshallian (not compensated) then, as long as the Willig conditions are met, the area below this and above the price line p_0, area a, gives the initial area of consumers' welfare. The area above supply curve S_0 and below p_0 is the producers' surplus, area c+b.

Assume the government reduces air pollution and good X is an agricultural product which benefits from this reduction. The supply curve for X would shift to the right as production increases at no extra cost to the farmer. The price of X falls to p_1 and the quantity increases to q_1. The consumer gains area b+f+g, which is the net benefit of the change to the consumers. The producers lose area b but gain area d+e, which means their net benefit can be negative. The pollution reduction decreases the cost of supplying the previous quantity q_0 and also allows output to increase to q_1. The quantity q_0-q_1 costs h to produce and increases benefits to the consumer by g, and to the producer by e. Before the pollution reduction this quantity cost h+e+g+k to produce, which was more than the consumers were prepared to pay.

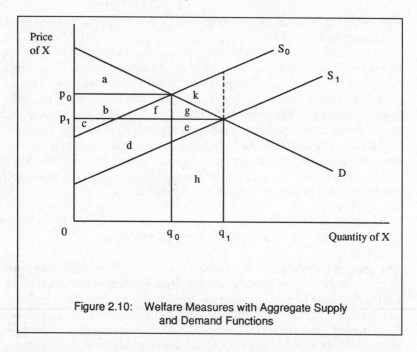

Figure 2.10:   Welfare Measures with Aggregate Supply
and Demand Functions

Aggregation over individuals makes some implicit assumptions about the distribution of income which the analyst may reject. In order to maintain a unique aggregate demand measure, the analyst assumes there is no change in the distribution of income associated with the data from which the demand curve is estimated. Also, the policy being considered must leave the distribution of income unaltered. Alternatively, the analyst may assume that the income elasticity of demand for the commodity is the same for all individuals. These assumptions are needed because any transfer of income from one individual to another will move the individual demand curves which will shift the aggregate demand curve unless the movments net out to zero. This shifting means there are as many aggregate demand curves as income distribution possibilities. Thus, a necessary assumption is that either income is not redistributed or the redistribution has no effect on demand. As neither condition is normally likely to hold, a weaker assumption is that income elasticities are similar among individuals and changes in income distribution are small.

Income distribution can also affect the relative prices from which the compensating and equivalent variations are measured; that is, welfare measurement can vary with income distribution. If the distribution of income in society is judged to be unfair, the relative prices and welfare measures which derive from it must be rejected as a basis for making social policy judgements. One solution to this problem is to accept the present distribution of income as the basis for deriving measures of social value.

2.4 WELFARE MEASURES AND SOCIAL CHOICE

This last section touches on the meaning of welfare measures for social choice; that is, how CBA information is to be used to make policy decisions. There is an important difference between the efficient allocation of resources and the distribution of income within society. The former is concerned with allocating scarce resources so as to produce goods and services, including environmental ones, demanded by individuals using the most efficient means. Allocative efficiency reflects the possibility of reallocating resources so as to achieve an increase in the net value of output produced by those resources. For example, the quantity of resources used for air pollution control might be increased without diminishing any other outputs.

In measuring the benefits of a pollution control policy in terms of producers' and consumers' welfare, the analysis is normally regarded as within positive economics because the concentration is on allocative efficiency. Haveman and Weisbrod (1975, p.44) state that:

> To determine allocative efficiency one must ignore considerations of which particular people are made better or worse off as resource allocation alternatives are considered. The issues of how alternative resource allocations affect the well-being of a particular people are captured by the distributional - or equity - goals.

Yet, the analysis of allocative efficiency can be designed so as to help the pursuit of equity goals. In the case of measuring the benefits from pollution control, the groups affected can be defined so as to provide information on the distribution of benefits useful to the policy decision-maker. For example, instead of total benefits a split can be made between consumers and producers, and these two groups can be further split into regions or income groups.

The acceptance of the current income distribution, and the assumption that it remains the same, are equivalent to relegating such decisions to a secondary position of concern. The acceptance of allocative efficiency as a goal requires a normative judgement, as does the choice of a particular income distribution. Demand analysis is dependent upon both preferences and the distribution of income and wealth, since both determine willingness and ability to pay. The choice to accept the underlying determinants of demand and concentrate on allocation is based upon the need to simplify the analyst's job. Allocative efficiency seems far less controversial than distributional equity. Welfare economists can still maintain their concern for equity and analyse it, but this will be separate from the benefit analysis.

This has certain implications for the welfare criteria used to decide whether a policy option will benefit society. There are several possible criteria, of which four are briefly discussed here. The first is Pareto Optimality, which requires that nobody be made worse off and at least one individual believes he/she is better off after a policy decision. The criticism of this is that most policy changes make some people better off and some people worse off simultaneously. Pollution control policies, for example, simultaneously impose costs and bestow benefits due to a change in the allocation of resources. As Pearce and Nash (1981 p.2) note:

> Quite simply, it is hard to imagine a policy which does not harm someone, even if it benefits others. The restrictiveness of the principle is even more obvious when it is remembered that CBA works with costs and benefits over time so that beneficiaries and losers are not just those comprising the affected parties in the immediate time-period.

Modern welfare economics is based upon the Kaldor-Hicks principle of *potential compensation*. That is, if the gainers from an action *could* compensate the losers, the action is an improvement regardless of whether compensation is actually paid. This implies two things: that benefits (i.e., the effects on gainers) exceed costs (the effects on losers); and that compensation is conceivable. (N.B., compensation does not have to be actually paid.) If benefits and costs stretch over time, then economic analysis will require that the present value of benefits, at some suitable discount rate, exceeds the present value of costs. The NPV criterion tests for exactly this. Also, inter-temporal compensation should be conceivable, a point analysed in Chapter 8.

When a government faces a range of projects, the Kaldor-Hicks principle is simply extended. Social welfare is improved by choosing those projects with the greatest net benefit, provided this net benefit is positive (i.e., is not a cost). Again, this is a restatement of the NPV rule: when faced with a series of projects (and a limited budget), choose projects in NPV order, with the highest NPV project being selected first.

Thus, if a project passes the NPV test and if compensation is feasible, meeting the Kaldor-Hicks compensation principle, pursuing such a project is defined as improving social welfare. Governments are assumed to correct significant, cumulative imbalances of gains and losses over time through the taxation system. In practice, the "possibility of compensation" part of the criterion is often forgotten. If compensation is actually paid, the principle is nothing more than the Pareto Criterion.

Freeman (1986) has claimed that the Pareto Criterion is widely rejected by economists as a guide to policy and plays no role in "mainstream" environmental economics. He stated further that the basis of CBA is the hypothetical compensation criterion, which "... is justified on ethical grounds by observing that if the gains outweigh the losses, it would be possible for the gainers to compensate fully the losers with money payments and still themselves be better off with the policy". Thus, the justification for the results of CBA (according to this view) is that they are potential Pareto improvements, although Pareto improvements themselves are rejected!

The only use of the potential compensation criterion is therefore to deny the need for compensation. The failings of such a recommendation and some of the claims made for the hypothetical compensation criterion have been well stated by Mishan (1969):

> Compensation is, after all, only hypothetical: it is consistent with making the poor yet poorer. Hence, to announce, as did Kaldor, Hicks, and others at that time, that an objective method of detecting increases in "wealth" or "efficiency" had been discovered, is to mislead opinion by use of persuasive words. Nothing had been discovered. Kaldor had merely coined a *definition* of efficiency, one whose ethical implications, as it happens, are hardly acceptable.

A persistent view among adherents of the positivist program has been that economists should avoid evaluation and prescription. Page (1988) points out that applied welfare economists have largely limited themselves to one normative idea, efficiency, which is often regarded as so universally appealing and analytically tractable that they scarcely think of it as normative at all. Thus, the potential compensation criterion is useful in separating efficiency and equity, but has meant that discussions of actual compensation have been avoided on the grounds that equity issues are outside of the economists' realm. Page has argued persuasively against this view and for the consideration of equity and other normative concepts besides efficiency in applied welfare economics, especially where intergenerational issues are involved.

The other two criteria work on the basis that the analysis should explicitly account for the distribution of benefits in society. Little (1950) put forward the idea that, in addition to a Kaldor-Hicks test, a judgement must be made as to whether the redistribution of wealth due to a policy is "good". This leaves the questions of what is "good" and who is to decide. The standard contention has been that the "decision-maker" judges these issues; that is, choices depend upon the political system. The final criteria, attributable to Bergson (1938), tries to make the idea of a "good" redistribution of wealth explicit by defining a social welfare function or social weighting. For example, the weights could be set to show the value judgement that the poor should benefit more than the rich (as suggested in Chapter 1). Of course, the weights still have to be set and this returns the criteria back to Little.

In summary, in carrying out a CBA the welfare economist can make an important contribution to the decision making process without introducing equity goals. This type of analysis, regarded as objective, could be used to approve or reject a policy on grounds of allocative efficiency, but must evoke an efficiency criteria. Most CBA practitioners judge the inclusion of equity goals to be outside the realm of economics. However, both equity and efficiency are subjectively chosen goals and the pursuit of one will affect the other.

2.5 CONCLUSIONS

As the theory now stands, the use of consumer surplus as a measure of welfare changes can be justified, as an approximation to the correct measures refined by Hicks, through the use of the Willig conditions. Producer's surplus is an output market measure of the welfare accruing to the owners of firms in the short run. As long as the assumptions which insure this is a measure of quasi-rent are met, the measure is theoretically justified. Controversy still surrounds certain aspects of the application of such measures, but they provide an input into the decision-making process for which there is no substitute at present.

REFERENCES

Bergson, A (1938) "A reformulation of certain aspects of welfare economics", *Quarterly Journal of Economics*, February 52: 314-344.

Currie J M, Murphy J A and Schmitz A (1971) "The concept of economic surplus and its use in economic analysis", *Economic Journal*, 81: 741-799.

Dupuit, J (1844) "On the measurement of the utility of public works", *Annales des Pontset Chausees*, 2nd Series, Vol. 8; reprinted in English in D Munby (editor), *Transport: Selected Readings*, Harmondsworth: Penguin Books Ltd, 1968.

Evans, A (1970) "Private good, externality, public good", *Scottish Journal of Political Economy*, February, 79-89.

Freeman, A M (1979) *The Benefits of Environmental Improvement: Theory and Practice*, London: John Hopkins Press.

Freeman, A M (1986) "The ethical basis of the economic view of the environment", *People, Penguins, and Plastic Trees: Basic Issues in Environmental Ethics*, edited by Donald Van De Veer and Christine Pierce, Belmont, CA: Wadsworth Publishing Company, 218-227.

Hausman, J A (1981) "Exact consumer's surplus and deadweight loss", *American Economic Review*, 71: 662-676.

Haveman, R H and Weisbrod B A (1975) "The concept of benefits in cost-benefit analysis: with emphasis on water pollution control activities", in H M Peskin and E P Seskin, *Cost Benefit Analysis and Water Pollution Policy*, Washington D C: The Urban Institute.

Henderson, A (1941) "Consumer's surplus and the compensating variation", *Review of Economic Studies*, February 8: 117-121.

Hicks, J R (1941) "The rehabilitation of consumers' surplus", *Review of Economic Studies*, February 8: 108-116.

Johansson, P (1987) *The Economic Theory and Measurement of Environmental Benefits*, Cambridge: CUP.

Just, R E, Hueth D L and Schmitz A (1982) *Applied Welfare Economics and Public Policy*, London: Prentice-Hall International.

Kreps, D (1990) *A Course in Microeconomics*, Princeton University Press.

Little, I M D (1950) *A Critique of Welfare Economics*, Oxford: Clarendon Press.

McKenzie, G W (1983) *Measuring Economic Welfare: New Methods*, Cambridge: CUP.

Mishan, E J (1947-48) "Realism and relevance in consumer's surplus", *Review of Economic Studies*, 15: 27-33.

Mishan, E J (1959) "Rent as a measure of welfare", *The American Economic Review*, June 49 no.3: 386-394.

Mishan, E J (1968) "What is producer's surplus?", *The American Economic Review*, December 58 no.5: 1269-1282.

Mishan, E J (1969) "Survey of welfare economics: 1939-1959", in *Welfare Economics: Ten Introductory Essays, 2nd edition*, New York: Random House.

Mitchell, R C and Carson R T (1989) *Using Surveys to Value Public Goods: The Contingent Valuation Method*, Washington D C: Resources for the Future.

Morey, E R (1984) "Consumer surplus", *American Economic Review*, 74: 163-173.

Page, T (1988) "Intergenerational equity and the social rate of discount", in *Environmental Resources and Applied Welfare Economics: Essays in Honour of John V Krutilla*, edited by V Kerry Smith, Baltimore: Resources for the Future, Johns Hopkins Press, 71-89.

Pearce, D W and Nash C A (1981) *The Social Appraisal of Projects: A Text in Cost-Benefit Analysis*, Basingstoke: Macmillan Education Ltd.

Randall, A and Stoll J R (1980) "Consumer's surplus in commodity space", *American Economic Review*, June 70 no.3: 449-457.

Shonkwiler, J S (1991) "Consumer's surplus revisited", *American Journal of Agricultural Economics*, May 410-414.

Willig, R D (1976) "Consumer's surplus without apology", *The American Economic Review*, 66 no.4: 587-597.

ENDNOTES

1. For a very careful development of the axioms of preference, see Kreps (1990).

2. At a level of consumption o-d, the total benefit of consuming the good is the area obcd, since this is the sum of all the incremental (marginal) values of each unit along the ray o-d.

3. See Just et al. (1982), p.87, for a willingness to pay interpretation.

4. The compensating variation equals the negative of the equivalent variation, and vice versa. That is, the compensating variation for a price fall equals the equivalent variation for a price rise, and vice versa.

5. For a proof, see Just et al. (1982), pp.89-92.

6. The surplus to a factor may persist under certain conditions. See Currie et al. (1971), pp.756-758.

7. Yet another measure is given in Just et al. (1982), pp.55-56.

8. If X is a non-excludable public good (such as water quality), then we would aggregate demand curves *vertically*. For an excludable private good such as wheat, demand curves are summed horizontally; see Evans (1970).

3 VALUING ENVIRONMENTAL GOODS (1): THE CONTINGENT VALUATION METHOD

3.1 INTRODUCTION

The Contingent Valuation Method (CVM) enables economic values to be estimated for a wide range of commodities not traded in markets. CVM was originally proposed by Davis (1963). The technique is now widely accepted by resource economists, following a great deal of empirical and theoretical refinements which took place in the 1970s and 1980s, mainly in the USA. In this chapter, the theoretical basis for CVM is described, its application discussed, and problem areas with the technique outlined. At the end of the chapter, a brief description of the closely related technique of contingent ranking is given.

3.2 THEORETICAL BASIS

As Chapters 1 and 2 have shown, economic value is measurable in relation to utility functions through the concepts of willingness to pay (WTP) and willingness to accept (WTA) compensation, as well as through the related measures of consumers surplus, compensating variation and equivalent variation. CVM works by directly soliciting from a sample of consumers their WTP and/or WTA for a change in the level of environmental service flows, in a carefully structured hypothetical market. WTP measures give an estimate of compensating variation for welfare-improving moves and of equivalent variation for welfare decreasing moves. However, if the resource is only available to the consumer in discrete quantities, then strictly speaking the compensating and equivalent surplus measures of value should be employed (see Chapter 2). Likewise, WTA replies give information about compensating variation for welfare-decreasing moves and equivalent variation for welfare-increasing moves. CVM thus provides, in principle, four exact welfare measurements.

3.3 THE APPLICATION OF CVM

Any CVM exercise can be split into six stages. These stages, as detailed below, are:

1. setting up the hypothetical market;
2. obtaining bids;
3. estimating mean WTP and/or WTA;
4. estimating bid curves;
5. aggregating the data, and
6. evaluating the CVM exercise.

Stage One: The Hypothetical Market
The first step is to set up a hypothetical market for the environmental service flow in question. For example, take a policy to restore old civic buildings in a city centre. Respondents might be told that the local government could engage in such restoration activities, describe what these would consist of and their effects, and explain that the operation could only go ahead if extra funds are generated. This sets up a *reason for payment* for services (the aesthetic quality of the built environment in this example), where no direct payment is currently exacted. How funds will be raised also needs to be described: the *bid vehicle* must be decided upon, e.g., property taxes, income tax, utility bills, trust fund payments or entry fees. In this example, the bid vehicle could be higher property taxes or contributions to a civic trust fund. The survey instrument (questionnaire) should also describe whether all consumers will pay a fee if the change goes ahead, and how this fee will be set. How the decision on whether to proceed with the project (the provision rule) should also be explained. The questionnaire should be pre-tested before the main survey occurs: this is often done using small "focus" groups assembled to discuss their reactions to a questionnaire prior to a pilot study. The information given to respondents about all aspects of the hypothetical market together with such information as is provided on the good being valued constitute the "framing" of the good.

Stage Two: Obtaining Bids
Once the survey instrument is set up, the survey is administered. This can be done either by face-to-face interviewing, telephone interviewing or mail shot. Telephone interviews are probably the least preferred method since conveying information about the good may be difficult over the telephone, partly due to a limited attention time span. Mail surveys are frequently used, but suffer from potential non-response bias and low response rates. Interviews with well-trained interviewers offer the most scope for detailed questions and answers, but a check on interviewer bias should be made. For a detailed account of alternatives for data collection, see Mitchell and Carson

(1989).
Individuals are asked to state their maximum WTP in order to have the environmental improvement go ahead (or, alternatively, their maximum WTP to prevent a deterioration in environmental quality occurring). They may also be asked to state their minimum WTA to go without the improvement or to put up with the deterioration. Taking WTP as an example, this figure may be derived in several ways:

(i)   As a bidding game: higher and higher amounts are suggested to the respondents until their maximum WTP is reached.

(ii)   As a closed-ended referendum: a single payment is suggested, to which respondents either agree or disagree (yes/no reply). Such replies must be analysed using a binary response technique such as logit analysis in order to derive an average value for WTP.

(iii)   As a payment card. A range of values is presented on a card which may also indicate the typical expenditure by respondents in a given income group on other publicly provided services. This helps respondents to calibrate their replies.

(iv)   As an open-ended question. Individuals are asked for their maximum WTP with no value being suggested to them. Respondents have often found it relatively difficult to answer such questions, especially where they have no prior experience of trading with the commodity in question.

Stage Three: Calculating Average WTP and/or Mean WTA
Once bids (WTA or WTP) have been gathered in, an average bid is calculated: typically both mean and median are reported. The median measure is unaffected by very large bids in the upper tail of the distribution (unlike the mean); median reported bids are almost always less than mean bids. At this stage "protest bids" are usually omitted from the calculation. Protest bids are zero bids given for reasons other than a zero value being placed on the resource in question. For example, a respondent may refuse any amount of compensation for loss of a unique environmental resource such as the Grand Canyon. Respondents may refuse to state a WTP amount because they do not wish to take part in the survey, or because they have an ethical objection to paying directly manner for environmental resource service flows. A decision must also be taken over how (if) to identify and treat outliers, that is, very large bids. For example, suppose 1000 people are asked their WTP for a water quality improvement. The first 999 bids collected have a maximum value of $200/year, but the 1000th bid is $10,000. Do we count this bid? If a mean measure of value is used, it will

be greatly increased by including this bid. Economic value is based on effective demand: thus if this bid represents a genuine (as opposed to a strategic) response and if the individual's income is commensurate with the bid, then there is no justification for excluding it. Such outliers are often excluded, however, having been identified by some rule of thumb such as the number of standard deviations away from the mean. If median WTP or WTA is reported, then outliers are less of a problem. Average bids are easily calculated if the payment card, open-ended value or bidding game approaches have been used. However, if a closed-ended referendum approach has been used, then a logit equation relating the probability of "yes" answers to each suggested amount must be estimated. The area under this curve gives mean WTP. Alternatively, the Cameron and James approach may be used to estimate mean WTP directly from a logit or probit equation (Cameron, 1988). Some closed-ended studies concentrate on median WTP instead of mean WTA.

Stage Four: Estimating Bid Curves

Investigating the determinants of WTP/WTA bids is useful in aggregating results (stage 5) and for assessing the validity of the CVM exercise. A bid curve can be estimated, using WTP/WTA amounts as the dependent variable and a range of independent variables. For instance, in the above example WTP bids might be regressed against income (Y), education (E) and age (A), as well as against some variable measuring the "quantity" of environmental quality being bid for (Q), if this varies across respondents then:

$$WTP_i = f(Y_i, E_i, A_i, Q_i) \qquad (3.1)$$

Then where i indexes respondents.

Bid curves are also useful to predict the valuation of changes in Q other than those suggested in the survey, and to test the sensitivity of WTP amounts to variations in Q. They also open up the possibility of predicting WTP amounts for changes in the level of some environmental variable X, where X and Q are both members of some set R, if stable and significant relationships can be found between Q and Y, A, E and other socioeconomic variables, and where the characteristics of Q can be mapped into those of X.

Stage Five: Aggregating Data

Aggregation refers to the process whereby the mean bid or bids are converted to a population total value figure. This figure should include all those components of value found to be relevant (see below), such as existence value and use value. Decisions over aggregation revolve around three issues.

First is the choice of the relevant population. This should have been decided when constructing the sampling frame from which the sample was drawn. The aim is to identify either (a) all those whose utility will be significantly affected by the action; or, (b) (which is the same or a smaller group), all those within a relevant political boundary who will be affected by the action. A decision must be made over the criteria to be used in deciding on who counts in (a) or (b). This group might be the local population, the regional population, the population of Scotland, or the population of the UK.

Second is moving from the sample mean to a mean for the total population. Several alternatives have been proposed. The sample mean could be multiplied by the number of households in the population, N. However, the sample might be a biased reflection of the relevant population; for instance, it might have higher income levels or show a lower level of educational achievement. If these variables have been included in the bid curve, an estimated population mean bid, μ, can be derived by inserting population values for the relevant variables in the bid curve. This number could then be multiplied by N. Loomis (1987) has argued that if the sample is unrepresentative of the population, then the bid curve used for this purpose should be estimated using Weighted Least Squares rather than Ordinary Least Squares.

Third is the choice of the time period over which benefits should be aggregated. This will depend on the setting within which the CVM exercise is being performed. If the present value of environmental benefit flows over time is of interest, then benefits are normally discounted. Where an irreversible environmental loss is involved, then the present value is calculated by taking a perpetuity. In all cases of benefit or cost flows over time where the time period is sufficiently long, society is confronted by the necessity of using current preferences to measure future preferences, as well as with the equity implications of discounting. These matters are taken up in Chapters 8 and 9.

Stage Six: Evaluating the CVM Exercise

This entails an appraisal of how successful the application of CVM has been. Did the survey result in a high proportion of protest bids? Is there evidence that respondents understood the hypothetical market? How much experience did respondents have of the good in question? How well did the hypothetical market capture all aspects of the environmental good? What assumptions were necessary to produce the mean and aggregate bid figures? How well were the problem areas associated with CVM handled? How do the bid figures compare with those obtained in other studies? For an illustration of how to appraise a CVM study, the reader is referred to Smith (1992).

3.4 PROBLEM AREAS ASSOCIATED WITH CVM

In the following sections (3.4.1 and 3.4.2) we introduce some of the problems associated with contigent valuation. These themes are picked-up again, and expanded on, in Chapter 7, which takes an overview of the question of the validity and reliability of the valuation methods described in this and the next three chapters.

3.4.1. Biased Estimates of Value

Bias exists in CVM responses if they systematically understate or overstate true value. Bias may result from a number of causes:

Strategic Bias
If respondents believe that bids will be collected, they may understate their WTP for a welfare-improving change because environmental goods are typically non-excludable in consumption (the free-rider problem). For example, consider ten households living around a lake which is being polluted by a sewage works. Water quality can only improve if the works are upgraded, but this means higher sewerage bills to the households. Each household has an incentive to understate its maximum WTP to have the works upgraded (through higher bills), since they know that any improvement in water quality will benefit them as much as it benefits the other households, since the benefits of water quality are non-excludable in consumption. So by paying nothing, the freerider enjoys some benefits from improvements so long as someone states a willingness to pay higher bills, which is then translated into positive and better water quality.[1]

The incentive to behave in this fashion could be reduced by stating that all will pay the average bid, or by stressing the hypothetical nature of the exercise and urging respondents to provide a true value, if they are able to formulate one. Alternatively, if respondents believe that their bids are purely hypothetical, they may overstate WTP for an environmental benefit, as this increases the probability of the improvement going ahead. Such behaviour can be reduced by suggesting (contrary to the action proposed to reduce free riding) that the survey results may indeed influence policy; they are therefore not purely hypothetical and might be collected (on the basis of average WTP) in order to provide the environmental gain in question.

Mitchell and Carson (1989) suggest four steps for minimizing strategic bias. These are:

- Remove all outliers (but see the earlier discussion of outliers).
- Stress that payment by others is guaranteed.
- Conceal others' bids.

● Make the environmental change dependent on the bid (that is, prevent the respondents from taking the change as automatically forthcoming irrespective of their bids).

Besides trying to reduce the likelihood of strategic bias, economists have been keen to test for its presence. With respect to the latter intent, two approaches dominate. First, one can examine the distribution of received bids and compare this with the hypothesized distribution of true bids (for example, Brookshire et al., 1976). Strategic behaviour is assumed to flatten the distribution as relatively more high and low bids are made (over and under-statement). Negative bids are excluded, so that negative valuations accumulate as zeros. This tends to skew the distribution. Brookshire et al. assume that the true distribution is normal, concluding from this that there is no strategic bias in their sample. However, the true distribution might equally be bi-modal. Bid distributions can also be found in Hanley (1988) and Hanley and Craig (1991), where the distributions are shown to be skewed but not bi-modal. However, even if one observed a concentration of very high and very low bids, this could be caused by other factors such as undetected protest bidding. Very high values may in any case cancel out very low values.

The second approach is to include questions to test for bias in the survey. This was done by Rowe et al. (1980), where respondents were offered the chance to revise their bids following information on the mean bid recorded in the sample. Only one respondent revised his bid (an Economics professor!).

Hoehn and Randall (1987) have argued that strategic bias can be eliminated by using a referendum format (yes/no responses) to parametrically increasing amounts. They show that truthful responses are always optimal in such a setting[2]. Also, free riding is a risky strategy if supply of the public good is uncertain, but demand is certain: respondents may thus believe that they risk foregoing the environmental improvement by understating its true value, even though, if the good were provided, they might be able to free ride. Milon (1989) and Bergstrom et al. (1989) find no statistically significant evidence of strategic behaviour occurring. Mitchell and Carson (1989) argue that strategic behaviour is more likely in mail surveys than in telephone or interview surveys, as respondents have more time for "strategizing" in the first case. They conclude that, on balance, strategic bias is of minor importance in well-designed CVM studies, especially as informational requirements for strategic behaviour are high. Recent findings from game theory and from experimental economics indicate that truth-telling may be optimal in revealing preferences over public goods in many circumstances (Evans and Harris, 1982).

The available evidence suggests that CVM studies are less prone to strategic behaviour than was once believed. However, this may apply less to WTA formats: asking individuals to state minimum compensation sums is clearly different to maximum WTP. As discussed later, WTA measures are problematic for other reasons as well.

Design Bias

The design of the CVM study includes the way information is presented to individuals, the order in which it is presented, the question format and the amount and type of information presented. There is a wide body of evidence to suggest that survey design can affect responses:

(i) Choice of bid vehicle: the bid vehicle used can influence the average bid. For example, consider a study to value the preservation of a wilderness area. Individuals may state a lower WTP if the bid vehicle is an entry fee as opposed to a payment into a trust fund. This might be because individuals resent paying in such a direct way for something "natural"; the payment debases the recreation experience. More protest bids may also be encountered with the entry fee. This would also be the case if the bid vehicle were an unpopular tax. Rowe et al. (1980) found that WTP to preserve landscape quality was higher when an income tax increase was suggested than when entry fees were used. The best recommendation is to avoid controversial payment mechanisms and/or choose the one most likely to be used in practice. This also improves the credibility of the hypothetical market (see below).

(ii) Starting point bias: in bidding games, the starting point given to respondents can influence the final bid tendered. This is either because of impatience on the part of respondents or because the starting point suggests what size of bid is appropriate (which is likely when respondents have no experience of trading with the resource in question). Payment card mechanisms are subject to a similar form of bias known as anchoring bias. Tests for starting point bias have produced mixed results. For example, Hanley (1989) found no evidence of starting point bias in a CVM study of WTP to reduce nitrate pollution in drinking water, a conclusion also reached by Thayer (1981); whereas Boyle et al. (1986) and Rowe et al. (1980) found it to be statistically significant.

(iii) Nature of information provided. In a hypothetical market, respondents combine information provided to them regarding the good to be valued and how the market will work, with information they already hold on that good. Their responses may be influenced by either hypothetical market or commodity-specific information given to them in the survey. This is an interesting, if troublesome, phenomenon which implys that WTP or WTA values are endogenous to the valuation process. Samples et al. (1986) found that bids from respondents to preserve different animal species varied significantly according to the information they were provided with by researchers. However, one may point out that valuations of all resources are determined by the information set which individuals have access to at any point in time;   Randall (1986) has argued that one should *expect* CVM answers to vary under different information sets, otherwise the technique would be shown to be insensitive to what should be significant changes in "commodity framing".

Recent work by, for example, Boyle (1989), Bergstrom et al. (1989), Hanley and Munro (1992) and Whitehead and Blomquist (1991), has cast more light on when changes in the information set can be expected to affect CVM estimates.   For example, Whitehead and Blomquist show both theoretically and empirically how information on related environmental goods can change the value of another good.   In their research, telling respondents about alternative wetland sites significantly altered WTP to protect the Clear Creek wetland in Kentucky.

The effects of information may be inappropriately labelled as "bias", depending on the way in which WTP is changed by the new information set. Information which improves the knowledge of an individual concerning the characteristics of a good can be regarded as informing a consumption decision.   Information which alters the preferences could be regarded as creating a bias.   The issue then concerns how far preferences can be regarded as exogenous to the valuation process.

Mental Account Bias
This issue raises one of the most potentially damaging criticisms of CVM. The issue revolves around a two-step decision-making process on the part of an individual. First, an individual decides how much income, wealth and time to expend on environmental goods in general within a given time period. This fixed total is then allocated across all environmental assets of interest and all environmental services to be consumed (forest visits, for example). Call the total environmental "budget" B, and the amount allocated to any asset i, B_i. Suppose we seek a CVM estimate of mean value for i. Mental account bias exists for an individual if he/she bids an amount $\hat{B}_i$, where $B > \hat{B}_i > B_i$. At the limit, $\hat{B}_i = B$ so that the whole budget is spent. Either case results in the CVM bid overstating true value. For example, a person's entire "species preservation budget" could be expended on blue whales, even though they care about preserving other species too. Evidence that such behaviour exists was provided by Seip and Strand (1990). However, mental account bias was found to be absent in a study of WTP to preserve landscapes in the Yorkshire Dales by Willis and Garrod (1991). Whilst mental account bias is unlikely to be a factor in all CVM surveys, the possibility of its presence should always be taken into account (Hoevenagel, 1990).[3]

Hypothetical Market Error
This is said to occur if the very fact that respondents are asked for valuations in a hypothetical market makes their responses differ

systematically from true values. If the effect leads to both over and under statement, then it is not bias we are faced with, but a random (that is, non-systematic) error term. Mitchell and Carson argue that this is the correct interpretation of the phenomenon.

Undoubtedly a CVM study cannot hope to replicate all the important features of real markets which lead to particular preference revelations. Missing are the opportunities for people to debate with each other the worth of something; to "learn by doing", where demands result from a series of purchasing decisions; and the fact that actual purchases are costly. CVM studies do not, in general, force actual trade-offs between more environmental quality and less of something else, the trade-off being purely hypothetical. A degree of reassurance can be obtained from findings in behavioural psychology and sociology. Surveys by Schuman and Johnson (1976) and Hill (1981) on the link between attitude and behaviour find that in almost all cases a positive link exists between the two, and that in some cases attitudes and intentions are good predictors of actions. Aggregate intentions are very reasonable guides to aggregate behaviour.

One of the best known tests for hypothetical market "bias" was Bishop and Heberlein's (1979) study of WTP and WTA for duck-hunting permits in Wisconsin. They found CVM estimates of WTP of $11-$21, and WTA estimates of $68-$101 per permit, depending on the bid format used. They then mailed actual cash offers to hunters and discovered an actual mean WTA of $63. This was substantially lower than the WTA CVM estimate, which was produced with a take-it-or-leave-it format. Bishop and Heberlein thus concluded that compensating variation WTA estimates were biased upwards. In a later experiment on deer-hunting permits in Wisconsin, Heberlein and Bishop (1986) found that in four out of six scenarios, hypothetical WTP and actual WTP were insignificantly different. Hypothetical offers were sometimes higher and sometimes lower than actual offers. Where a take-it-or-leave-it format was used, then in both cases bids in the CVM study were insignificantly different from those actually tendered. Note, however, that WTA formats were not used in this experiment, and that on the whole WTA scenarios may suffer from greater credibility problems than WTP ones.

In conclusion, the extent to which hypothetical market "bias" occurs seems to depend on how questions are asked in the CVM study, on how realistic respondents feel the hypothetical market to be, and on whether WTP or WTA formats are used. This leads onto the next problem area: which measure of welfare should be chosen?

3.4.2 Choice of Welfare Measure

The two measures of welfare change used by economists, as we saw in Chapter 2, are WTP and WTA. In a seminal paper, Willig (1976) showed that these two measures would be very close to each other if the ratio of consumer's surplus to income (expenditure) was sufficiently small, and if the income elasticity of demand for the good was sufficiently low. Where these conditions did not hold, precise limits on the difference between the two measures could be calculated. Whilst Bockstael and McConnell (1980) criticized the applicability of Willig's findings to environmental benefit applications, many early CVM studies took the position that the two measures should give the same result. Randall and Stoll (1980) extended Willig's theorem (which was derived for price changes) to the quantity changes more commonly encountered in environmental valuation (and thus to the surplus measures of Chapter 2). They derived an expression for adjusting WTP into WTA amounts, and vice versa:

$$WTA - WTP = \alpha M^2 / Y \qquad (3.2)$$

where α is the "price flexibility of income", M is Marshallian consumer's surplus and Y is income. Using this equation, WTA and WTP can be shown to be very close (+/- 5%) under most conditions likely to be encountered in CVM work.

However, empirical work showed that (i) WTA formats gave a proportionately high number of protest bids; and that (ii) in most cases, stated WTP was significantly lower than stated WTA (see, for example, Rowe et al., 1980; Hammack and Brown, 1974; and Hanley, 1988). Moreover, experimental work by Knetsch and Sinden (1984) and Gregory (1986) found that WTA exceeded WTP: the difference in CVM measures could not therefore be put down to some weakness of the technique, although subsequent experimental work found that WTP and WTA converged with repeated trials, with WTA bids being revised downwards (e.g., Coursey et al., 1987). Three reasons why WTA > WTP are:

(i)   Actual WTA > actual WTP because of "loss aversion". Individuals value a given reduction in entitlements more highly than an equivalent increase in entitlements (Knetsch, 1989).

(ii)   Income and substitution effects. Income constrains WTP bids (unless limitless borrowing is possible), whereas WTA bids are unconstrained. Moreover, Randall and Stoll's method of calculating the difference due to income effects is now thought to be flawed. Hanemann (1986) showed that the α parameter used in equation (3.2) above is in fact a ratio of the income elasticity of demand for the good being valued η, and the elasticity of substitution between that good and all other goods, σ. Plausible values for η and σ imply quite large differences between WTA and WTP. If substitution possibilities are few, then WTA>>WTP (Hanemann, 1991). Recent experimental evidence would seem to support this conclusion (Shogren et al., 1992).

(iii)   Hoehn and Randall (1987) have argued that risk averse consumers who are given only one chance to value the good (rather than the repeated valuations that occur in a normal market) will on average overstate WTA and understate WTP, since they are unsure how much they value the good and so wish to avoid bidding an amount greater than its true value may turn out to be.

In addition to these reasons for a substantial discrepancy between WTA and WTP, recent research has shown that WTA formats are particularly prone to a large frequency of protest bids and/or a large frequency of outliers. The former because people are unwilling, on ethical grounds, to accept monetary compensation for the loss of an environmental benefit. Alternatively, people may be unable to believe in the proposed situation if WTA amounts are used for environmental gains (compensation for a gain foregone). The latter is due, in the case of environmental loss, to a kind of reverse protest bid: I feel very unhappy with the notion of compensation, so I state a (ridiculously) large amount. Therefore, although it can be argued that compensating surplus measures are preferable for cost-benefit analysis (since they take the status quo as the reference position), and that we can obtain these for welfare-decreasing moves only by measuring WTA, a consensus is emerging that, in most situations, WTP measures should be used, with the understanding that they probably underestimate WTA amounts in most cases.[4]

The phenomena of refusal-to-play and extreme-bidding found in contingent valuation studies may be symptomatic of a fundamental difference in philosophical beliefs. Neo-classical utilitarianism operates with a teleological outlook, whereas a considerable number of individuals may exist who hold to deontological philosophies (these terms are explained below). Utilitarianism has two main features: the principle of consequentialism and of utility. Consequentialism regards the rightness or wrongness of an act as being determined by the results that flow from it. The utility principle holds some specific type of state (for example, pleasure or happiness) as the only thing that is intrinsically good. The problem which economists are confronting seems to go beyond the utilitarian framework (Spash, 1992).

Teleological ethical theories place the ultimate criterion of morality in some non-moral value (e.g., welfare, utility, happiness) that results from acts. Such theories see only instrumental value in such acts, but intrinsic value in the consequences of these acts. In contrast, deontological ethical theories attribute intrinsic value to features of the act, themselves. For example, lying is wrong even when it produces better consequences than any other alternative.

Thus, individuals who regard the world from a deontological perspective will express absolute values beyond any possible trade. These could be an expression of the rights of animals to welfare or the rights of humans to life. Freeman (1986) has suggested that lexicographic preferences may be taken as a belief in such rights. When preferences are lexicographic, the individual cannot be compensated for the loss of a quantity of one good by increases in the quantity of one or more other goods, no matter how small the former or how large the latter. However, this approach reduces the difference between payment offered and compensation demanded to an anomaly within utilitarianism rather than a fundamental difference in philosophical outlook. In the context of intergenerational issues, the expression of a deontological belief system will conflict with the standard neo-classical approach. That is, the extent to which society accepts the current generation's moral judgement on the weights to be attached to future generations' welfare will be determined by factors other than utility and capital productivity. More specifically, if it is accepted that future generations have fundamental human rights, these must be upheld on their own grounds and not purely because of the utility they create now (Spash, 1993). We return to intergenerational rights at several points in forthcoming chapters.

3.5 CVM AND NON-USE VALUES

One advantage of CVM over other valuation techniques is the capacity of CVM to estimate non-user values. Individuals may derive utility from the existence of a recreational resource, even if they themselves do not physically visit that site. Thus, hunters capture use value from marshlands by hunting ducks, but someone who never visits these marshlands may still value their preservation.

In early CVM studies, the total value (TV) of a resource was thought to consist of four separable components:

$$TV = E(CS) + OV + XV + BV \qquad (3.4)$$

where $E(CS)$ is expected consumer's surplus (that is, use value), OV is option value, XV is existence value and BV is bequest value. Option value, a sort of insurance premium to ensure the supply of the environmental good, was thought to be positive for risk averse individuals facing supply uncertainty, following Weisbrod (1964). However, given demand uncertainty, option value may be negative. According to Shogren and Crocker (1990), option value is only definitely positive when there is no demand uncertainty, and where supply uncertainty can be completely removed by the proposed resource allocation. Bequest value and existence value were first suggested by Krutilla (1967), and may arise from either selfish or altruistic motives. Their existence is suggested by the public's WTP to preserve, for example, the blue whale and rain forests. Walsh et al. (1984) tried to estimate all of the elements of total value shown above for the preservation of wilderness areas in Colorado. They found that the sum of non-use values (XV + BV + OV) was around 40% of total value. Ignoring such non-use values would therefore, clearly lead to an under-estimation of the value of a resource such as wilderness. Further empirical evidence on the importance of non-use values can be found, for example, in Navrud (1988), where non-use benefits accounted for 63% of the total value of improving water quality, and in Bowker and Stoll (1988).

Current practice with respect to the components of total value is to categorize them into option price and existence values (with no distinction being made between E(CS) and OV, or between XV and BV). Option price is defined as the relevant measure of user benefit under both supply and demand uncertainty. Brookshire et al. (1983) report WTP option price estimates for wildlife encounters under varying degrees of supply uncertainty, given both certain and uncertain demand by hunters. Option price increases as supply uncertainty declines. Pure existence values were also estimated and found to be significant elements of value.

In measuring different components of total value, two practices should be avoided. These are:

(i)   Asking each respondent to bid separate amounts for each element of benefit, since this invites double counting and increases the likelihood of hypothetical market bias/error.

(ii)   Asking respondents to decompose an already-given total bid into bid categories, since this has been found to suffer from methodological difficulties.

Responses may be separated into groups of users and non-users according to information elicited in the course of the interview. This allows the calculation of separate user and non-user bids. With respect to option price, each respondent can be given a range of supply possibilities and asked to bid on them individually. These ranges would partially overlap across respondents. The degree of demand uncertainty a respondent was operating under when questioned can also be discovered by direct questioning[5]. We return to the important subject of existence values in Chapter 14.

3.6 CONCLUSIONS

As will be evident from the preceding material, results from CVM studies are heavily dependent on how well the study is designed, carried out and interpreted. Given that these tasks are performed well, then CVM is a useful technique for estimating economic values for some non-market resources. This conclusion has been reached by (i) examining the results of individual CVM surveys; (ii) experimenting with the degree of repeatability of CVM results; and (iii) using other methodologies alongside CVM to value the same resource. All these approaches are discussed in Chapter 7.

Rowe and Cheshunt (1983, p.70) give the following description of what constitutes a "good" CVM study:

> It must be informative; clearly understood; realistic by relying on established patterns of behaviour and legal institutions; have uniform application to all respondents; and, hopefully, leave the respondent with a feeling that the situation and his responses are not only credible but important.

The conditions and procedures under which CVM operates best can be summarized as follows:

(i)   The hypothetical market must be both credible and realistic.

(ii)   The payment vehicle used and/or the welfare measure (WTP or WTA) should not be controversial or invoke ethical opposition (that is, it should be neutral).

(iii)   Respondents should be presented with sufficient information regarding the resource in question and the means of payment for their bid to be an informed one.

(iv)   Ideally, respondents should be familiar with the resource in question, and have some experience of trading in it.

(v)   Where possible, WTP measures should be sought, as respondents often have difficulty with the notion of accepting monetary compensation for changes in environmental service flows. This is especially true for welfare-increasing moves.

(vi)   A big enough sample size should be chosen to permit the desired level of confidence intervals and reliability.

(vii)   Tests for bias, should be included and strategies adopted to minimize strategic bias in particular.

(viii) Protest bids should be identified.

(ix)   It should be ascertained whether the sample has characteristics similar to those of the population, and adjustments made if necessary.

(x)   A bid curve, should be estimated and parameter signs checked to see whether they accord with a priori expectations. A minimum value of 15% for the adjusted R is recommended by Mitchell and Carson.

Recently, the National Oceanic and Atmospheric Administration of the USA commissioned a "Blue Ribbon" panel of experts to consider the use of CVM in assessing damages due to oil spillages (under the Oil Pollution Act, 1990). This panel consisted of a number of famous economists, such as Nobel Prize winners Kenneth Arrow and Robert Solow. The panel was also asked to investigate the concept of existence value. The panel's report (NOAA, 1993) is a qualified support for CVM. The panel state that existence values are a theoretically meaningful aspect of value. As regards the ability of CVM to estimate such values, the panel noted five main problem areas:

1. CVM results can be inconsistent with rational choice (the "embedding" problem, discussed in Chapter 7);

2. CVM can suffer from mental account bias, especially when respondents are not adequately informed as to substitutes;

3. The issue of the population over which to aggregate benefits;

4. The effects of providing information; and

5. Warm glow effects (see Chapter 7).

However, the panel felt that so long as certain guidelines were followed, CVM results could be judged as both meaningful and useful indicators of natural resource damages. These guidelines are that (i) WTP, not WTAC, measures should be sought; (ii) mail-slot surveys should be avoided; (iii) respondents should be given full information on the resource change (including information on substitutes), and be asked how well they understand this information; (iv) open-ended responses should be rejected in favour of closed-ended referendum formats; (v) random sampling of the population of interest; (vi) respondents should be reminded about the need to reduce expenditure on some item on their budget in order to be able to pay their stated bid; and (vii) careful pre-testing survey instruments should be carried out. For further details on the panel's recommendations, readers are referred to their report.

APPENDIX 3.1: THE CONTINGENT RANKING METHOD

N.B.   This section contains material of a significantly greater level of difficulty than in the rest of the chapter: it can be omitted if desired with no loss of continuity.

Contingent Ranking (CR) has its theoretical basis in the random utility maximization model due to McFadden. Respondents are asked to rank different combinations of environmental quality (for example, differing noise levels, N) and "access costs", C, from most preferred to least preferred. A question might thus take the form:

Please rank the following possible situations:

1. Ambient noise levels of about 80 decibels, and a local tax level of £2,000/yr.
2. Noise levels of 120 dbs and a tax of £1,750/yr.
3. Noise levels of 140 dbs and a tax of £1,500/yr.

If respondents order these alternatives from most to least preferred, then under certain restrictions, this yields sufficient information, when combined with socio-economic data, to evaluate a change in, in this case, noise levels. It can be argued that such a ranking procedure is easier for people to handle conceptually, when faced with the situation of putting a money value on a non-market good, relative to the procedure involved in contingent valuation. However, there are numerous problems associated with the technique, which we discuss following an outline of the procedure involved in a CR study. The first step is to set up a series of alternatives to be ranked. Evidence shows that using too many (>4?) options confuses respondents and reduces the value of information gained from the study. The relationship between decision variables (here, N_i and C_i) must be decided. Next, define an indirect utility function[6] such as V^a, which is linear, must be defined:

$$V^a = \alpha_1 N_i + \alpha_2 C_i \tag{A3.1}$$

If noise falls by one unit ($\Delta N=1$) with utility held constant, C can also fall, in amount α_1/α_2. This amount (which is positive, since both parameters are assumed to be negative) is WTP in this simple model for a one unit fall in N.

If other factors such as income are to be included, then they must enter interactively with the choice variables N and/or C. For example, if income Y is thought relevant, then we could estimate:

$$V^b = \beta_1 N_i + \beta_2 C_i + \beta_3 (C/Y)_i \tag{A3.2}$$

The welfare measure of a change in the environmental variable N is now calculated by taking the total differential of the indirect utility function, setting $dV=0$ (that is, constant utility). This gives, for equation (A3.2):

$$WTP = \frac{\beta_1 dN}{\beta_2 + \dfrac{\beta_3}{Y}} \tag{A3.3}$$

The maximum likelihood estimator used to estimate these equations will depend on assumptions about the stochastic component of the utility function. Typically, this component is assumed to have a Weibul distribution; thus a maximum likelihood logit model routine will give the maximum likelihood values for the β parameters above.

Contingent Ranking has been used to study visibility benefits in both rural areas, such as, Mesa Verde National Park (Rae, 1983), and urban areas, such as, Cincinatti (Rae, 1981). It has also been used to estimate the value of a reduction in traffic fumes in Philadelphia (Lareau and Rae, 1985) and water quality improvement benefits on the Monogahela (Desvouges and Smith, 1986). Problems with the contingent ranking method are as follows:

1. The information obtained concerns ordinal measures of WTP, unlike the cardinal measures obtained by CVM. Thus, contingent ranking (CR) requires a larger sample than CVM.

2. CR is subject to bid vehicle bias.

3. The CR estimate of value will depend on: (i) the number of alternatives to be ranked; (ii) the range over which any variable is specified; and (iii) how variables such as income, age and sex are introduced into the indirect utility function (that is, what interactions are specified). As Lareau and Rae (p.730) comment:

   If prices are too low, respondents order alternatives by focusing mainly on the environmental attribute, while if prices are too high, respondents order alternatives according to the price attribute; precise trade-off estimates cannot be determined in either situation.

4. To produce estimates commensurate with exact welfare measures, the way in which respondents rank alternatives must be specified.

5. The technique is statistically more demanding than CVM.

6. The probability of selecting a particular alternative, and of ranking alternatives in a particular order, has to be assumed to be independent of excluded alternatives. This implies that valuation of one environmental good has to be assumed to be independent of the valuations of other environmental goods: an assumption, as Lareau and Rae point out, is of doubtful authenticity.

REFERENCES

Bergstrom J, Stoll J and Randall A (1989) "Information effects in contingent markets" *American Journal of Agricultural Economics* 71: 685-691.

Bishop R and Heberlein T (1979) "Measuring values of extra market goods: Are indirect measures biased?" *American Journal of Agricultural Economics* 61 (5): 926-930.

Bockstael K and McConnell K (1980) "Calculating equivalent and compensating variation for natural resource facilities" *Land Economics* 56 (1): 56-62.

Bowker J M and Stoll J (1988) "Use of dichotomous choice nonmarket methods to value the whooping crane resource" *American Journal of Agricultural Economics* 70: 372-381.

Boyle K (1989) "Commodity specification and the framing of contingent valuation questions" *Land Economics* 65: 57-63.

Boyle K, Bishop R and Welsh M (1986) "Starting Point Bias in Contingent Valuation Surveys" *Land Economics* 61: 188-194.

Brookshire D, Eubanks L and Randall A (1983) "Estimating option price and existence values for wildlife resources" *Land Economics* 59 (1): 1-15.

Brookshire D, Ives B and Schulze W (1976) "The valuation of aesthetic preferences" *Journal of Environmental Economics and Management* 3 (4): 325-346.

Brookshire D, Randall A and Stoll J (1980) "Valuing increments and decrements in natural resource service flows" *American Journal of Agricultural Economics* 62 (3): 478-488.

Cameron T (1988) "A new paradigm for valuing non-market goods using referendum data" *Journal of Environmental Economics and Management*.

Cameron T and James M "Efficient estimation methods for use with closed ended contingent valuation survey data" *Review of Economics and Statistics* 69: 269-276.

Davis R (1963) "Recreation planning as an economic problem" *Natural Resources Journal* 3 (2): 239-249.

Desvouges W and Smith V K (1986) *Measuring Water Quality Benefits* Boston: Kluwer Nijhoff Publishing.

Desvouges W, Smith V and Fisher A (1987) "Option price estimates for water quality improvements" *Journal of Environmental Economics and Management* 14: 248-267.

Desvouges W, Smith V and McGivney M (1983) "A comparison of alternative approaches for estimating recreation and related benefits of water quality improvements" Washington: EPA.

Evans R and Harris F (1982) "A Bayesian analysis of the free rider meta-game" *Southern Economic Journal* 49: 137-149.

Fisher A and Raucher R (1984) "Intrinsic benefits of improved water quality" in V K Smith (editor) *Advances in Applied Economics* Greenwich, Conn.: JAI Press.

Freeman A M (1986) "The ethical basis of the economic view of the environment" in D van der Veer and C Pierce (editors) *People, Penguin and Plastic Trees: Basic Issues in Environmental Ethics* Belmont, CA: Wadsworth Publishing Co.

Gregory R (1986) "Interpreting measures of economic loss" *Journal of Environmental Economics and Management* 13: 325-337.

Hammack J and Brown G (1974) *Waterfowl and Wetlands: Towards Bioeconomic Analysis* Baltimore: Johns Hopkins Press.

Hanley N (1988) "Using contingent valuation to value environmental improvements" *Applied Economics* 20: 541-549.

Hanley N (1989) "Problems in valuing environmental improvements resulting from agricultural policy changes: The case of nitrate pollution" Discussion paper no. 89/1, Economic Dept, University of Stirling.

Hanley N and Craig S H (1991) "Wilderness preservation and the Krutilla Fisher model: The case of Scotland's Flow Country" *Ecological Economics* 4: 145-164.

Hanley N and Munro A (1992) "The effects of information in contingent markets for environmental goods: A survey and some new evidence" Institute for Economic Research, Queens University, Discussion Paper 848.

Heberlein T and Bishop R (1986) "Assessing the validity of contingent valuation: Three experiments" *Science of the Total Environment* 56: 99-107.

Hill R (1981) "Attitudes and behaviour" in M Rosenberg and R Turner (editors) *Social Psychology: Sociological Perspectives* New York: Basic Books.

Hoehn J and Randall A (1987) "A satisfactory benefit cost indicator from contingent valuation" *Journal of Environmental Economics and Management* 14 (3): 226-247.

Hoevenagel R (1990) "The validity of the contingent valuation method: Some aspects on the basis of three Dutch studies" Paper to the European Association of Environmental and Resource Economists" conference, Venice, 1990.

Kahneman D and Knetsch J (1992) "The purchase of moral satisfaction" *Journal of Environmental Economics and Management* 22(1): 57-70.

Knetsch J (1989) "The endowment effect and evidence of nonreversible indifference curves" *American Economic Review*, December 1277-1284.

Knetsch J (1990) "Environmental policy implications of disparities between willingness to pay and compensation demanded" *Journal of Environmental Economics and Management* 18: 227-237.

Knetsch J and Sinden J (1984) "Willingness to pay and compensation demanded: Experimental evidence of an unexpected disparity" *Quarterly Journal of Economics* 94 (3): 507-521.

Krutilla J (1967) "Conservation reconsidered" *American Economic Review* 57: 787-796.

Lareau T and Rae D (1987) "Valuing WTP for diesel odour reductions: An application of the contingent ranking technique" *Southern Economic Journal* 728-742.

Loomis J (1987) "Expanding contingent value sample estimates" *Land Economics* 63 (4): 396-402.

Milon, J (1989) "Contingent valuation experiments for strategic behaviour" *Journal of Environmental Economics and Management* 17: 293-308.

Mitchell R and Carson R (1989) *Using Surveys to Value Public Goods: the Contingent Valuation Method* Washington DC: Resources for the Future.

NOAA (1993) Report of the NOAA panel on contingent valuation. Mimeo dated 12th January 1993, National Oceanic and Atmospheric Administration.

Rae D (1983) "The value to visitors of improving visibility at Mesa Verde and Great Smoky National Parks" in R Rowe and L Chestnut (editors) *Managing Air Quality and Scenic Resources at National Parks and Wilderness Areas* Boulder, Co.: Westview Press.

Randall A (1986) "The possibility of satisfactory benefit estimation with contingent markets" in R Cummings, D Brookshire and W Schulze (editors) *Valuing Public Goods: an Assessment of the Contingent Valuation Method* Totowa, NJ: Rowan and Allanheld.

Randall A and Stoll J (1980) "Consumers surplus in commodity space" *American Economic Review* 70 (3): 449-455.

Rowe R and Chestnut L (1983) *The Value of Visibility: Economic Theory and Applications for Air Pollution Control*, Cambridge MA: Abt Books.

Rowe R, d'Arge R and Brookshire D (1980) "An experiment on the economic value of visibility" *Journal of Environmental Economics and Management* 7: 1-19.

Samples K, Dixon J and Gowen M (1986) "Information disclosure and endangered species valuation" *Land Economics* 62 (3): 306-312.

Schuman H and Johnson M (1976) "Attitudes and behaviour" in A Inkeles (editor) *Annual Review of Sociology* Paolo Alto, Annual Reviews Inc.

Seip K and Strand J (1990) "Willingness to pay for environmental goods in Norway: A contingent valuation study with real payment" Memorandum 12, Dept. of Economics, University of Oslo.

Shogren J and Crocker T (1990) "Adaptation and the option value of uncertain environmental resources" *Ecological Economics* 2(4): 301-310.

Shogren J, Shinn S, Hayes D and Kliebenstien J (1992) "Experimental evidence on the divergence between measures of value" Mimeo, Economics Dept., Iowa State University.

Smith V K (1992) "Arbitrary values, good causes and premature verdicts" *Journal of Environmental Economics and Management* 22(1): 71-89.

Spash C L (1992) "The rights and wrongs of intergenerational externalities" Mimeo, Dept. of Economics, University of Stirling.

Spash C L (1993) "Economics, ethics, and long term environmental damages" *Environmental Ethics* 15 (2): 117-132.

Walsh R, Loomis J and Gillman R (1984) "Valuing option, existence and bequest demands for wilderness" *Land Economics* 60 (1): 14-29.

Weisbrod B (1964) "Collective consumption services of individual consumption goods" *Quarterly Journal of Economics* 78 (3): 471-477.

Whitehead J and Blomquist G (1991) "Measuring contingent values for wetlands: Effects of information about related environmental goods" *Water Resources Research* 27: 2523-2531.

Willig R (1976) "Consumers surplus without apology" *American Economic Review* 66: 589-597.

Willis K and Garrod G (1991) "Landscape values: A contingent valuation approach and case study of the Yorkshire Dales National Park" Working paper 21, Countryside Change Centre, University of Newcastle-upon-Tyne.

ENDNOTES

1. See Johannson (1991, p.105) for more details on free riding and public goods.

2. Although, as Mitchell and Carson point out, this application of Zeckhauser's political referendum model does not strictly carry over since more than 'vote' is cast.

3. The related problem of embedding is discussed in Chapter 7, the work of Kahneman and Knetsch (1992) being particularly relevant in this regard.

4. For an account of the importance of systematic WTP/WTA divergences, see Knetsch (1990).

5. For instance, by asking them to assess the probability of their visiting a particular forest sometime in the future.

6. The indirect utility function is written with utility as a function of prices and income. It can be derived by substituting Marshallian demand functions into a conventional direct utility function.

4 VALUING ENVIRONMENTAL GOODS (2): THE HEDONIC PRICING METHOD

4.1 INTRODUCTION

Hedonic pricing (HP) derives from the characteristics theory of value, developed by Lancaster (1966), Griliches (1971) and Rosen (1974), with the first HP studies being published in the late 1960s and early 1970s (for example, Ridker and Henning, 1967; Anderson and Crocker, 1971). The method identifies environmental service flows as elements of a vector of characteristics describing a marketed good, typically housing. HP seeks to find a relationship between the levels of environmental services (such as noise levels or total suspended particulate levels), and the prices of the marketed goods (houses). HP has been used to value such things as noise levels around airports (O'Byrne et al., 1985), earthquake risks (Brookshire et al., 1985), urban air quality (Brookshire et al., 1982) and amenity values of woodland (Willis and Garrod, 1991).

In this chapter, the theoretical basis for HP is first considered, followed by an explanation of the method by which HP analyses are carried out. The chapter concludes by noting some of the problems associated with the technique.

4.2 THE CHARACTERISTICS THEORY OF VALUE

The characteristics theory of value, sometimes referred to as the Lancaster-Rosen approach, states that any given unit within a commodity class can be described by a vector of characteristics, z. For example, the commodity class could be housing, and the unit a particular house. The price for which a given unit can be sold is a function of these characteristics. Differentiating the unit price with respect to the quantity of any characteristic gives the implicit price of that characteristic. Individuals maximizing utility will rearrange their purchases of the commodity until the marginal rate of substitution[1] between a composite commodity (which represents everything

74

else they buy), x, and each characteristic, $z_i(i=1...n)$, is equal to the implicit price of that characteristic[2]. Consumers will bid an amount $B_i[z,(.)]$ for an increase in the characteristic. If the market reaches equilibrium, then every consumer will be in a position where the marginal bid, $\delta B_i/\delta z_i$, is equal to the implicit price (that is, marginal cost) of the characteristic (Palmquist, 1991).

For example, house prices should reflect the capitalized value of environmental quality to the home-owner. The representative individual is assumed to have a utility function that is *weakly separable*. This, in general terms, means that the marginal rate of substitution between two goods, a and b appearing in an individual's utility function, is independent of the quantities of all other goods. The implication in HP is that, if the representative individual's utility function is weakly separable in housing, then a demand curve for environmental quality can be estimated ignoring the prices of all other goods (see Freeman, 1979). *Weak complementarity* is also assumed. That is, if the level of purchases of the private good (here, housing, h) is zero, then the marginal willingness to pay for, or marginal demand price of, environmental quality is also zero. Thus, HP is incapable of estimating non-user values and can only "pick-up" those elements of environmental quality change reflected by house prices.

4.3 HOW THE METHOD WORKS

This section follows Freeman (1979), which is an excellent introduction to early work on non-market good valuation. The first step in any HP study is to decide which environmental quality variable is of interest, and then to ascertain whether sufficiently disaggregated, spatial data are available, along with data on house prices and housing characteristics. Once this has been verified, the typical HP exercise proceeds in two stages: estimation of a hedonic price function and estimation of a demand curve for some element of environmental quality.

Stage One: Estimation of Hedonic Price Function
In this stage, the relationship between the environmental variable of interest and a related marketed good is estimated, including as explanatory variables all other characteristics thought to be relevant in determining the price of this marketed good. The choice of these explanatory variables is potentially crucial, for reasons that will become apparent. For example, house prices (P_h) within a city might depend on: site characteristics (S_i), such as the number of rooms, the size of garden and whether a garage is provided or not; neighbourhood characteristics (N_j), such as ethnic composition, crime rate and number of schools in the area; and environmental quality variables (Q_k), such as air quality and noise levels. The following hedonic price

equation can be estimated using ordinary least squares (OLS):

$$P_h = P\ (S_i, N_j, Q_k) \quad [\ i=1..m,\ j=1..n,\ k=1..l\ ] \tag{4.1}$$

This equation allows implicit prices for each characteristic to be calculated. If (4.1) is linear, these implicit prices will be constants. However, linearity will only occur if consumers can "re-package" characteristics. As Rosen (1974) has observed, this is improbable. Householders cannot buy one characteristic of a given house (garden size, say) and combine it with a different characteristic of a second house (e.g. number of rooms) when making their purchase. Therefore, (4.1) is expected to be non-linear, giving implicit prices dependent upon the quantity of each characteristic consumed. But which non-linear form is most appropriate? In Figure 4.1, one possible partial relationship between house prices and some measure of environmental quality, Q_l (air quality), is shown. As may be seen, as the air quality level increases, the price of a house rises (higher levels of Q_l are thus desirable, ceteris paribus), but at a decreasing rate. The marginal cost of air quality thus falls as the level of air quality rises. An alternative possibility, not shown in Figure 4.1, is that house prices rise at an increasing rate as air quality rises; this means that the marginal costs of air quality are increasing. Both scenarios are plausible.

The implicit price of a given environmental characteristic is obtained from equation (4.1) by partially differentiating (4.1) with respect to the characteristic of interest. For example, for Q, the implicit price would be:

$$\delta P_h / \delta Q_l = P\ (S_i, N_j, Q_k) \tag{4.2}$$

This implicit price $\delta P / \delta Q$ is called the *rent differential*, r, and is a measure of the value of a marginal change in the environmental quality variable Q_l. In equation (4.2), it is shown to be a function of the levels of all the variables in the hedonic price equation. Simplifying matters, under certain conditions the implicit price will depend only on the level of that characteristic. In Figure 4.1, the shape of the function relating house prices to Q_l indicates that the implicit price falls as the level of air quality rises, as mentioned above.

The rent differential shows the marginal cost of buying an increase in the quality variable Q_l and (if the housing market is functioning perfectly) the marginal benefit of a one unit increase in the quality variable (Freeman, 1974). A perfectly functioning market has perfect information flows. Also, all individuals trading in the market are able to adjust their buying behaviour, moving along the rent differential curve $\delta P_l / \delta Q_l$ until the marginal value to each of an improvement in environmental quality is equal to the marginal cost of that improvement, defined by the implicit price. In Figure

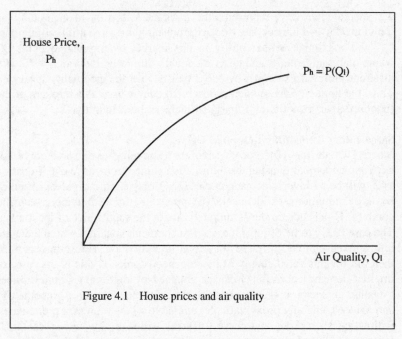

Figure 4.1   House prices and air quality

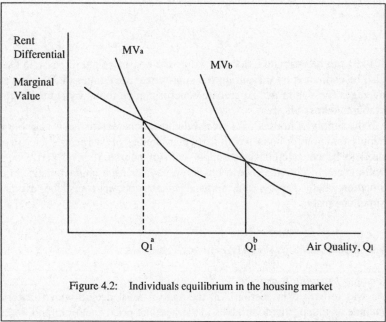

Figure 4.2:   Individuals equilibrium in the housing market

4.2, the function MV_a represents the marginal valuation of air quality by individual "a", which declines due to diminishing marginal utility. Individual "a" will maximize his/her utility in this market by moving to point Q^a_1 where marginal benefits and costs are equal. Similarly, individual "b", with different preferences shown by MV_b, will choose the air quality level Q^b_1. Thus, the implicit price (which is observed) can be used as a measure of the (unobservable) benefits of a marginal increase in air quality.

Stage Two: Estimating a Demand Curve

Stage Two of the HP process involves estimating a demand curve for environmental quality using the information gained from stage one. Equation (4.2) will be an inverse demand curve[3] for Q_1 only if all individuals affected by noise pollution are identical. The procedure for estimating a demand curve for Q depends on the assumptions about the supply side of the market. The case likely to be of most interest is a short-run situation where there are only a fixed number of houses in any air quality class. House-buyers must then bid for this fixed supply of heterogeneous units. If this is the case, an implicit demand curve for Q can be obtained by regressing implicit prices r against Q, socio-economic variables thought relevant such as income (Y) and age (A), and any proxy variables available which represent preferences. Estimating such a demand curve for areas within a city, with these areas indexed by "i", gives the inverse demand curve:

$$r_{1i} = P (Q_1, Y_i, A_i) \qquad (4.3)$$

If (4.3) can be estimated, then the value of a non-marginal increase in Q_1 can also be estimated by measuring the appropriate area under (4.3), using area averages for Y_i and A_i. Aggregate benefits can be found by summing these amounts across all areas.

If the supply of houses with given bundles of characteristics is variable, the supply function for houses with particular bundles of characteristics will also need to be considered. This supply will, of course, depend partly on the willingness of potential house-buyers to pay for each characteristic. In this situation, both supply and demand in the market must be estimated simultaneously.

4.4 PROBLEMS WITH THE HP METHOD

Omitted Variable Bias

As was remarked in section 4.3, the analyst must decide which factors to include as independent variables in the hedonic price equation (and, indeed, in the demand curve). This selection process can give rise to problems. If a variable which has a significant effect on house prices, and which is correlated with some or all of the included variables, is omitted from the hedonic price equation, this will influence the coefficients of the estimated variables. This leads to biased estimates for these coefficients and for the implicit prices (for a recent application, see Atkinson and Crocker, 1992).

Multi-Collinearity

Several of the independent variables included in the hedonic price equation may be closely correlated with each other. For example, if a house is sited near a quarry, as dust levels increase so do noise levels. Such multi-collinearity can result in a number of problems. These include imprecise coefficient estimates (high standard errors), and intuitively "wrong" signs on variables, even though the R^2 may be high (Maddala, 1979). Multi-collinearity can also bring about considerable instability in parameter estimates and, if serious, can reduce the confidence attached to model predictions (Stewart, 1984).

Choice of Functional Form

What functional form should be chosen for the hedonic price equation? We have argued above that the hedonic price equation is unlikely to be linear. Indeed, if it were linear, a demand equation could not be estimated because the implicit price for air quality would be constant. However, economic theory does not suggest which non-linear form is to be preferred. Garrod and Allinson (1991) have argued that there is unlikely to be one universally preferred functional form, and that, even for a given data set, criteria for functional form selection may be conflicting. These criteria, which are both statistical and practical, include (i) requiring as few parameter estimates as possible (parsimony); (ii) requiring that the parameters have clear economic interpretations; (iii) choosing the form which economizes on computing time; (iv) explaining the observed data well; and (v) making good predictions (for example, that the form chosen correctly predicts the change in house prices from a reduction in noise levels (Garrod and Allinson, p.3).

Functional forms that predict well (for example, flexible forms) may not have sensible interpretations for all the parameters to be estimated. Cropper et al. (1988) compared alternative functional forms in terms of the difference between predicted marginal values and actual marginal values. These actual values were observable in their study as they applied Monte Carlo analysis to a simulated data set: once a utility function has been specified in such analysis, then actual welfare measures can be calculated. Cropper et al. found that linear and linear Box-Cox functional forms performed best on this criterion.

Market Segmentation

Housing markets are often segmented on grounds such as ethnic composition, rental versus owner-occupied, and price bracket. Failing to recognize such segmentation in an HP study, when it is present in reality, will result in biased coefficients in the hedonic price function; segmentation implies that demand parameters vary across segments. The HP analyst must recognize such segmentation and estimate separate hedonic price equations for each segment. But deciding how to divide up the housing market of a city can be a difficult problem. Michaels and Smith (1990) solved this problem by asking realtors (estate agents) in Boston to segment the housing market in that city. On the basis of price brackets, four distinct sub-markets were identified. Separate hedonic price equations were then estimated for each segment in order to value the disutility of living close to hazardous waste sites.

Expected versus Actual Characteristic Levels

In using the HP approach to value environmental attributes, current levels of environmental quality are assumed to influence house prices. However, house prices can also be influenced by expected changes in quality levels. For instance, the prospect of a by-pass in a busy residential zone can keep prices higher than in the absence of such expectations. The implicit price would fail to measure the valuation of current noise levels alone. If expectations are important, excluding them from the HP equation leads to omitted variable bias.

Restrictive Assumptions

HP gives an accurate estimate of the value of environmental quality only if (continuing the house price/air quality example): (i) All buyers in the housing market are perfectly informed of air quality levels at every possible housing location. (ii) All buyers in the market are able to move to utility maximizing positions (otherwise, marginal cost is not equivalent to marginal WTP). (iii) The housing market is in equilibrium; the vector of implicit prices is such that the market clears at all times. Clearly, these assumptions will never fully describe reality. Furthermore, the assumption of weak complementarity implies that only those environmental improvements that have an impact on the property market will be measured.

Finally, Kask and Maani (1992) have pointed out that HP applications to the value of changes in risky environmental events (such as the Brookshire et al. study of earthquake risks in California) are likely to produce biased estimates of consumer benefits of avoiding or reducing such risk. In choosing whether or not to buy a home in a safe area of San Fransisco people are engaging in self-protection. When paying a premium for such a house, they reduce the probability of being located in an earthquake zone and thus reduce the expected loss from an earthquake. A problem arises in that individuals' subjective values of such losses are likely to be either less than or greater than the scientific (or endowed) probability of such events. This occurs for two reasons. First, studies have shown that people consistently over-value very low probability events, and consistently under-value high probability events (Lichtenstein et al., 1978; Viscusi and Magat, 1987). Second, people may have too little information, or information of too low a quality, to arrive at "correct" probabilities. The implication, as Kask and Maani show, is that hedonic prices may either over-estimate or under-estimate welfare changes (according to whether a low or high objective probability event is being considered, and to the amount and quality of information available to individuals).

4.5   CONCLUSIONS

As has been pointed out in the preceding section, there are many problems associated with the HP technique. Perhaps the most important of these are the assumptions made about the related market (the housing market, in this chapter). However, the method does make use of data on actual behaviour, unlike the contingent valuation method described in Chapter 3. Although this chapter on HP has concentrated on house prices and environmental quality levels, the technique is applicable to other goods. HP can be used to estimate the implicit price of any observable characteristic of any good, so long as the weak complementarity assumption holds. HP could therefore be used to estimate the value of the "green premium" on environmentally-friendly consumer goods, or the value of environmental risk on human health through wage differentials. Results from hedonic wage studies on the value of risk are mentioned in Chapter 6.

REFERENCES

Anderson G and Bishop R (1986) "The valuation problem" in D Bromley (editor) *Natural Resource Economics* Boston: Kluwer-Nijhoff.

Anderson R J and Crocker T D (1971) "Air pollution and residential property values" *Urban Studies* 8: 171-180.

Atkinson S and Crocker T (1992) "Econometric health production functions: Relative bias from omitted variables and measurement error" Journal of Environmental Economics and Management 22 (1): 12-24.

Brookshire D, Thayer M A, Schulze W D and d'Arge R C (1982) "Valuing public goods: a comparison of survey and hedonic approaches" *American Economic Review* 72: 165-178.

Brookshire D S, Thayer M A, Tischirhart J, and Schulze W D (1985) "A test of the expected utility model: Evidence from earthquake risk." *Journal of Political Economy* 93, 369-389.

Cropper M, Deck L and McConnell K (1988) "On the choice of functional form for hedonic price functions" *Review of Economics and Statistics* 70: 668-675.

Freeman A M (1974) "Air pollution and property values: a further comment" *Review of Economics and Statistics* 56: 554-566.

Freeman A M (1979) *The Benefits of Environmental Improvement*. Washington DC: Resources for the Future.

Garrod G and Allinson P (1991) *The Choice of Functional Form for Hedonic House Price Functions*. Discussion paper 23, Countryside Change initiative, University of Newcastle-upon-Tyne.

Griliches Z (1971) *Price Indexes and Quality Change*. Cambridge MA: Harvard University Press.

Kask S and Maani S (1992) "Uncertainty, information and hedonic pricing" *Land Economics* 68 (2): 170-184.

Lancaster K J (1966) "A new approach to consumer theory" *Journal of Political Economy* 74: 132-157.

Lichtenstein S, Slovic P, Fischoff B, Layman M, and Combs B (1978) "Judged frequency of lethal events" *Journal of Experimental Psychology* 4 (6): 551-578.

Maddala G S (1979) *Econometrics* Tokyo: McGraw Hill

Michaels R and Smith V (1990) "Market segmentation and valuing amenities with hedonic models: the case of hazardous waste sites" *Journal of Urban Economics* 28: 232-242.

O'Byrne P, Nelson J and Seneca J (1985) "Housing values, census estimates, disequilibrium and the environmental cost of airport noise" *Journal of Environmental Economics and Management* 12: 169-178.

Palmquist R (1991) "Hedonic methods" in J B Braden and C D Kolstad (editors) *Measuring the Demand for Environmental Quality* Amsterdam: Elsevier.

Ridker R G and Henning J A (1967) "The determinants of residential property values with special reference to air pollution" *Review of Economics and Statistics* 49: 246-257.

Rosen S (1974) "Hedonic prices and implicit markets: product differentiation in pure competition" *Journal of Political Economy* 82: 34-55.

Stewart J (1984) *Understanding Econometrics* London: Hutchison.

Viscusi W and Magat W (1987) *Learning about risk: consumer and worker responses to hazard information* Cambridge, Ma.: Harvard University Press.

Willis K and Garrod G (1991) "The Hedonic Price method and the valuation of countryside characteristics" Countryside Change Centre working paper 14, University of Newcastle-upon-Tyne.

ENDNOTES

1.   That is, the rate at which an individual is willing to exchange one commodity for another: the slope of an indifference curve.

2.   Here we assume that the price of x is normalized at one.

3.   An inverse demand curve has price, or marginal willingness to pay, on the left-hand side, and quantity and socio-economic variables, other prices, etc. on the right-hand side.

5 VALUING ENVIRONMENTAL GOODS (3): THE TRAVEL COST METHOD

5.1 INTRODUCTION

The Travel Cost Method (TCM) can claim to be the oldest of the non-market valuation techniques. It originated in a letter from the economist Harold Hotelling to the director of the US Park Service in 1947, but was formally introduced to the literature by other economists, namely Wood and Trice (1958) and Clawson and Knetsch (1966). The basic method is frequently known as the Clawson-Knetsch approach. TCM is predominantly used in outdoor recreation modelling, with fishing, hunting, boating and forest visits among the most popular applications. The method is widely used by government agencies in the USA, and increasingly in the UK, e.g. by the Forestry Commission (Willis and Benson, 1989). In this chapter, we will look at how to apply the method, and at the problems that arise in doing so, at a number of variants on the basic technique, and at recent research which attempts to explain variations in travel cost estimates found in the USA.

5.2 THE BASIC METHOD

The TCM seeks to place a value on non-market environmental goods by using consumption behaviour in related markets. Specifically, the costs of consuming the services of the environmental asset are used as a proxy for price. These consumption costs will include travel costs, entry fees, on-site expenditures and outlay on capital equipment necessary for consumption. The method assumes *weak complementarity* between the environmental asset and consumption expenditure. This, as will be recalled from the preceding chapter, implies that when consumption expenditure is zero, the marginal utility of the public good is also zero. So if travelling to a forest becomes so expensive that no one goes any more, the marginal social cost of a decrease in the quality of that forest is also zero. The TCM cannot estimate non-user values. An implicit assumption made in most travel cost studies is that the representative visitor's utility function is "separable" in the recreation activity being modeled. This means that, if the activity of interest is fishing, then the utility function is such that demand for fishing trips can be estimated independently of demand, say, for cinema trips (alternative leisure activities) or for heating oil (alternative marketed non-leisure goods). A full discussion of separability in travel cost models is given by Fletcher et al. (1990).

Travel costs (C) depend for a given site "j" on several variables:

$$C_{ij} = C \ (DC_{ij}, \ TC_{ij}, \ F_i) \quad i=1...n, \ j=1...m \qquad (5.1)$$

Here, DC are distance costs for each individual "i", dependent on how far he/she has to travel to visit the site and the cost per mile of travelling. TC are time costs: these depend on how long it takes to get to the site and the value of an individual's time. F is the fee, if any, which is charged for entrance to site j. Travel costs (C) are included in a trip generating function (TGF), which predicts how many visits (V) will be undertaken by any individual i to site j. Also included in the TGF for an individual would be socio-economic characteristics such as income, education and age level, as well as variables giving information on the type of trip. Examples of this case are dummy variables on whether a visit to the site is the sole purpose of that individual's journey from home, and whether the individual is on holiday or a local day-tripper.

The alternative to the individual TCM as described above is the zonal TCM. This was the version first employed by Wood, Trice, Knetsch and Clawson. The zonal approach entails dividing the area surrounding the site to be valued into "zones of origin". These may be concentric rings around the site, but are more likely to be selected with regard to local government administrative districts (such as counties or states). This is because the zonal TCM must also include population levels for each zone of origin in order to predict trips per zone, and such population data are more readily available at the local government level than for concentric rings around a site. The number of zones used can be quite large; Hanley (1989), for instance, used 57 zones. The TGF for the zonal model is:

$$V_{zj} = V \ (C_{zj}, \ Pop_z, \ S_z) \quad z=1...Z \qquad (5.2)$$

where V are visits from zone z to site j, Pop is the population of zone z and S_z are socio-economic variables such as income averaged for each zone. The dependent variable is often expressed as (V_{zj} / Pop_z), or trips per capita.

Once a TGF such as (5.2) has been estimated using multiple regression, a demand relationship is estimated by simulating what would happen to visits per annum (individual TCM) or visits from each zone in the zonal model as

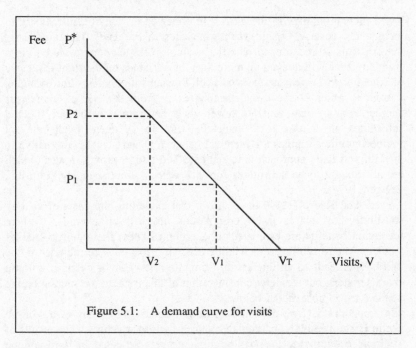

Figure 5.1:   A demand curve for visits

the "fee" is increased. In this way, a demand curve is traced out for each site. The fee is driven up until visits either go to zero or to less than one (depending on the functional form of the TGF). This is shown in Figure 5.1, where total existing visits from all zones are V_T. The TGF is used to trace out the demand curve D, which shows that visits will be made to the site so long as the cost of the visit stays below P^*. For example, at a fee of P_1, visits are predicted to fall from V_T to V_1, and a further increase in the fee to P_2 reduces visits to V_2. The reader should note that these fee/visit combinations (with the exception of the zero additional fee/V_T combination) are all predictions, based on the observed relationship between travel costs and visits. The key assumption behind the demand curve is that as the travel costs, defined in equation (5.1), increase the number of visits fall.

Measuring the area under this second stage demand curve gives an estimate of consumers' surplus. This value is most usually reported as consumers' surplus per visit. If the log of visits is regressed on travel costs etc, then this has the convenient property that the reciprocal of the travel cost coefficient gives consumers' surplus per visit. Travel cost models are often estimated for particular sites, such as Hanley's (1989) study of Achray Forest in Central Scotland. However, the approach can also be applied to groups of sites, for example, Willis and Benson's work on UK forests (1989), the study by Sellar et al. (1985) of lakes in East Texas, and the Smith and Desvouges (1986) study of US Army Corps of Engineers' water-based recreation sites in the USA. In either case, researchers may try to include the costs of visiting substitute sites in the TGF (Hof and King, 1982). This is because, to take the example of a single site study, visits from any zone will depend on more than the variables on the right-hand side of equation (5.2); that is, the availability of substitute sites. For example, a zone j_1 which is the same distance away from the site of interest as another zone j_2 may generate fewer visits per capita to the site if good substitutes are closer to j_1 than they are to j_2, even if all relevant socioeconomic variables are identical between j_1 and j_2. The alternative to the Hof and King approach is to estimate TGFs for a group of sites (which are all thought to be substitutes for each other), simultaneously (Burt and Brewer, 1974).

Smith and Kaoru (1990) have shown that excluding the costs of visiting substitute sites biases travel cost results upwards on average. Where recreation benefits are estimated for a group of sites, site quality variables (such as water cleanliness or wildlife diversity) may also be included in the TGF. This leads to an interest in estimating the value of changes in these characteristics, but we defer consideration of this issue to the section on the hedonic travel cost model below.

In Appendix 5.1, we present data from a zonal TCM study of a wildlife site in Eastern England particularly valued by bird watchers. The results of a simple econometric analysis of this data are presented in terms of the TGFs that can be recovered and of the consumers' surplus estimates (readers might like to try and replicate these results).

5.3 PROBLEMS WITH THE TRAVEL COST METHOD

The basic problems are:

(i)   the choice of dependent variable,
(ii)   multipurpose trips,
(iii)   holiday-makers vs. residents,
(iv)   calculation of distance costs,
(v)   the value of time,
(vi)   statistical problems.

(i) Choice of Dependent Variable
Two basic options exist for choosing the dependent variable. These are (1) visits from a given zone; and (2) visits made by a given individual. Option (2) is usually implemented by collecting data on visits per annum for each respondent (VPA). Option (1) is frequently expressed as visits per capita, V/Pop.

There is no consensus in the literature as to which option is preferable on theoretical grounds. Brown et al. (1983), for instance, advocate V/Pop, whilst Common (1988) advocates VPA. Fletcher et al. (1990) note several problems with V/Pop, especially that this measure is unlikely to be theoretically consistent with consumer theory. However, VPA data may suffer from recall error in some situations, particularly in "informal" recreation settings, but work better for fishing and hunting trips. Unfortunately, consumers' surplus estimates for a given site or class of sites have been shown to vary substantially according to which measure is used for the dependent variable. This is shown in Table 5.1 using data from Willis and Garrod (1991) concerning a sample of UK forests. Willis and Garrod concluded that using individual visits per annum (VPA) instead of zonal visits reduced the non-market recreation value of UK estate of the Forestry Commissions from £53.00 million to £8.66 million.

Table 5.1 Recreation benefits from UK forests, 1988

Forest Site	Consumers' Surplus (£ per day-trip)	
	Zonal Model	VPA Model
Brecon	2.60	0.66
Buchan	2.26	0.20
Cheshire	1.91	0.06
Lorne	1.44	0.96
New Forest	1.43	0.12
Ruthin	2.52	0.88

Source: Willis and Garrod (1991), p.41.

(ii) Multi-Purpose Trips

A convention is followed in travel cost analyses which distinguishes "meanderers" from "purposeful visitors". The former describes those for whom a visit to the site in question is only part of the purpose for their journey. The latter term describes those for whom a visit to the site is the sole purpose of their trip. Consider people visiting Glencoe, a national park site in Scotland about 40 miles from the town of Fort William. Clearly, some of the travel cost for the meanderers to Glencoe should be excluded from the minimum value they place on a day out in Glencoe, because they are also going to visit, say, Fort William during the same trip. Some of their travel costs should be apportioned to Glencoe, but how much? There are two options. The first is to ask people to score the relative importance of a visit to Glencoe; that is, relative to their enjoyment of the entire trip. This score, expressed as a number between 0 and 1, can be used to weight their total travel cost (e.g., Hanley and Ruffell, 1992). Second, meanderers may be excluded from the TCM analysis and a per visit consumers' surplus figure, based on these functions, computed. This average visitor consumers' surplus can then be aggregated across all visitors. This assumes, however, that meanderers, on average, value the site no less highly than purposeful visitors.

(iii) Holiday-makers and Residents

A similar problem occurs here to that discussed under (ii) above. Suppose that our sample of visitors to Glencoe contains people who have travelled from temporary holiday accommodation to the site. Their valuations could be measured by looking at these daily travel costs. However, the argument could be put forward that part of the reason for their visit to Scotland was the existence of sites like Glencoe. If this is true, then some of their travel costs from their permanent residence to Scotland should be allocated to the Glencoe valuation exercise, but how much? A weighting scheme could be employed, such as in (ii) above, but this is even more difficult in the present case. An alternative is to exclude holiday-makers and to assume during aggregation that their average valuation of the site is no less or no more than that of day-trippers. A third option is to treat holiday-makers no differently from day-trippers and consider only their daily travel costs. This, however, will probably bias the total value figure downwards.

(iv) Calculation of Distance Costs

After data has been collected on the distance travelled by respondents to the site in question, this variable is converted into a "cost of distance travelled" variable. This involves setting a price per mile, which requires choosing between two options: (1) use petrol costs only as an estimate of marginal cost, or (2) use "full cost of motoring" figures, to include an allowance for depreciation, insurance, etc. Consumers' surplus figures will depend on the choice. For example, in the Achray Forest study by Hanley (1989), using full cost data gave a total consumers' surplus figure of £402,023 per annum, whilst using petrol costs only gave a figure of £160,744. Individuals, in maximizing utility, are assumed to compare the marginal utility with the marginal costs of consumption; this makes option (1) more attractive, since option (2) is a measure of average costs.

(v) The Value of Time

In the household production function approach to recreation demand modelling, consumers combine several inputs to "produce" recreation service flows (see Deaton and Muellbauer, 1980). Principal among these inputs are visits, equipment and time. Time is expended both in travelling to a site and whilst recreating on the site. As a scarce commodity, time clearly has an implicit (or shadow) price. Much attention in the recreation demand literature focuses on how this price should be estimated. If individuals are giving up working time in order to visit a site, the wage rate is the correct opportunity cost. However, most recreation time is spent at the expense of alternative recreational activity, because most individuals are constrained by their contracts as to working hours. This means the opportunity cost will be measured with reference to the value, at the margin, of other recreation activities foregone. Ideally, a separate value would be calculated for each individual because each will have a different set of alternatives and differing valuations of these options. The difficulty and cost of collecting such data rule out this option.

Therefore, authors have searched for a uniform proxy value. One of the earliest suggestions is due to Cesario (1976) who, after reviewing empirical evidence, suggested a value of one-third of the hourly wage rate. McConnell and Strand (1981) and Common (1973) estimated a value for time by a simulation process, choosing that value which maximized the explanatory power of the trip generating function, i.e., the R^2 value. Smith and Desvouges (1986) compared results from the Cesario, McConnell/Strand and full-cost (hourly wage) alternatives for 23 recreation sites in the USA. They found that the full cost and Cesario alternatives were rejected (at the 10% level) in 7 cases, but that the McConnell/Strand method fared worse in terms of the variance of estimates it produced. In the UK, the Department of Transport calculates values for leisure time obtained from revealed and stated preference techniques. Based on these Department of Transport calculations, Hanley and Ruffell (1992) used an average figure of £0.00/hour for those respondents stating that they "...enjoyed the drive to the forest...", and a value of £2.68/hour for those who indicated that they disliked the drive.

Chevas et al. (1989) provide more recent estimates of the value of time. They distinguish between the opportunity cost measure of travel time and the "commodity value" measure of travel and on-site time. Time has a positive commodity value if its consumption directly generates positive utility. On-site time clearly has a positive value, whilst travel time may have a positive or negative value. They use a household production function approach to estimate this commodity value for recreational boating in East Texas, looking at travelling time alone. They find the commodity value of travel time to be small but positive. The value varies across sites, reaching a maximum of $0.41/hour. Assuming the value of travel time is the difference between the opportunity cost and the commodity value gives a net value. If this net value is significantly lower than the hourly wage rate it must be largely due to labour market constraints rather than to positive commodity value, which is small. The fact that the commodity value varies across sites is unsurprising, as it depends on the characteristics of the most frequently used approach routes to a site.

(vi) Statistical Problems

The dependent variable is both censored and truncated. Truncated means that as only visitors to the site are recorded, there is no information on the determinants of the decision to visit the site. Also visits are only recorded during the sampling period and may thus incorrectly describe the preferences of those visiting at other times of year. Censored means that less than one visit cannot possibly be observed. This implies that the dependent variable (visits) is censored at one, and that OLS (Ordinary Least Squares) estimates of demand parameters will be biased (Smith and Desvouges, 1986). The solution to truncation problems is to use a Maximum Likelihood (ML) estimator instead of OLS. Smith and Desvouges show how parameter and consumers' surplus estimates vary according to whether OLS or ML estimation routines are used. Their data show that OLS gives larger consumers' surplus estimates than ML.

A variety of functional forms for the TGF can be found in the literature. The choice of functional form is important, as changing the functional form can produce large changes in consumers' surplus estimates from a given data set. This point is illustrated in Table 5.2, which is taken from Hanley (1989). The most popular forms are linear, quadratic, semi-log and log-log. As mentioned, economic theory is unclear as to the preferred choice here. On statistical grounds R-squared values should not simply be compared across the different forms, as they involve different dependent variables (i.e., log or non-log). One relevant approach is to transform the dependent variable by dividing each observation by the geometric mean of the series. The resulting series is then regressed against the independent variables, and the equation with the lowest residual sum of squares chosen. Another approach is to use only log transforms of the dependent variable (that is, to restrict choice to semi-log and log-log). Such a log transform is also one way of coping with error terms that have non-constant variance (heteroscedasticity). Log-log and semi-log forms can be compared using R-squared. Finally, functional forms can be compared on the criterion of which best predicts observed visitor numbers across a range of sites (Willis and Garrod, 1991).

Table 5.2 Influence of TCM Functional Form on Consumers' Surplus

Functional Form	Consumers' Surplus (1988 £/visit)
1. $V/P = a - b\ TC + g\ TC^2$ Quadratic	0.32
2. $V/P = a - b\ \ln(TC)$ Semi-log (independent)	0.56
3. $\ln(V/P) = a - b\ TC$ Semi-log (dependent)	1.70
4. $\ln(V/P) = a - b\ (\ln TC)$ Log-log	15.13

V/P = visits per capita from each zone
TC = travel costs from each zone
a,b,g = parameters to be estimated

5.4 THE HEDONIC TRAVEL COST MODEL

The Hedonic Travel Cost model attempts to place values on the characteristics of recreational resources. Thus, society might wish to try to value an increase in the cleanliness of a fishing river, or a decrease in the area of old-growth woodland in a public forest. A number of variants of the Hedonic Travel Cost Model (HTC) have been used, starting with that of Brown and Mendelsohn (1984). This version has been applied recently to forest characteristics by Englin and Mendelsohn (1991). The method is implemented as follows. First, respondents to a number of sites (e.g., forests) are sampled to determine their zone of origin. The levels of physical characteristics (such as broadleaved/conifer areas and the percentage of forest as open space) are recorded for each site. Next a travel cost function is estimated for each zone:

$$C(Z) = c_0 + c_1 z_1 + c_2 z_2 + \ldots\ldots c_m z_m \qquad (5.3)$$

where $C(Z)$ are travel costs, z_1 is distance to site, $z_2\ldots z_m$ are characteristics, and $c_0\ldots c_m$ are coefficients to be estimated. Equation (5.3) is specified as linear, since marginal costs for each characteristic are assumed to be outside of an individual's control (exogenous). A separate regression is performed for each zone of origin, so that each will have a vector of coefficients $\{c_0\ldots c_m\}$ associated with it. For a given characteristic m, the utility maximizing individual will choose visits such that the marginal cost of the characteristic (the coefficient c_m) is just equal to the marginal benefit to him/her. These marginal costs will vary, for a given characteristic, across zones of origin. As the forest is assumed to be a public good (and thus consumption of its recreational opportunities is non-rival), the marginal social value is the sum of all individual (zonal) marginal values. In Englin and Mendelsohn (1991), some of these marginal values are negative, implying that the individual would drive further to have less of the good. This is plausible for undesirable characteristics (such as clear-cut), or when the individual is over-satiated with a desirable characteristic.

The second stage of the Brown-Mendelsohn approach is to estimate a demand curve for each characteristic. This is done by regressing site characteristic levels (the dependent variable) against the predicted marginal cost of that characteristic (which is implicitly the marginal value as explained above), and socioeconomic variables for each zone of origin. A separate regression is run for each characteristic. The expectation is that the coefficient on the marginal cost variable will be negative, so that as the level of a characteristic rises, people are unwilling to pay as much for each further increment. Englin and Mendelsohn find this to be so for ten out of eleven characteristics modeled.

Two alternatives have been proposed to the Brown-Mendelsohn approach to HTC. One, associated with Vaughan and Russell (1982) and also used by Smith et al. (1983), involves either a two-step or one-step method. In the two-step version, visits from each site are regressed on socio-economic characteristics of the visiting population. In the second step, these coefficients are then regressed on site characteristics. An alternative, one-step approach is to include interaction terms between forest characteristics (Z) and socio-economic variables (X), and regress visits on these interaction terms, plus the Z and X variables. Finally, site characteristics can be used as simple shift variables in the TGF for a number of sites where data is pooled across all sites. Changes in consumers' surplus due to changes in the level of a given characteristic z_1 are then measured by the area between two second-stage demand curves, when z_1 changes. This is the approach used by Loomis et al. (1986) to value changes in water quality due to hydro-electric developments.

However, the HTC method has dropped somewhat out of favour with environmental economists due to a number of problems, highlighted in a survey paper by Bockstael et al. (1991) see also Smith and Kaoru (1987). First, the marginal value of a characteristic in the HTC method is given by the extra costs individuals are prepared to spend to enjoy, for example, a river with a higher amenity value than a less-visited, lower amenity site closer to home. Yet these relative values (that the clean river costs more to visit than the dirty river) are an accident of nature, in that the clean river just happens to be further away. Bockstael et al. give the example of the valuation of two characteristics of lakes, namely scenic beauty and fish catch. If fish catch increases with distance from a major population centre but scenic beauty simultaneously declines, then a positive price (value) for scenic beauty will not be found. Many authors have in fact found negative prices for characteristics which would be expected to have positive marginal values. These difficulties have led some researchers to seek an alternative method of valuing site characteristics, with current research interest being centred on the random utility model of recreation demand; see Fletcher et al. (1990) for details.

5.5 CONCLUSIONS

The travel cost model is now well established as a technique for valuing the non-market benefits of outdoor recreation resources. However, as noted above, there are many problems associated with the technique and, as with hedonic pricing, applications are limited. Only recreational resources which necessitate significant expenditure for their enjoyment can have user values estimated. For example, no estimate could be made for the value of a park in the middle of a city which is visited only by pedestrians. However, the outdoor recreation resources to which TCM can be applied are an important subset of environmental assets. How much faith should be put in TCM estimates of their value? This is considered in Chapter 7, but we can note here some findings from a "meta-analysis" of US travel cost studies by Smith and Kaoru (1990). Smith and Kaoru looked at 77 US travel cost studies for which consumers' surplus per visit figures were calculable. They then tried to explain these figures, econometrically, by relating them to factors such as the treatment of substitute sites, the treatment of the opportunity cost of time, the type of recreational activities being undertaken (e.g., hunting, swimming), the type of site (e.g., river, wetlands, forest), and functional form. In this way, they were able to explain 43% of the variation in consumers' surplus figures across the studies and also predict the effect on consumers' surplus of, for example, employing a particular functional form or treatment of travel time. Thus, the consumers' surplus figures from travel cost studies are unlikely to be random numbers with no link to the value of a site. However, current research does not tell us how close travel cost estimates come to "true" user value.

APPENDIX 5.1 TCM DATA FOR BLACKTOFT SANDS

The data given below were gathered for a wildlife site in Eastern England. Distances were converted into travel costs using a marginal cost per kilometre of £0.07 and assuming an average party size of 2.13 persons/party (the figure from the sample). Time costs, both on-site and travelling, were set at zero. The regression equation estimated was:

Ln V/P = -1.807 (27.97) - 0.307 (7.17) TravCost

Figures in parentheses are absolute values of the t-statistics. The travel cost variable is thus significant at the 95% level, and correctly signed (i.e. negative). The R^2 value was 49%. Second-stage demand curve analysis showed that, in order to drive total visits to less than one, the fee had to rise by £14.65, with zone 55 being that with least elastic demand. This implies a consumers' surplus per visit of £2.89. Assuming a positive time value equal to £2.61 per hour increased consumers' surplus per visit to £9.65.

Zone	Visits	Distance from Site (km)	Zone Income	Zone Population
1	64	3.6	16316	7200
2	11	10.9	11727	7200
3	21	9.3	15912	12700
4	22	12.0	18421	16900
5	1	18.0	6250	3700
6	4	24.0	14125	3300
7	5	20.4	10800	10000
8	1	26.0	11250	38900
9	24	30.3	14185	115900
10	6	36.0	15000	37000
11	1	38.0	16250	1300
12	2	25.0	14375	6500
13	7	25.1	18036	63200
14	10	41.0	20875	67400
15	2	37.0	11375	5700
16	1	50.0	32500	700
17	1	22.0	11250	1500
18	1	50.0	37500	700
19	1	60.0	22500	21000
20	1	48.0	11250	3300
21	1	50.0	11250	4800

22	1	70.0	11250	1300
23	1	90.0	8750	9700
24	1	80.0	13750	1100
25	1	90.0	*	6200
26	1	52.0	16250	3100
27	1	116.0	32500	31700
28	1	70.0	6250	14300
29	1	100.0	13750	29400
30	2	74.0	15750	197300
31	2	128.0	21875	179900
32	1	120.0	11250	82000
33	1	112.0	6250	33600
34	4	59.0	17187	100900
35	1	120.0	11250	99500
36	1	228.0	11250	92100
37	2	262.0	38750	147300
38	1	338.0	*	77900
39	2	355.0	18125	117400
40	1	386.0	37500	75300
41	1	138.0	11250	131400
42	2	213.0	13750	80800
43	1	224.0	8750	133500
44	1	306.0	37500	93200
45	1	286.0	18750	77000
46	1	236.0	27500	120600
47	1	330.0	6250	116800
48	1	278.0	16250	96500
49	1	500.0	11250	152108
50	1	336.0	8750	74500
51	1	436.0	13750	86600

52	1	528.0	13750	10100
53	1	340.0	8750	130500
54	1	344.0	42500	216700
55	4	312.0	13125	6713300
56	1	50.0	8750	500

Notes: Distances are for a round-trip; population figures are rounded; income figures are zonal averages from the sample, evaluated at mid-points of pre-tax household income groups.

REFERENCES

Bockstael N, McConnell K and Strand I (1991) "Recreation" in J Braden and C Kolstad (editors) *Measuring the Demand for Environmental Quality* Amsterdam: Elsevier.

Brown G and Mendelsohn R (1984) "The hedonic travel cost model" *Review of Economics and Statistics* 66: 427-433.

Brown W, Sorhus C, Chou Yang B and Richards J (1983) "Using individual observations to estimate recreation demand functions: a caution" *American Journal of Agricultural Economics* 65: 154-157.

Burt O and Brewer D (1974) "Estimation of net social benefits from outdoor recreation" *Econometrica* 39: 813-827.

Cesario F (1976) "Value of time in recreation benefit studies" *Land Economics* 52: 32-41.

Chevas J P, Stoll J and Sellar C (1989) "On the commodity value of travel time in recreational activities" *Applied Economics* 21: 711-722.

Clawson M and Knetsch J (1966) *Economics of Outdoor Recreation* Baltimore: Johns Hopkins University Press.

Common M (1973) A Note on the Use of the Clawson Method *Regional Studies* 7: 401-406.

Common M (1988) "Individual observations, per capita observations and zone averages in the specification and estimation of trip generating functions" mimeo Canberra: ANU.

Fletcher J, Adamowicz W, and Graham-Tomasi T (1990) "The travel cost model of recreation demand" *Leisure Sciences* 12: 119-147.

Hanley N (1989) "Valuing rural recreation benefits: An empirical comparison of two approaches" *Journal of Agricultural Economics* 40 (3): 361-374.

Hanley N and Ruffell R (1992) The Valuation of Forest Characteristics. Discussion Paper 849, Institute for Economic Research, Queens University.

Hof J and King D (1982) "On the necessity of simultaneous recreation demand equation estimation" *Land Economics* 58: 547-552.

Loomis J, Sorg C and Donnelly D (1986) "Economic losses to recreational fisheries due to small head hydro development" *Journal of Environmental Management* 22: 85-94.

McConnell K (1985) The Economics of Outdoor Recreation, in A Kneese and J Sweeney (editors) *Handbook of Natural Resource Economics* Amsterdam: Elsevier.

McConnell K and Strand I (1981) "Measuring the cost of time in recreation demand analysis" *American Journal of Agricultural Economics* 153-156.

Sellar C, Stoll J and Chevas J P (1985) "Validation of empirical measures of welfare change" *Land Economics* 61 (2): 156-175.

Smith V K and Desvouges W (1986) *Measuring Water Quality Benefits* Boston: Kluwer

Nijhoff.

Smith V K, Desvouges W and McGivney M (1983) "Estimating water quality benefits: an econometric analysis" *Southern Economic Journal* 50: 422-437.

Smith V K and Kaoru Y (1987) "The hedonic travel cost model: A view from the trenches" *Land Economics* 63 (2): 179-192.

Smith V K and Kaoru Y (1990) "Signals or noise? Explaining the variation in recreation benefit estimates" *American Journal of Agricultural Economics* May 419-433.

Vaughan W and Russell C (1982) "Valuing a fishing day: an application of the varying parameter model" *Land Economics* 58 (4): 450-463.

Willis K and Benson J (1989) "Recreation value of forests" *Forestry* 62 (2): 93-110.

Willis K and Garrod G (1991) "An individual travel cost method of evaluating forest recreation" *Journal of Agricultural Economics* 42 (1): 33-42.

Wood S and Trice A (1958) "Measurement of recreation benefits" *Land Economics* 34:195-207.

6 VALUING ENVIRONMENTAL GOODS (4): PRODUCTION FUNCTION APPROACHES

6.1 INTRODUCTION

This chapter is concerned with approaches which link environmental quality changes to changes in production relationships. Like hedonic pricing and travel costs, these approaches are indirect means of non-market good valuation. In fact, as will become apparent, the travel cost technique can be regarded as a special case of the production function approach. These production functions may relate either to firms producing goods or services, or to households producing services that generate positive utility. This latter description of households' behaviour may seem odd at first sight. However, one can view households as combining certain commodities to produce other commodities. For example, a rural household may combine the quality of water in its well with water treatment equipment to produce drinking water. An increase in the level of a pollutant in the well (nitrates, say) will cause the household either to cut its water consumption or, more likely, to increase its purchases of water treatment equipment. Alternatively, the household may spend time and energy boiling water if the pollutant is a pathogen.

Firms also combine environmental attributes with purchased inputs to produce commodities. For example, a farm combines air quality (Q_1) and water quality (Q_2) with purchased inputs to produce soybeans. The production function for a representative farm might look like

$$X^s = f (L, K, I, Q_1, Q_2) \qquad (6.1)$$

where L and K are labour and capital inputs, I is a vector of purchased inputs such as fertilizers and pesticides, and X^s is the output of soybeans. If we assume that $\delta X^s/\delta Q_1$ is positive, then a *decrease* in air quality will, *ceteris paribus*, reduce output levels. Put another way, to maintain a given level of X^s, the amounts of other inputs must be increased. The value of a change in Q_1 could thus be estimated by valuing this impact on production.

A similar approach could be adopted for changes in Q_2.

All the approaches outlined in this chapter share the characteristic that changes in expenditures are due to the need to substitute other inputs for changes in environmental quality. We consider two such approaches: avoided cost and dose-response methods. Linking the two is the evaluation of human morbidity and mortality, a crucial issue which often determines project approval and environmental standards.

6.2 THE AVOIDED COST APPROACH

6.2.1 How it Works

When a change in environmental quality occurs, households are able to react. In the case of decreasing quality, expenditures will be made to mitigate the effects and protect the household from welfare reductions. The value of an improvement in environmental quality can be inferred directly from reductions in expenditures on defensive activities; that is, from reductions in averting expenditure (AE) (Courant and Porter, 1981). If AE and environmental quality are perfect substitutes, an approximation of the exact welfare effects on households of a change in pollution levels is provided by the associated change in AE (Smith, 1991).

An example is an increase in aircraft noise due to a new airport. In the absence of intervention, households will engage in averting behaviour, such as moving away from the area (an impact measurable via hedonic pricing) or noise-proofing their home. In theory, the benefits of a policy to reduce aircraft noise (by insisting on quieter jets, for instance) could be obtained from avoiding the costs of AE. However, such a procedure would almost certainly produce an underestimate of the benefits of such a policy to households. This is because AE and peace and quiet, in this instance, are imperfect substitutes. If AE and environmental quality (Q) were perfect substitutes, a household could, in effect, purchase a desired level of Q through AE. However, even for direct users, AE and Q are rarely perfect substitutes; for example, the household cannot easily noise-proof the garden. Thus, savings in AE would underestimate the benefits of a reduction in noise levels, since some aspects of noise pollution cannot be offset by AE (unless the individual moves house).

Other difficulties can exist with regard to the AE measure of changes in environmental quality. Investments in defensive equipment may be difficult to reverse, preventing households from moving to the position where the marginal costs and marginal benefits of pollution avoidance are equated. The analyst must make sure that changes in AE are caused entirely by the environmental change of interest, and not some other factor. Finally, AE may generate benefits other than pollution avoidance. Double glazing not only cuts noise levels but also reduces heat losses and thus saves on energy bills. This would make AE an overestimate of the cost of increased noise levels.

Bartik (1988) shows that, under certain conditions, defensive expenditures provide both an upper and a lower bound to the exact welfare measures of equivalent and compensating variation. This is illustrated by Figure 6.1 (adapted from Bartik). Environmental quality Q may be bought by undertaking defensive expenditure, which is a function of the price of averting behaviour, P. P in turn depends on the level of pollution, Z. Q^m and Q^h_0 are, respectively, the Marshallian demand curve for Q (which might be peace and quiet), and the Hicksian demand curves for Q given the pre-change utility level V_0. If pollution is reduced to say Z_0 from Z_1, then the household can reduce defensive expenditures. This reduction is shown as area "a" provided the household wants to stay at its pre-change level of environmental quality, Q_0. The compensating variation measure of the fall in pollution is [a+b]. The equivalent variation measure will exceed this, as it relates to the post-change utility level, V_1 and will measure [a+b+c+d]. However, if the savings in defensive expenditure necessary to reach the post-change level of Q are measured, the area will be even larger [a+b+c+d+e]. The *observed* change in defensive spending will be none of these measures, but rather the area [a+g+h].

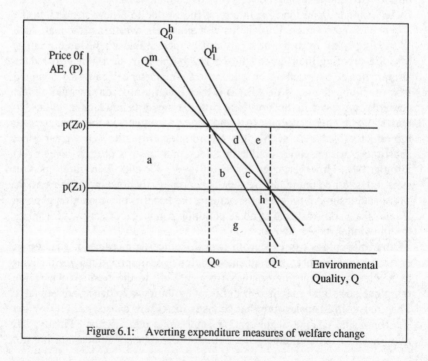

Figure 6.1: Averting expenditure measures of welfare change

Does an *ex ante* perspective on the welfare change mean averting expenditure can be used as a lower bound on WTP for environmental quality? Courant and Porter (1981) show that, in general, the answer is no, but this depends on the nature of the consumers' utility function. Suppose there is only one measure of environmental quality, air quality (A), and two goods, soap (S) and a composite good X (representing all other goods purchased). The soap can be used to offset the decrease in air quality, so that a given level of "cleanliness" C can be achieved for any given level of A, if expenditure on S is high enough. In Case One:

$$U = U (C,X) \text{ and } C = C (S,A).$$

Given this framework, Courant and Porter show that the change in AE underestimates the WTP for the change in air quality, and that AE may stay constant if A increases.[1] Case Two is where air quality enters directly into the utility function:

$$U = U (C,X,A).$$

Now the relationship between changes in AE and changes in welfare are indeterminate, since they depend on the precise complementarity/ substitutability relationships between C, X and A (Courant and Porter, 1981 p.328).

Harrington and Portney (1987) argued that AE measures of changes in environmental quality are most likely to be a lower bound on WTP, a conclusion also reached by Shortle and Roach (1989). This is true even when pollution enters the utility function directly so that, in the Courant/Porter notation, $U = U(A,C,X)$. Jacobs (1991) argues that the AE method (which he refers to as the "avoided cost approach") dropped out of favour after the Roskill Commission's CBA carried out for the UK government on the site for a third London airport in the early 1970s. This CBA used the cost of rebuilding a medieval church as the economic cost of destroying the original. However, as will be apparent from the references cited above, academic work on AE has continued, especially in the USA, with recent applications to drinking water contamination in Pennsylvania reported by Abdalla et al. (1992) and Musser et al. (1992).

6.2.2 An Application

A contentious area where the AE approach has been utilized is in valuing human morbidity and mortality. The main alternative to using AE is to measure the (net or gross) productivity of an individual and then discount lifetime earnings (output) over the expected life span (Lave and Seskin, 1977). This method has been used to produce values for human life for the

UK National Radiological Protection Board and the UK Department of Transport. However, there are several problems with this approach: (i) as people get older their economic value declines, (ii) the unemployed and parents at home can be attributed zero economic value, and (iii) the customary measure of value in economics, revealed preference, is ignored. Moreover, the value of life under this "human capital" approach is highly dependent on the discount rate used. Under the related "net output" approach, the present value of consumption is deducted from the present value of output, implying that the retired have *negative* values!

The AE route might appear more attractive, since it measures how much people actually pay to reduce the risk of being injured, sick or dying. However, AE will measure the reductions in these risks only if both the marginal cost of AE and the effect of such expenditure on risk reduction are known. There is also a dilemma here regarding the fact that AE represents individuals' guesses, however well informed, about the effectiveness of the expenditure. Should some adjustment be made for prediction of errors?

Examples of AE studies of human life include Blomquist (1979) and Dardin (1980). Blomquist looked at the expenditure on car seat belts in the UK (before they became compulsory). This produced a best estimate of £530,000 million per statistical life (1991 £s)[2]. Dardin looked at spending on smoke detectors and produced a figure of £370,000 (1991 £s). The AE approach has also been used to estimate the benefits of reduced morbidity. A recent example is a study of the value of reduced risks of skin cancer by Dickie et al. (1991). A sample of adults in San Diego and Wyoming was questioned to discover their stated WTP for an imaginary product that would cut the risk of getting skin cancer caused by exposure to the sun (a problem relating to stratospheric ozone depletion). By quantifying people's perceptions of risk, both with and without the imaginary product, the mean WTP for a 1% reduction in lifetime risk was calculated at between $4.44 and $2.70 per adult at a 5% discount rate, depending on age.

Both figures for the value of a *life* as revealed by individuals seem very low if compared to estimates from hedonic wage studies or from contingent valuation. Using the former approach involves separating out the part of wages that is a return for risk. Using this method, Marin and Psacharopoulos (1982) produced a value (1991 £s) of £2.5 million, whilst Meng and Smith (1990) estimated the value of life at £3.84 million. In contingent valuation studies, individuals are asked to bid for improvements in safety provisions which reduce the risk of being killed, for example, whilst driving. Using this approach, Jones-Lee et al. (1985) calculated a figure of £2.45 million (1991 £s).

So why do AE measures give such relatively small values? Cropper and Freeman (1991) give two main reasons. First, the actual marginal cost of AE may be difficult to measure. For example, the financial expenditure on seat belts would underestimate the actual marginal cost since it fails to allow for the wearer's discomfort and inconvenience. More seriously, individuals will engage in AE so long as the marginal cost is less than the marginal benefit (a reduction in the risk of death). Therefore AE costs will almost certainly underestimate benefits for all but the marginal user. Second, the value of risk function may be subject to sharp discontinuities. An individual's WTP to go from a 0.9 to a 0.8 risk of death may be $1 million, while their WTP to go from certain death to a 0.9 probability may be infinite!

Finally, some authors (Moore and Viscusi, 1988) recognize that an altruistic value exists for human life: people are WTP something to reduce the probability of others being killed. Including such altruistic motives can increase the value of a statistical life by nearly half; see Jones-Lee et al. (1985). For a comprehensive account of such altruism, see Jones-Lee (1992).

6.3 DOSE-RESPONSE FUNCTIONS

Dose-response methods seek a relationship between environmental quality variables and the output level of a marketed commodity. Output may be defined either in quantity terms (for example, cubic metres of wood produced from a forest) or in quality terms (damage to buildings from acid deposition). The most common examples relate to air quality impacts on agricultural production (for example, Adams et al. 1989; Adams et al. 1982) and pollution impacts on fisheries (for example, Kahn and Kemp, 1985; Kahn, 1991; Silvander and Drake, 1991).

The technique takes natural science information on the physical effects of pollution and uses this in an economic model. Thus, the method can be split into two parts: (i) the derivation of the pollutant dose and receptor response function, and (ii) the choice of economic model and its application. In the remainder of this section, the example of air pollution effects on agricultural crops is used (a topic picked up again in Chapter 10).

A change in pollution levels alters the elements in, and form of, the set of alternatives which constrain agricultural production choices and so affects the decisions of the farmer in the pursuit of maximum profits. To assess the gain or loss of benefits resulting from such a change requires the analysis of biological processes, technical possibilities, their interactions with producer decisions and the effect of resulting production changes on consumer welfare. Biological or production response data provide a link between pollutant dose and the performance parameters of a crop system. The response relationship, as discussed in Chapter 10, may be quantified directly from biological experimentation, indirectly from observed producer output and behavioural data (secondary data), or from some combination of data sources. Procedures based upon producer data (for example, production or cost functions) are preferable from the viewpoint of economic analysis (Adams, 1983) and can avoid the need for explicit dose-response functions. Attempts have been made to apply cost and production functions to the regional assessment of crop losses from ozone (Mjelde et al., 1984; Spash, 1987), but data and statistical difficulties have restricted their applicability. At present, explicitly calculated dose-response functions are most commonly applied in economic assessments of environmental stress to agriculture.

6.3.1 Valuation of Agricultural Crop Yield Changes

Various methods have been applied to evaluate the benefits from reducing crop losses caused by air pollution. Three main categories of economic approach can be defined: traditional models, optimization models and econometric models. The econometric techniques tend to rely upon knowledge of more advanced economic concepts and as a result will be difficult for some readers to comprehend. Such readers can omit the last part of this section without loss of continuity.

The Traditional Model

The "traditional" type model is a simple method of approximating a monetary value for crop yield changes. The model has various names in the literature: the historical approach, the naive model, the biologists' approach and the *ad hoc* approach. Until the late 1970s the traditional model was the most prevalent type of monetary crop loss assessment being applied in the US (Adams et al., 1984). The model multiplies estimates of a physical crop change, based on current acreage in production, by the current price of the crop. This implies a simple response assumption that resource use and prices, and thus consumer surplus, remain constant.

In regional crop loss assessments, assuming that the market price will be unaffected by yield increases is particularly tempting because the size of the increase is assumed to be small relative to the national market. However, this can cause serious errors in benefit estimates where the crop in question is regionally concentrated in production; for example, a substantial decrease in corn yield in the Corn Belt area of the United States could not realistically be assumed to leave prices unaltered. Unlike other methodologies, the traditional model cannot drop the constant price assumption, cannot measure changes in consumers' surplus and ignores distributional impacts.

Some analysts claim that the traditional model is justified as a first order approximation to the change in consumers' surplus arising from a policy change, and hence has some economic relevance (Kopp et al., 1984). However, studies comparing the traditional model and more comprehensive techniques have found the former to overestimate benefits by 20-100% (Adams et al., 1982; Adams, 1983; Adams and McCarl, 1985). Since the traditional model can measure only quasi-rent (see Chapter 2 for a definition), that is, it holds consumer surplus constant, the difference is even more dramatic. When considering only producer effects, the estimates of the traditional procedure are up to four times greater than other economic techniques.

The advantage of the traditional model is that the informational requirements are relatively modest, allowing a quantitative measure of damages to be calculated quickly and inexpensively (Adams and Crocker, 1980). Yet the results from, and the procedure of, the model are largely discounted by economists as being an unrealistic abstraction that ignores well-documented price effects and is incapable of addressing distributional consequences (Hamilton et al., 1984).

Optimization Models

There are two types of optimization model: Linear Programming (LP) models and Quadratic Programming (QP) models. Both require extensive data sets and are normally established as computer programs due to their complexity. Both LP and QP are similar in their approach. They both require the following: an objective function capable of being maximized or minimized; alternative methods or processes for obtaining the objective; and resource and other constraints. They describe the world as it *should be,* given certain assumptions that is, they are normative models.

The LP model can be set up as cost minimizing or profit maximizing. In the former case, the cost minimizing set of production activities is selected to produce specific goods, given constraints on critical inputs (for example, land). Leung et al. (1978) identify the basic assumptions of the LP model:

(i)   Linear production relationships; that is, constant input-output coefficients.
(ii)   Linear relationships are inequalities; a productive activity can use less than or equal to, but not more than, the amounts of resources available.
(iii)   Linear objective function.
(iv)   Specification of process relationships, as opposed to estimation in an econometric model.
(v)   Additivity.
(vi)   Perfect divisibility of inputs and outputs.[3]
(vii)   Finiteness; there is a limit to the number of alternative activities and resource restrictions that can be allowed.
(viii) Single-value expectations; that is, certainty.

In LP, biological dose-response functions can be used to alter the quantity of output produced from the set of inputs required for each production activity, and so can mimic the effect of varying air pollution (for example, tropospheric ozone) concentrations. Both LP and QP assume an infinitely elastic supply curve for variable inputs and constant returns to scale. The quantity demanded is exogenously fixed when cost minimization is the objective of LP, while price is exogenously fixed when profit maximization is the objective. In QP, price and quantities are endogenously determined. This forms the main difference between the two models.

Optimization models can give details on benefit distribution and model the complex inter-relationships of an economy, allowing indirect effects to be considered. However, when discrepancies arise between the model solutions and reality the cause will be uncertain. Such discrepancies could be due to incorrect or inaccurate modelling of production activities, improper constraints or just the fact that the real world operates suboptimally due to market interference or distortions (Oury, 1971). Optimization models are generally poor predictive tools, but can be improved in this respect by recursive programming (Leung et al., 1978).

Econometric Models
In contrast to the normative optimization models, econometric models, by the very nature of the data base used to develop them, reflect historical reality over space and time. This applied work is objective in the sense that the results can be rigorously examined using accepted scientific and statistical methods,[4] although ideological bias can be expected both in the selection of questions investigated and in the inferences drawn from factual evidence.

Econometric models cannot capture the effects of new technologies developed outside the time (or space) span of the data; nor can they estimate the effect on production of institutional rearrangements which market prices fail to reflect. That is, the institutional setting is taken as given. Following Kopp et al. (1984), three categories of econometric models for assessing crop loss from air pollution can be defined; namely, aggregate supply/ demand models, microtheoretic supply/demand models, and neo-classical econometric production, cost or profit function models.

Aggregate supply/demand models require little in the way of theory, except for some general specification of the variables affecting price and a decision as to whether the system is simultaneous or recursive. The model may be recursive in that each equation of the system can be solved in turn because each has an ordering in time; thus the solved value can enter the next equation as a predetermined variable. For example, a farmer may use current production methods and crop mixes to help decide his or her subsequent year's production; that is, production is determined first and then prices are determined; the model is not simultaneous.

Microtheoretic supply/demand models specify an objective function for the firm, under perfectly competitive conditions, which is then estimated empirically. This basis in neo-classical theory requires strict adherence to the underlying assumptions. Microtheoretic approaches capture both the physical engineering aspects of production and the behavioural aspects of producers. The parameters of the model can be made functions of pollution concentrations so that changes in those concentrations are reflected by changes in the parameters and shifts in the supply function. The microtheoretic approach has the ability to incorporate biological information or to estimate the parameters of biological functions directly from observed producer behaviour. In the latter case, the approach becomes a neo-classical econometric model and is independent of an explicit dose-response function.

In recent years econometric approaches have moved away from the use of production functions. The problem with using such production functions lies in the need to specify the functional form of the production function; for example, Cobb-Douglas. This prior specification of the production technology can cause unsatisfactory restrictions (in terms of behavioral assumptions) on the firm's output supply and input demand functions. Thus, the "dual" approach has been offered as an alternative which avoids many of these estimation problems (Dixon et al., 1984).

Assume the production unit is a farm which employs multiple input factors to produce multiple outputs, and that a specific technology is given which describes the physical transformation of inputs into outputs (that is, a production function). Any physical effects upon production attributable to an environmental variable (for example, air pollution) must impact production through an alteration in the farm's production possibilities. The farm's production possibilities are restricted by fixed factors of production, managerial capacity, expectations, the state of technology and the natural environment.

The production function picks out the maximum output as a function of inputs, while a transformation function picks out the maximum net output vector (Varian, 1984). Thus a transformation function serves as a measure of technical inefficiency for the farm with multiple outputs. The dual approach allows cost, revenue and profit functions to form the focus of empirical estimation by establishing correspondences with the farm's production possibility set. This duality insures that any impact realized upon the farm's production possibilities due to the effect of an environmental set of variables will be mirrored in the transformation function. In addition, the production possibilities of a farm facing a multiple output technology (for example, grain and straw) can be fully described by a transformation function. Two dual approaches to production which have been applied to agricultural crops are the profit function and the cost function (see Spash, 1987). An overview of the relationship between production and dual approaches in the agricultural context can be found in Capalbo and Antle (1988).

In addition to the direct economic impacts of air pollution on producers and consumers, indirect impacts can also be important. Indirect impacts are those changes induced by alterations in the pollutant-affected product which occur in other markets and sectors of the economy; for example, the disruption of livestock production as a result of ozone damage to forage crops. A comprehensive economic model would include all such indirect welfare changes in the assessment of benefits.

6.4 CONCLUSIONS

This chapter has looked at ways of valuing environmental effects using production function-based approaches. The notion of a household production function leads to an averting expenditure measure; this can be an overestimate or underestimate of welfare effects depending on the reference level of utility and the degree of substitutability. When the *ex ante* welfare level is the reference one and when AE is an imperfect substitute, then AE measures underestimate the benefits of reducing pollution. AE also seems to produce relatively low values for human life when compared to hedonic wage and contingent valuation results.

Dose-response models offer a means of measuring the economic costs of a number of important pollutants, including acid depositions and tropospheric ozone. But controversies over the appropriate way in which to model responses (apart from a recognition of the obvious inferiority of the "traditional" model) mean that widely varying estimates of economic damages can emerge.

REFERENCES

Abdalla C, Roach B and Epp D (1992) "Valuing environmental quality changes using averting expenditures" *Land Economics* 68: 163-169.

Adams, R M (1983), "Issues in assessing the economic benefits of ambient ozone control: Some examples from agriculture" *Environment International* 9.

Adams, R M and Crocker T D (1980) "Analytical issues in economic assessments of vegetation damages" in P S Teng and S V Krupa (editors) *Assessment of Losses which Constrain Production and Crop Improvement in Agriculture and Forestry* Proceedings of E C Stakman Commemorative Symposium, Misc Publication No. 7, Agricultural Experimentation Station, University of Minnesota.

Adams, R M and Crocker T (1991) "Materials damages" in J Braden and C Kolstad (editors), *Measuring the Demand for Environmental Quality* Amsterdam: North Holland.

Adams, R M, Crocker T D and Thanavibulchai N (1982) "An economic assessment of air pollution damages to selected annual crops in Southern California" *Journal of Environmental Economics and Management* 9: 42-58.

Adams, R M, Glyer J, Johnson S and McCarl B (1989) "A reassessment of the economic effects of ozone on US agriculture" *Journal of the Air Pollution Control Association* 39: 960-968.

Adams, R M, Hamilton S A and McCarl B A (1984) *The Economic Effects of Ozone on Agriculture* Corvallis, Oregon: Environmental Research Laboratory, US Environmental Protection Agency.

Adams, R M, Hamilton S and McCarl B (1986) "The benefits of pollution control: the case of ozone and US agriculture" *American Journal of Agricultural Economics* 68: 886-893.

Adams, R M and McCarl B A (1985a), "Assessing the benefits of alternative oxidant standards on agriculture" *Journal of Environmental Economics and Management* 12: 264-276.

Adams, R M and McCarl B A (1985b) *The Effects of Acid Deposition on Agriculture: Summary and Recommendations* Corvallis, Oregon: Department of Agricultural and Resource Economics, Oregon State University.

Bartik, T (1988) "Evaluating the benefits of non-marginal reductions in pollution using information on defensive expenditures" *Journal of Environmental Economics and Management* 15: 111-127.

Blaug, M (1982) *The Methodology of Economics* Cambridge University Press.

Blomquist, G (1979) "Value of life saving: Implications of consumption activity" *Journal of Political Economy* 87: 540-588.

Capalbo, S M and Antle J M (editors) (1988) *Agricultural Productivity: Measurement and Explanation* Washington DC: Resources for the Future.

Courant, P and Porter R (1981) "Averting expenditures and the cost of pollution" *Journal of Environmental Economics and Management* 8: 321-329.

Cropper, M and Freeman A M (1991) "Environmental health effects" in J Braden and C Kolstad (editors) *Measuring the Demand for Environmental Quality* Amsterdam: North Holland.

Dardin, R (1980) "The value of life: new evidence from the marketplace" *American Economic Review* 70: 1077-1082.

Dikie M, Gerking S and Agee M (1991) "Health benefits of PMP control: The case of stratospheric ozone depletion and skin damage risks" in J B Opschoor and D W Pearce (editors) *Persistent Polluants: Economics and Policy* Dordrecht: Kluwer Academic.

Dixon, B L, Garcia P, Mjelde J W and Adams R M (1984) Estimation of the Cost of Ozone on Illinois Cash Grain Farms: An Application of Duality (Urbanna: Agricultural Economics Staff Paper No.84 E-276, University of Illinois).

Hamilton, S A, McCarl B A and Adams R M (1984) "The Effect of Aggregate Response Assumptions on Environmental Impact Analysis" (Corvallis: Department of Agricultural and Resource Economics, Oregon State University).

Harrington, W and Portney P (1987) "Valuing the benefits of health and safety regulation" *Journal of Urban Economics* 22: 101-112.

Jacobs, M (1991) *The Green Economy: Environment Sustainable Development and the Politics of the Future* London: Pluto Press.

Jones-Lee, M (1991) The evaluation of the consequences of accidents as a basis for preventitive measures. Presented to Conference of World Health Organization and Swiss Foundation for Alcohol Research, Switzerland.

Jones-Lee, M (1992) "Paternalistic altruism and the value of a statistical life" *Economic Journal* 102(410): 80-90.

Jones-Lee, M, Hammerton M and Phillips P (1985), "The value of safety: results from a national sample survey" *Economic Journal* 95: 49-72.

Kahn, J (1991) "Atrazine pollution and Chesapeake fisheries" in N Hanley (editor) *Farming and the Countryside: an economic analysis of external costs and benefits* Oxford: CAB International.

Kahn, J and Kemp W (1985) "Economic losses associated with the degradation of an ecosystem" *Journal of Environmental Economics and Management* 12: 246-263.

Kopp, R J, Vaughan W J and Hazilla M (1984) Agricultural Sector Benefits Analysis for Ozone Methods Evaluation and Demonstration. North Carolina: Research Triangle Park, US Environmental Protection Agency, 1984.

Lave, L and Seskin E (1977) *Air Pollution and Public Health* Baltimore: Johns Hopkins Press.

Leung, S K, Reed W, Cauchois S and Howitt R (1978) *Methodologies for Valuation of Agricultural Crop Yield Changes: A Review* Sacramento, California: Eureka Laboratories.

Marin, A and G Psacharopoulos (1982) "The reward for risk in the labour market" *Journal of Political Economy* 90: 827-853.

Meng R and Smith D (1990) "The valuation of risk and death in public sector decision making" *Canadian Public Policy* 16: 137-144

Mjelde, J W, Adams R M, Dixon B L and Garcia P (1984) "Using Farmers' Actions to Measure Crop Loss Due to Air Pollution" *Journal of Air Pollution Control Association* 31: 360-364.

Moore, M and Viscusi K (1988) "Doubling the estimated value of life: results using new occupational fatality data" *Journal of Policy Analysis and Management* 7: 476-490.

Oury, B (1971) "Supply estimation and predictions by regression and related methods" in E O Heady (editor) *Economic Models and Quantitative Methods for Decision and Planning in Agriculture: Proceedings of an East-West Seminar* Iowa State University Press.

Shortle J and Roach B (1989) "A diagramatic analysis of defensive expenditures" Staff Paper 171, Department of Agricultural Economics, Pennsylvania State University.

Silvander, U and Drake L (1991) "Nitrate pollution and fisheries protection in Sweden" in N Hanley (editor) *Farming and the Countryside: an economic analysis of external costs and benefits* Oxford: CAB International.

Smith, V K (1991) "Household production functions and environmental benefit estimation" in J Braden and C Kolstad (editors) *Measuring the Demand for Environmental Quality* Amsterdam: North Holland.

Spash, C L (1987) Measuring the Tangible Benefits of Environmental Improvement: An Economic Appraisal of Regional Crop Damages Due to Ozone. Unpublished MSc Dissertation, University of British Columbia, Canada.

Varian, H R (1984) *Microeconomic Analysis 2nd edition* New York: W W Norton and Co.

ENDNOTES

1.	Courant and Porter also derive conditions under which the change AE over-estimates WTP.

2.	These conversions into 1991 pounds sterling are taken from Jones-Lee (1991).

3.	Although there are ways of relaxing these particular assumptions in LP (step-wise and integer programming routines).

4.	The dichotomy of positive and normative is not as clear-cut as is often suggested, especially by economists. For an excellent discussion of these issues, see Blaug (1982) Chapter 5.

7 HOW GOOD ARE OUR VALUATION METHODS?

7.1 INTRODUCTION

In the preceding chapters, we have considered four different ways of placing values on environmental service flows: the contingent valuation method (CVM), the travel cost method (TCM), hedonic pricing (HP) and production function approaches. Several crucial questions need to be addressed concerning how good these methods are at valuing the environment. For instance, how much faith can be placed in the value estimates generated by such methods? Are the results acceptable for inclusion in the CBA procedure?

Such questions have already been approached by detailing the problem areas facing each technique individually. For CVM, the many possible sources of bias and choice of welfare measure are problematic. In the HP method, there are difficulties over the functional form selected and the necessary restrictive assumptions about how the related market works. In the TCM chapter, the treatment of holiday-makers, substitute sites and multi-purpose visits were shown to be crucial to the consumers' surplus figures generated. The averting expenditure method was criticized as resulting, in some cases, in underestimates of damage suffered or avoided due to imperfect substitutability; there is also a problem over model choice in dose-response approaches.

Another point already brought out is that only CVM is an inclusive method. The other methods are restricted to measuring a limited class of environmental impacts. Outdoor recreational resources such as forests, lakes and wetlands are most suitable for the application of TCM, but even then only the direct use values of actual users are considered. For HP, a relationship must be found between the environmental impact of interest and the price of some marketed good or service. Dose-response methods will only measure that part of a change in environmental quality (e.g., air quality) that reduces production of marketed outputs (e.g., timber) for given levels of resource inputs (e.g., land area, fertilizer applications, labour inputs).

However, the extent to which CVM can be generalized is easily overstated. According to the "Reference Operating Conditions" (see Appendix 7.1) identified by Cummings et al. (1986), CVM works best in only a limited range of circumstances. Primary among these are that respondents are already familiar with the resource to be valued (or can become familiar with it during the course of the survey); that the hypothetical market is realistic; and that respondents already have some experience in trading the resource in question. However, what is unknown are the quantitative (as opposed to qualitative) penalties if these conditions are violated.

In addition to these operating conditions, further restrictions on the applicability of CVM can occur, because it has been noted to work better in *ex ante* settings as opposed to *ex post* settings. Suppose the benefits of restoring and landscaping an area of derelict buildings in the middle of a city are to be estimated. Figure 7.1 shows environmental quality as initially being at E_0 and increasing to E_1 due to the project. Assume this project is yet to commence and that a CVM exercise is to be carried out to estimate the welfare change it would generate. This CVM study might show people an artist's impression of the site after landscaping and suggest that the project will go ahead only if a civic improvement trust, entirely funded by public donations, is set up to carry out the work. This gives an estimate of

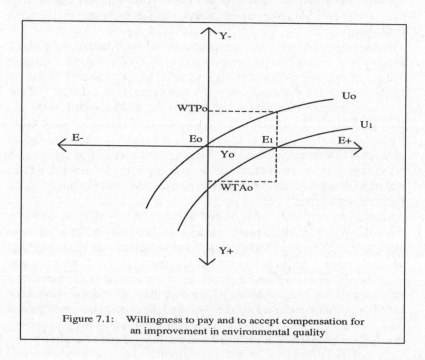

Figure 7.1:   Willingness to pay and to accept compensation for
an improvement in environmental quality

the compensating surplus measure of welfare gain, being WTP for a welfare-improving move. In Figure 7.1 this is the distance $[(Y_0 - (Y_0 - WTP_0)]$, where $\{Y_0, E_0\}$ is the initial, or reference, level of welfare on indifference curve U_0 for environmental quality E_0 (i.e., without the improvement equal to E_1), and with household income equal to Y_0. Alternatively, an equivalent surplus measure of welfare gain could be estimated by asking people what would be the minimum local property tax rebate they would require to allow the site to be left derelict, rather than have it improved. ("The city council could spend its budget surplus this year on either a property tax rebate or on improving the quality of this site.") This is the distance $[Y_0 - (Y_0 + WTA_0)]$ along indifference curve U_1.

However, if the project has already been completed, then estimating the two measures of the welfare change are more troublesome. The WTP version will now be WTP to prevent the city council "un-doing" all its restoration work, an unbelievable scenario. An alternative would be: "What sum of money do you think the council should have spent on the improvement, on a per household basis?". The WTA measure becomes: "What minimum local tax rebate would you have accepted rather than have this project go ahead?". Again, as the improvement may already be visible to respondents, this makes the CVM scenario more unrealistic and thus reduces the credibility of the estimates generated.

More generally, there are a number of ways of evaluating such "credibility". Credibility can be considered from within the structure of CBA where the basic premises are accepted or from outside this structure. In the former case three main factors might be considered as determining credibility:

(i)   How repeatable are the results generated by a methodology?

(ii)   How valid are these results?

(iii)   What esteem does the method hold within the academic community?

If a method is applied to the same data set over a number of trials and if the results are statistically the same (insignificantly different), the method has passed a *Repeatability* test. The limited evidence on repeatability is reviewed in section 7.2. *Validity* is a more slippery concept: three definitions of the term are used and the evidence with regard to each examined in section 7.3. *Esteem* or the degree to which valuation methods are held in high regard by academics is difficult to judge. If academic journals are taken as judging the quality of research by peer review, then the fact that studies using all the methods discussed have been published is a sign of their quality. In passing, we can note that the most commonly found articles in recent years concern CVM, TCM and HP, approximately in that order. The averting expenditure and production function types of approaches have received relatively little attention. This shows how using journal publications as a barometer makes academic excellence difficult to distinguish from ease of application, from controversy generated by a method or from simple popularity. Esteem is also shown when methods are adopted for teaching environmental economics and are recognized by government and non-governmental organizations. However, this respectability factor is excluded from further discussion due to the difficulties of developing suitable measures and the lack of any studies.

These measures of credibility judge the valuation techniques from within the framework of CBA. However, credibility can be defined in a broader context where, for example, the methodology itself is questioned. Thus, in section 7.4 the wider limitations of all the methods are reviewed.

7.2 REPEATABILITY

Repeatability has been peripheral to the research interests of economists involved in non-market goods valuation. The aim is to replicate the results by running the method under exactly the same circumstances, in the same way as a natural scientist would repeat an experiment to test results. This kind of test has mainly been conducted for CVM studies and can be difficult to apply where replication is inexact.

Examples of replication by the same researchers include the following. Sodal (1988) obtained CVM estimates of the value of moose hunting in Norway which were insignificantly different from the findings of an earlier Swedish study. Mitchell and Carson (1989) reported that similar values for freshwater improvement benefits were estimated using CVM in 1980 and again in 1984. Bishop and Heberlien found similar values using CVM for WTP for deer-hunting permits in Wisconsin in 1983, 1984 and 1986 (Heberlien, 1986). These results showing "stability over time" are encouraging; however, sample populations varied in all these cases.

Perhaps more important are test-retest studies, where the same sample of people are given the same questionnaire at different time periods. Jones-Lee et al. (1985) found statistically insignificant differences in mean bids for the same sample of people tested and then retested one month later. More recently, Loomis (1989) found no significant difference in CVM estimates of WTP to improve water quality in Mono Lake, in the Sierra Nevada mountains, when he re-surveyed the original sample after a lapse of nine months. Loomis (1989, p.83) concluded that "...the test-retest results ...support the contention that the contingent valuation method provides reliable estimates of total willingness to pay for both visitors and (the) general (public) ...". Test-retest results for CVM were also reported by Laughland et al. (1991).

Unfortunately, some series of studies that might be expected to yield comparable results (such as TCM measures of forest recreation) are strictly incomparable. For example, Willis and Benson (1989a, 1989b) conducted extensive TCM work on UK forests in 1987 and 1988. A selection of their estimates are given in Table 7.1. However, since they failed to re-survey any forest over the two years, the results are difficult to compare. Differences in consumers' surplus per visit depended principally on the varying forest and visitor characteristics across the forests surveyed. That is, the samples are of different populations and the goods are different.

Similar problems arise in comparing the results of the production function approach. Spash (1987) reviewed regional studies of the economic crop losses due to tropospheric ozone pollution and found numerous variations which would affect comparability even if the region were the same. These variations include different economic models, different dose-response models, the type and number of crops, the nature of the supply shift, the inclusion of cross-crop substitution, and the type of benefit areas affected (i.e., producers' and/or consumers' surplus).

Table 7.1 Travel Cost Estimates Across UK Forests

Forest Site	Year	Consumers' Surplus (£ 1988, per visit)
Hamsterley, County Durham	1987	1.64
Dalby, North York Moors	1987	1.93
Grizedale, Lake District	1987	1.34
Clateringshaws, Borders	1987	2.41
Forest of Dean, Symonds Yat	1987	2.24
Thetford, East Anglia	1987	2.66
New Forest, Bolderwood	1988	1.43
Inverliever, Loch Awe	1988	3.31
Coed Taf, Brecon	1988	2.60
Bennachie, Buchan	1988	2.26
Glen Trool, Borders	1988	1.61
Ruthin, Clwyd	1988	2.52

Source: Willis and Benson (1989a, 1989b).

7.3 VALIDITY

Three definitions of validity can be identified as useful with regard to non-market good valuation: construct validity, theoretical validity and convergent validity.

7.3.1 Construct Validity

Construct validity refers to how well a valuation method explains the values generated.

If the CVM method is considered first, construct validity can be tested by analysing whether bids can be explained in terms of the good being valued and of the characteristics of the sample or population. If variations in bids can be explained in this way they represent more than mere random numbers and thus pass the construct validity test. This amounts to asking if both a bid curve which has theoretically correct signs (e.g., is income positively signed) and a "reasonable" R^2 value can be estimated. Surveying the CVM literature and taking account of econometric reasoning for cross-sectional data, Mitchell and Carson (1989) come up with a minimum value of 15% for R^2, adjusted for degrees of freedom.[1] Whilst the literature contains several examples of CVM studies with lower R^2 values (e.g., Hanley, 1989), this is one possible rule of thumb.

When considering the construct validity of CVM, there are two reasons to begin to worry even if the above tests are passed. The assumption is that CVM bids are representative of the economic market value of a good and are not merely random numbers. However, there is recent evidence that this may be false because of *ordering* and *embedding* effects.

Kahneman and Knetsch (1992) report on an effect due to the order in which the WTP responses are elicited when several goods are being valued. The same good will elicit a higher WTP if it is first in the list rather than valued after others. As the order in which goods are listed is arbitrary, so is the resulting WTP. They found that people's WTP for improved rescue equipment and personnel varied significantly depending upon whether it was valued (i) alone; (ii) after the more inclusive category of public good of improved disaster preparedness; or (iii) after both the even broader categories of improved environmental services and improved disaster preparedness. Tolley and Randall (1983) also found ordering effects for improved visibility in the Grand Canyon.

The embedding effect was noted by Kahneman (1986, p.191) in a study of the WTP to preserve the quality of fishing in the lakes of Ontario. Kahneman found no significant differences between the WTP for lakes in one small area of the province (Muskoka) and that for all similar lakes in the province. In the same study reported above, Kahneman and Knetsch (1992) showed how the generality of the class of good could be expanded or reduced without significantly influencing the WTP bid. For example, a good might be classified as bread or more broadly as food. If one was asked to bid for bread, the amount would be expected to be smaller than the amount bid for food over a given time period. In the study by Kahneman and Knetsch three samples bid on the three goods described above. Thus each sample group had a different good as the first WTP question. The result was that the WTPs for improved environmental services (including preparing for disasters), for improved disaster preparedness and for improved rescue equipment were found to be insignificantly different from each other. In other words, the median (and mean) response was the same irrespective of the generality of the good! Kahneman and Knetsch concluded that WTP is approximately constant for public goods that differ greatly in inclusiveness. An explanation they advance is that CVM results represent a "warm glow" from the moral contribution to the welfare of society represented by a good cause such as the environment, rather than the actual values people place on a specific environmental good. Their findings are damaging to the credibility of applying CVM to public goods, typically supplied by government or charities, as such commodities are susceptible to the warm glow effect. This would restrict CVM to commodities that could in principle be supplied privately (such as wildlife, through hunting permits). Unsurprisingly, Kahneman and Knetsch's results have been much criticized by some CVM practitioners, e.g., Mitchell (1991) and Smith (1992).

Evidence supporting the existence of embedding has also been presented by Diamond et al. (1992) for alternative levels of wilderness protection, and by Desvouges et al. (1992) for the protection of alternative numbers of migratory wildfowl. However, evidence has also been put forward recently to dispute the validity of the Diamond and Desvouges studies, failing to find statistically significant levels of embedding (Imber et al., 1991; Carson, Flores and Hanemann, 1992; Loomis and Larson, 1992). The debate on embedding is thus currently unresolved.

What does construct validity mean for the other methods? For TCM, it means being able to estimate a trip-generating function with coefficient signs that are consistent with the theory behind the method, and a "reasonable" R^2. In TCM work, especially where a zonal approach is used, quite high R^2 values are commonly recorded. For example, Willis (1991) achieved R^2 values of between 75% and 99%. Studies using visits per annum as the dependent variable typically yield lower R^2 values. Smith and Kaoru (1990) report the results of a meta-analysis of TCM studies in the USA.[2] Their objective was to explain the variation in the consumers' surplus per visit measured across 77 TCM studies. They found that differences in (i) econometric procedure, (ii) the treatment of substitute sites, (iii) the valuation of time, and (iv) the resource being valued (for example, fishing compared to informal beach recreation) can explain much of the variation in TCM estimates of consumers' surplus per visit. They were able to explain up to 43% of the variation in this way. Whilst Smith and Kaoru's results largely ignore non-US work, they do give some reassurance that consumers' surplus per visit figures are not merely random numbers.

In the case of HP, a similar criterion can be adopted. That is, the HP function should provide a good explanation of house prices and have coefficient signs which are intuitively plausible. A good example of managing to meet these criteria is the HP study by Brookshire et al. (1982). They looked at air quality in Los Angeles and estimated separate house price equations for two pollutants, NO_x and Total Suspended Particulates (required due to multicollinearity problems). An R^2 value of 89% was obtained for the equation predicting the partial effect of NO_x levels on house prices. All the variable coefficients, except that for the neighbourhood crime rate, were significant at the 95% level and had the expected signs. Also, all the variables were significant and correctly signed for the Total Suspended Particulates equation.

7.2.2 Theoretical Validity

This means that results generated by the methods should be consistent with economic theory. This interpretation of validity is clearly related to construct validity. Considering CVM, WTP and WTA bids are clearly theoretically justified on the grounds that they are approximations for the Hicksian variation and surplus measures detailed in Chapter 2. For a period in the 1970s, an anomaly appeared to be present in the finding that WTP bids were consistently lower than WTA bids (as discussed in Chapter 3). One explanation given is that, due to loss aversion, WTP and WTA should be expected to differ significantly (Knetsch, 1989). CVM is therefore producing theoretically correct results if, for example, it shows WTP to set up a new wildlife reserve as being less than WTA to allow an existing, similar reserve to be closed. Similarly, following the work by Hanemann (1991) on substitution effects, CVM would be expected to produce a bigger gap between WTP and WTA when few substitutes exist for the environmental good being valued. The problem these examples raise for theoretical validity is that the theories tested are being changed by the test results. As new evidence appears, it is incorporated into the existing theory. The reason this is problematic is that once a ruling paradigm (theoretical system) is in place, it becomes entrenched despite the evidence of its failings.

7.2.3 Convergent Validity

Convergent validity relates to the extent to which different methods for valuing a given environmental change produce similar results. If a CVM study gives a result similar to a hedonic price or travel cost study, then at least the analysis is converging on one answer. Whether this is the correct answer may be unknowable but, without a reason to believe that the two methods should be converging on some other magnitude, it is reasonable to take the convergence of any two methods on the value of a given good as a desirable sign. However, defining convergence can itself be difficult. Many decisions must be made in the course of implementing any one of the methods, and the fact that there are cases where the correct choice is unknown means that more than one estimate is available from each technique. This makes comparisons vague. For example, Sellar et al. (1985) and Smith and Desvouges (1986) both produce more than one value estimate from each technique being compared (in these cases, TCM and CVM). Sampling, data analysis and survey instrument design all introduce possible bias and error into the calculation of a WTP amount. Authors engaged in convergent validity studies have therefore sought to find estimates which come within some specified or implicit bounds of other estimates. Cummings et al. (1986), in the most comprehensive critical review of such work for CVM, use a +/- 50% criterion (in terms of the acceptable overlap in consumers' surplus estimates).

We now describe some evidence from convergent validity studies.

1. CVM Compared to HP

The best known work here is by Brookshire et al. (1982), mentioned above. They use HP and CVM to measure WTP for air quality improvements in Los Angeles. Having first demonstrated that the HP estimate should exceed the CVM estimate, they produce a range of figures (for different districts and air quality changes) which support this hypothesis. For example, for a move from poor to fair air quality, they calculated an HP estimate of $49.92 per month and a CVM estimate of $14.54. These results failed to falsify their hypotheses, which were (i) that both CVM and HP values should be significantly different from zero for the air quality improvements modelled; and (ii) that the HP measures should exceed the CVM measure. A further comparison was made by Brookshire et al. (1985) between HP and CVM estimates of WTP for information on earthquake hazards in California. This gave a CVM figure of $5,920 for maximum WTP to move outside earthquake-prone zones, i.e., areas notified as "Special Studies Zones" (SSZs) by the US Geological Survey. By comparison an HP estimate of $4,650 was obtained for the price differentials attributable to houses located outside of SSZs. Finally, d'Arge and Shogren (1989) produced closely comparable results for CVM and HP for access to water frontage in holiday accommodation.

2. CVM Compared to TCM

This constitutes the largest body of material on convergent validity. Many authors have used both methods to value recreational/wilderness resources.

In the UK, Hanley (1989) estimated user benefits at the Queen Elizabeth Forest Park. He produced a CVM figure of £181,250 and a range of TCM results. Using petrol costs to convert distance data and ignoring any money cost of leisure time, the preferred TCM estimate (semi-log form) was £160,744. Both of these values were thought to be under-estimates. Hanley and Harley (1989) looked at user benefits for Loch Garten bird reserve in the Highland Region. They produced a CVM figure of £121,600 and a preferred TCM estimate of £110,982 (semi-log form), again using petrol costs to convert distance travelled. Thayer (1981) looked at WTP for landscape in the Jemez Mountains of New Mexico. He obtained a TCM estimate of $1.85-$2.59 per visitor day, compared with a CVM estimate of $2.54.

Table 7.2 TCM vs. CVM

Lake Site	Willingness to Pay (1985 US Dollars per Visit)			
	TCM	CVM Open-ended[1]	CVM Open-ended[2]	CVM Close-ended
Conroe	32.06	-0.87[3]	-8.65[3]	39.38
Livingston	102.09	6.21[3]	1.09[3]	35.21
Somerville	24.42	11.17[3]	NA	NA
Houston	13.07	5.40	2.28[3]	13.81

[1]Mean value.
[2]Derived by integrating under the bid curve.
[3]Significant difference at 95% level compared to other value estimates for same lake.
NA = not available.
Source: Sellar et al. (1985).

Improvements to water quality have been the subject of CVM work in the USA. Smith and Desvouges (1986) looked at the Monongahela River in Pennsylvania. They considered two water quality changes which resulted in improved recreational opportunities: boatable to game fishing, and game fishing to swimmable. For the former, the simple travel cost estimate was $7.16 per capita, whilst CVM gave estimates varying from $4.21 to $30.88 depending on the format used (e.g., according to the starting point). Sellar et al. (1985) produced a wide range of TCM and CVM estimates for recreational boating in East Texas, finding that estimates are insignificantly different in 2 out of the 4 lakes surveyed, depending on the set of values chosen. The open-ended CVM method performed badly relative to the closed-ended method; see Table 7.2. The values shown are WTP for an annual ramp permit for a boat less actual annual expenditure (i.e., consumers' surplus). The open-ended CVM method yielded negative consumers' surplus figures in two cases (implying partly that respondents were ill-informed about their existing expenditures).

7.4 WHAT DO OUR VALUE MEASURES MEASURE?

In CBA, "value" is an expression of the preferences of individuals, customarily shown by their behaviour in markets and backed up by the ability to pay. The non-market valuation methods attempt to get around the problem of the non-existence of markets and, as shown, have successfully produced economic values for some of the service flows provided by the environment. However, all four methods are very much rooted in the CBA tradition, with a theoretical foundation in neo-classical welfare economics. This has implications for the type of environmental values being estimated. Four broad areas of concern are the anthropocentric nature of economic value, the effect of information on values, the implications of aggregating value across individuals, and the reductionist methodology.

Anthropocentric Values
A service flow will have economic value only if it enters at least one individual's utility function or one firm's production function. Thus, if there is an element of the natural capital stock (a view, an insect, a river) that fails either of these criteria, then it has no economic value. If no-one knows about it, no-one can express a preference to conserve it. More controversially, if no-one cares about this element, then it has no economic value unless it enters into the production function of something people do care about.

Under the CBA system, intrinsic value exists only in humans and not in animals, plants and other natural resources. This is contrary to the view of some utilitarians who regard animals as having intrinsic value. Bentham (1789), the forefather of modern economic utilitarianism, attributed intrinsic value to animals on the grounds that they could suffer pain and feel pleasure. The exclusion of all non-anthropocentric things from holding intrinsic value means that their value derives solely through usefulness to human individuals. CBA is therefore based on an anthropocentric definition of value, which excludes the intrinsic value of a fish, an eagle or the whole biosphere. This viewpoint can cause drastically different policy prescriptions when considering environmental problems such as how to maintain natural capital (Spash and Clayton, 1992).

Value and Information

Economic value is measured by the summation of individual preferences; for valuation to lead to an optimal allocation of resources, individuals should be perfectly informed.   In reality, values, rather than preferences, are aggregated, irrespective of how badly informed individuals are of the effects of changes in the supply of goods and services. Suppose a forest is being valued. Preservation of the forest will halt soil erosion and thus preserve the ability of farmers downstream to carry on farming. Unfortunately, these farmers are ignorant of this and when asked to state or reveal their preference for preservation, bid a low amount. An ecologist is aware of these problems, but her or his money vote may be overwhelmed by the combined money votes of the ill-informed farmers.

Of course this argument is clearly capable of rebuttal: the farmers' aggregate WTP would rise if they were told about the threat to their livelihood. The farmers are merely ill-informed and cannot be expected to make the "right" choice without complete information. This, however, is avoiding the real issue which is what level of information do these farmers require to be "informed", and how should this information be delivered to them? In a complex world with specialist knowledge required to understand ecosystem functioning, a degree in ecology would be useful before they made an informed decision. The difficulty is one raised in Chapter 3, that preferences are both informed *and* formed by information.

Another problem is that even if the farmers are ignorant of the threat posed by deforestation, their action in implicitly allowing the forest to be felled has an opportunity cost which is the value of future agricultural production foregone because of the loss of soil. This future loss has economic value which (discounted, of course) an economist would use in a CBA. This raises the awkward issue of which measure (stated WTP or opportunity cost) should be utilized when the two differ.

Aggregating Values

A further issue may be identified, that of democracy in decision-taking. Suppose a quarry is planned for one of the Western Isles in Scotland. This will provide jobs for locals in an area of high unemployment. However, it will result in the eradication of a colony of a particular rare flower. The islanders, asked to state their preference for preserving the plant by stopping the quarry, bid very low amounts, even though they are well-informed as to the effects of the project. Mainlanders also bid low, on the grounds that they can see the plant on the mainland anyway. Only a few botanists are up in arms, yet their combined WTP is too small to stop the quarry passing the CBA test.[3] This is an example of CBA acting as the economic version of democracy: the preferences of the many are remorselessly outweighing the preferences of the few. Only by weighting the botanists' bids much more highly than those of the islanders will the project fail the CBA test. But this amounts to saying that the preferences/utility of botanists are more important than those of the general public: a controversial point. We return to the notion of democracy and CBA in Chapter 14.

What if a CVM survey were conducted asking people their minimum WTA sums to put up with the destruction of the flowers in the preceding situation? Although islanders might bid low or zero amounts, the botanists might bid extremely high amounts, so high in fact that the project fails the CBA test. Have we thus given a higher weight to the welfare of the botanists? Not really: all we have done is altered the prior allocation of property rights, so that the botanists must be compensated for the loss of the flowers, rather than paying to acquire the right to protect them. The prior definition of property rights is thus crucial. Some might object that allocating property rights to the few (the botanists) is undemocratic, since the many (the islanders) wish the project to go ahead. Yet society often places more weight on the welfare of those possessing prior rights to a resource (e.g., landowners) who may deplete or destroy that resource despite the loss of benefit to the many.

Reductionism
The concept of the value of something being the summation of individual preferences, especially where such preferences are ill-informed as to the environmental interconnections between individuals and their actions, is also inconsistent with the ecological paradigm of the whole being greater than the sum of its parts. Norgaard (1989) has criticized conventional economics as being very unsuited to study environmental problems due to this *atomistic* approach, which contrasts with the *holistic* approach of ecologists. However, the reader should note that this attack applies beyond conventional economics, which has borrowed the reductionist methodology from the natural sciences. Norgaard's criticisms of neo-classical economics receive more attention in Chapter 9.

7.5 CONCLUSIONS

Three measures of validity have been suggested, each of which can be used to assess the worth of non-market good valuation techniques. Some of the evidence reported in sections 7.2 and 7.3 can be viewed as encouraging, but this is clearly an area where more work must be done. The temptation would appear to be very strong for grabbing techniques from the shelf and applying them, in contrast to testing their validity. Section 7.4 suggests several criticisms of the notion of economic value. The message here is to realize the context within which CBA results operate. In other words, the CBA outcome is but one piece of relevant information in taking a decision. How much weight is given to CBA in any decision is impossible to generalize upon; this is the subject of further deliberations in Chapter 14 where all aspects of the environmental application of CBA are considered together.

APPENDIX 7.1 CVM REFERENCE OPERATING CONDITIONS

The "Reference Operating Conditions" of Cummings et al. (1986) have been summarized by Desvouges et al. (1987) as follows:

ROC1. Participants (in the CVM survey) must understand and be familiar with the commodity to be valued.

ROC2. Participants must have had or be allowed to obtain prior valuation and choice experience with respect to consumption levels of the commodity.

ROC3. There must be little uncertainty (about the operation of the hypothetical market).

ROC4. Willingness to Pay and not Willingness to Accept Compensation measures should be elicited.

REFERENCES

d'Arge R and Shogren J (1989) "Non-market asset prices: a comparison of three valuation approaches" in H Folmer and E van Ireland (editors) *Valuation and Policy Making in Environmental Economics* Amsterdam: Elsevier.

Bentham J (1789) *An Introduction to the Principles of Morals and Legislation* New York: L J LaFleur, 1948.

Brookshire D, Thayer M, Schulze W and d'Arge R (1982) "Valuing public goods: a comparison of survey and hedonic approaches" *American Economic Review* 71: 165-177.

Brookshire D, Thayer M, Tschirhart J and Schulze W (1985) "A test of the expected utility model: evidence from earthquake risks" *Journal of Political Economy* 93 (2): 369-389.

Carson R, Flores N and Hanemann W (1992) "On the nature of compensatable value in natural resource damage assessment" Paper to ASSA Conference, New Orleans.

Cummings R, Brookshire D and Schulze W (1986) *Valuing Public Goods: An Assessment of the Contingent Valuation Method* Totowa, NJ: Rowman and Allenheld.

Desvouges W, Johnson F, Dunford R, Boyle K, Hudson S and Wilson K (1992) "Measuring natural resource damages with contingent valuation: Tests of validity and reliability" in Cambridge Economics *Contingent Valuation: A Critical Assessment* Cambridge, Ma..

Desvouges W, Smith V K and Fisher A (1987) "Option price estimates for water quality improvements: a contingent valuation survey of the Monogahela River" *Journal of Environmental Economics and Management* 14: 248-267.

Diamond P, Hausman J, Leonard G and Denning M (1992) "Does contingent valuation measure preferences? Experimental evidence" in Cambridge Economics *Contingent Valuation: A Critical Assessment* Cambridge, Ma..

Hanemann M (1991) "Willingness to pay and willingness to accept: how much can they differ?" *American Economic Review* June: 635-647.

Hanley N (1989) "Valuing rural recreation benefits: an empirical comparison of two approaches" *Journal of Agricultural Economics* 40: 361-374.

Hanley N and Harley D (1989) "Economic benefit estimates for nature reserves: methods and results" Discussion paper 89/6, Dept. of Economics, University of Stirling.

Heberlien T (1986) "Measuring resource values: the reliability and validity of dichotomous contingent valuation measures" Paper to American Sociological Association meeting, New York, August.

Imber D, Stevenson G and Wilks L (1991) "A contingent valuation of the Kakadu Conservation Zone" Resource Assessment Commission Research Paper No. 3, Australia.

Jones-Lee M, Hammerton M and Philips P (1985) "The value of safety: results from a national sample survey" *Economic Journal* 95: 49-72.

Kahneman D (1986) "Comments by Professor Daniel Kahneman" in R Cummings, D Brookshire and W Schulze *Valuing Public Goods: An Assessment of the Contingent Valuation Method* Totowa, NJ: Rowman and Allenheld pp.185-194.

Kahneman D and Knetsch J L (1992) "Valuing public goods: the purchase of moral satisfaction" *Journal of Environmental Economics and Management* 22 no.1: 57-70.

Knetsch J (1989) "Environmental policy implications of disparities between willingness to pay and compensation demanded measures of value" *Journal of Environmental Economics and Management* 18: 227-237.

Laughland A, Musser W and Musser L (1991) "An experiment on the reliability of contingent valuation" Staff Paper 202, Department of Agricultural Economics, Penn State University.

Loomis J (1989) "Test-retest reliability of the contingent valuation method: a comparison of general population and visitor responses" *American Journal of Agricultural Economics* February: 77-84.

Loomis J and Larson D (1992) "Total economic values of increasing grey whale populations" Division of Environmental Studies and Dept. of Agricultural Economics, University of California, Davis CA..

Mitchell R (1991) "Using surveys: the methodological debate in the USA" Paper to the EAERE conference, Stockholm, 1991.

Mitchell R and Carson R (1989) *Using Surveys to Value Public Goods* Washington DC: Resources for the Future.

Norgaard R (1989) "The case for methodological pluralism" *Ecological Economics* 1: 37-58.

Sellar C, Stoll J and Chevas J-P (1985) "Validation of empirical measures of welfare change" *Land Economics* 61: 156-175.

Smith V K (1992) "Arbitrary values, good causes and premature verdicts" *Journal of Environmental Economics and Management* 22: 71-89.

Smith V K and Kaoru Y (1990) "Signals or noise? Explaining the variation in recreation benefit estimates" *American Journal of Agricultural Economics* May: 419-433.

Sodal D P (1988) "The recreational value of moose hunting" Mimeo, Agricultural University of Norway.

Spash C L (1987) Measuring the Tangible Benefits of Environmental Improvement: An Economic Appraisal of Regional Crop Damages due to Ozone. Unpublished M.Sc. dissertation, University of British Columbia pp.224.

Spash C L and Clayton A M H (1992) "Strategies for the Maintenance of Natural Capital" Paper to the International Society for Ecological Economics Conference, Stockholm, August.

Thayer M (1981) "Contingent valuation techniques for assessing environmental impacts: further evidence" *Journal of Environmental Economics and Management* 8: 27-44.
Tolley G S and Randall A (1983) "Establishing and Valuing the Effects of Improved Visibility in the Eastern United States" Report to US Environmental Protection Agency.
Willis K (1991) "Recreational value of the Forestry Commission estate in Great Britain" *Scottish Journal of Political Economy* 38: 58-75.
Willis K and Benson J (1989a) "Recreational values of forestry" *Forestry* 62 (2): 93-110.
Willis K and Benson J (1989b) Values of user-benefits of forest recreation: some further site surveys. Report to Forestry Commission.

ENDNOTES

1. If R^2 is 15%, then 15% of the variation in WTP bids is explained by the independent variables included in the bid curve.

2. Meta-analysis, in this case, refers to regressing estimates of consumers' surplus per visit (obtained from a large number of empirical studies) against variables indicating the methodological steps taken in obtaining these estimates, along with dummy variables representing the type of resource being valued.

3. This argument assumes that all individuals have approximately equal levels of disposable income.

8 DISCOUNTING AND THE ENVIRONMENT

8.1 INTRODUCTION

One of the major items of controversy with respect to the application of CBA to environmental management is the idea of discounting (introduced in Chapter 1) and the derivation of the discount rate. This is understandable because of the implications of discounting for benefits and costs which accrue in the distant future. Decisions concerning whether to undertake projects with long-term benefits (for example, growing oak trees) or with long-term costs (for example, storing nuclear waste) frequently turn on the choice of discount rate. The further into the future benefit and cost streams occur, the lower their present value. Thus, as far as current decision-makers using the net present value (NPV) criterion are concerned, growing oak trees becomes unattractive and creating and storing nuclear waste seems less onerous. As the discount rate is increased, this time bias increases.[1]

In this chapter the justifications for and arguments about discounting are explained and explored. In the first part of the chapter the emphasis of neo-classical economists on intergenerational efficiency is shown to be the driving force behind discounting. Within this area much discussion has concerned the choice of discount rate. After reviewing this literature, we argue that in choosing the discount rate, economists take an ethical view about the claims of future generations. The ethical position has received little attention or justification. Four justifications for discounting future claims are considered and rejected. In the second part of the chapter the implications of discounting for intergenerational transfers and equity are analysed and found to favour an appeal to alternative ethical systems. The alternative approach adopted by environmental economists is to come to ethical terms with the future by studying the policy implications of various ethical principles. However, the principles employed are found to possess too many attributes of utilitarianism to do justice to the belief that future people may be harmed by our present policies and have a *right* to be free

127

from such harm. The acceptance of such a right entitles future people to either compensation in the form of transfers or a veto over certain policies.

8.2 THE CHOICE OF A DISCOUNT RATE

Discounting is performed to calculate the present value of a stream of costs and benefits associated with a project or policy. If benefits exceed costs in every time period, the present value is positive for any discount rate. Generally, however, the choice of the social discount rate is crucial in determining whether the present value is positive or negative.

The process of discounting the future is defended by economists as reflecting the way people behave and value things. Both consumers, via a positive rate of time preference,[2] and producers, via the opportunity cost of capital, are observed to treat the future as less important than the present. Consumers lend money and expect to be rewarded for their abstinence from consumption; for example, savings accounts earn interest. Producers earn more interest on earlier cash receipts by loaning them to others in the economy and tying into their productivity, making earlier profits more valuable.

Neo-classical economists have shown how, in a simplified world, a unique discount rate is determined by the market. The social welfare function in the neo-classical world is utilitarian. This may be written as W^u, where:

$$W^u = W(U_1 + U_2 + \dots U_n) \tag{8.1}$$

and $U_1 \dots U_n$ are the total utilities of the t generations (t running from 1 to n). This function implies that marginal utilities must be equated across time if equation (8.1) is to be maximized. If future utility is to be discounted at some positive utility discount rate δ ($0 < \delta < 1$), then this is referred to as "pure time preference". Thus, in continuous, infinite time (8.1) becomes:

$$W^u = \int_{t=t_0}^{\infty} e^{-\delta} u_t \, dt \tag{8.2}$$

where t now runs to infinity.[3] The problem of directly measuring utility can be avoided by making utility a function of consumption at time t, C:

$$W^u = \int_{t=t_0}^{\infty} e^{-\delta} U_t(C_t) \, dt \tag{8.3}$$

Another argument, why a positive marginal rate of time preference exists for the rational individual, is that as incomes rise, marginal utility declines, so that, in equation (8.3), $\delta U/\delta C$, which can be written as U_C, > 0 but $\delta^2 U/\delta C^2$, which can be written as U_{CC}, < 0. Thus, the richer are future generations, the less value they will place on each extra pound's worth of consumption. The value of our time preference rate now depends on three things:

(i)   the pure time preference rate, δ,
(ii)   the elasticity of marginal utility, $\eta(C_t)$, and
(iii)   the rate of change of consumption, $(\dot{C}_t/C_t)$.

Calling our new rate the consumption rate of interest, i_t, we have:

$$i_t = \delta + \eta(C_t)\frac{\dot{C}}{C_t} \quad \text{where}$$

$$\eta(C_t) \equiv -\frac{U_{cc}(C_t)C_t}{U_c(C_t)} > 0$$

(8.4)

As Dasgupta (1982) notes, even if we have zero pure time preference, future costs and benefits are still discounted (i_t is positive) if consumption is growing.

Individual rates of time preference determine decisions over present consumption and savings. Aggregate savings provide a supply of loanable funds. Deferring current consumption increases future income via the marginal productivity of capital. Under perfect competition, savings and investment schedules intersect to define a unique equilibrium where the marginal rate of return on capital equals the marginal rate of time preference. That is, a single discount rate prevails.

8.2.1 The Social Rate of Discounting

Marginal Rate of Time Preference
The discount rate that society would choose to express its time preference can be different from the marginal rate of time preference. There are three main reasons for the social rate, s, being less than the individual rate, i; that is, for $s_t < i_t$:

(i)   According to Marglin (1963), society would choose to save more collectively than the sum of individuals' savings decisions. This is essentially because saving now (and investing now) provides external consumption benefits in the future, which will be under-supplied by the free market due to the free rider problem. Governments should therefore make up for this deficit by applying a lower discount rate to public investments than the private sector applies to private projects.

(ii)   Individuals as members of a society have different inter-temporal preferences than the same individuals have in their roles as consumers, to the extent that they attach a lower discount factor to future costs/benefits in the former than in the latter role. This may be especially true for environmental costs and benefits. Governments, acting as disinterested processors of citizen wants, should therefore use a lower discount rate than the rates revealed by individuals in their saving decisions. Indeed, citizens may express their desire for a lower social discount rate politically.

(iii)   The suitability of the market-determined discount rate for long-term, public policy decisions is brought into question by the fact that only the time preferences of the present generation enter into the process. Individuals with finite life expectancies are likely to act differently in their private consumption decisions from a society that has a collective commitment to life in perpetuity. Thus, the supply of loanable funds for investment is influenced by private time preferences that diverge from a collectively determined rate of social time preference. A higher discount rate than is socially optimal will occur and the level of investment will be too low to make adequate provision for future generations (Ramsey, 1928; Pigou, 1932). This "defective telescopic faculty" leads to what has been called the "super-responsibility" argument for government intervention. Removing δ from equation (8.4) clearly reduces the value of i_t. As future generations have no vote in current decisions with long-run consequences, the state has a duty to take their preferences into account. Marglin rejects this as being undemocratic. In addition, removing the fear of death motivation for discounting is insufficient to make $\delta=0$, since the impatience motive still exists.

Opportunity Cost of Capital

The social discount rate will be lower than the market return on capital, r, due to taxation. This means that the private sector will undertake too little investment from society's point of view. In particular, projects with long-term benefits, such as the development of alternative energy systems, will be under-supplied. This also implies that both renewable and non-renewable resources will be depleted too fast. For empirical evidence that r > i, see Feldstein (1977). For experimental evidence that i > s, see the experiment on management strategies for soil erosion control by Pope and Perry (1989).

Weighted Discount Rate

Several authors, such as Harberger and Haveman, have argued that the social discount rate should be a weighted average of the consumption rate of interest and the rate of return on capital in the private sector. The weights are to be determined by the proportions of investment funding coming from displaced consumption and displaced private sector investment respectively. Lind (1982) argues that such an approach is needlessly complicated. He advocates adjusting all cost/benefit flows to take account of their impact on private investment using a shadow price of capital. These adjusted flows are then discounted at the consumption rate of interest. More recently Lind (1990) has gone on to state that, in a world of increasing capital mobility, the opportunity cost of funds to the public sector is unaffected by the crowding out argument.[4] Instead, the real cost of borrowing on the world market should be used by the public sector. For example, in the USA at present, this implies a real rate of about 2%, which was indeed the rate adopted by the US Congressional Budget Office in 1986 (Hartman, 1990). Where capital is rationed, however, at either the total public sector or agency level, then Quirk and Terasawa (1991) have suggested that the rate of return on the marginal (excluded) project is appropriate, giving a rate of 10% for the USA when their paper was written.

8.2.2 A Zero Discount Rate?

Economic arguments about the choice of a social rate of discount can be split into the following categories:

(i)   an infinite social discount rate should be used;
(ii)   the intergenerational (between generations) discount rate should be greater than zero but less than infinity;
(iiia) the intra-temporal (within a generation) and intergenerational discount rates should be the same; or,
(iiib) the appropriate social discount rate is zero; and
(iv)   a negative inter-temporal discount rate should be used.

Lemons (1983) has placed the philosophical viewpoints on whether a duty to posterity exists into three categories:

(i)   no moral obligations beyond the immediate future exist;
(ii)   moral obligations to the future exist, but the future is assigned less weight than the present; and
(iii)   rights and interests of future persons are the same as those of contemporary persons.

This is an incomplete ranking and should also include:

(iv)   moral obligations to the future exist, and the future is assigned more
         weight than the present.[5]

As Spash (1993) has argued, these two sets of categories show an obvious
correlation between the economic and philosophical perspectives. The
acceptance of discounting as the proper approach to inter-temporal
distribution requires, as Page (1977) has noted, an unavoidable moral
judgement. A zero social discount rate, where intergenerational decisions
are involved, would prevent future environmental damages from implicitly
being ignored.

Olson and Bailey (1981) argue that using a zero value for δ is irrational
if capital (the means of obtaining consumption) is productive and there is a
demand for investment funds. If there is no time penalty to prevent
abstention and a positive reward to foregoing current consumption, which at
the limit is infinite, then consumption will never rise above the subsistence
level. Unless what they term "... drastically diminishing marginal utility
holds ..." then "... the case for positive time preference is absolutely
compelling". However, we can note a point of divergence here for
discounting in environmental management, since not all *natural capital* is
productive and reproducible.

Heal (1986) also finds a zero discount rate to be inter-temporally
inefficient. He models an economy with a single non-renewable resource.
In finite time, the problem is to:

$$\cdot \text{ Max } \quad U(C_t) = \sum_{t=0}^{T} \lambda_t \, U(C_t) \tag{8.5}$$

subject to

$$\sum_{t=0}^{T} C_t \leq \bar{S} \tag{8.6}$$

Here, λ_t is the discount factor, or $(1 + \delta)^{-t}$, using our terminology, and S is
the total size of the non-renewable resource. If we set $\delta=0$, then $\lambda_t = 1$, and
the optimal solution implies $C_t^* = \bar{S}/T$, if U(C) is concave. However, as we
let T=∞, then $C_t^*=0$. So the optimal solution in the limit is for consumption
to be zero in each time period, which is obviously not optimal in any
intuitive sense. This result, however, only holds in this simple "cake-eating"
model.

8.2.3 Justifications for Discounting

Only at the extreme of an infinite discount rate would no future effects of current actions be taken into account. More commonly an arbitrary but positive rate is used in cost-benefit analysis. Thus, the future is held to matter, but how far this is so depends on the rate chosen. Four general justifications for discounting the future effects of present actions can be identified.[6]

First, the very temporal location of our descendants disqualifies them from equal treatment with current members of the body politic. Yet does this mean future people should be treated as if they were already dead? The current generation does affect the probability that future individuals' needs for drinkable water and desire for clean air will be satisfied. Assuming the existence of a given population, when should the effective dividing line be drawn between now and the less important future?[7] Factors, such as age, temperament or interest, change the chosen dividing point into present and future time. Failing to acknowledge the importance of environmental degradation in the future, just because psychologically it is thought of as separated from the present, is totally arbitrary (Dower, 1983).

Second, the argument has been made that we should restrict our attention to those aspects of our actions for which preferences are known and exclude unknown future preferences. This argument is similar in line of reasoning to the need for personal identity in making hypothetical intergenerational contracts (Parfit, 1983; Norton, 1982). That is, no coherent sense can be given to making persons better or worse off if the specific persons are different *ex ante* and *ex post*. This argument relies on the assumption that all rights come from individuals and therefore the identity of individuals is central to their rights. Thus, individuals cannot claim to have been harmed by the actions of their predecessors which leave them in poverty (for example) because their existence is contingent upon the events causing their poverty. As long as future individuals do not regret their existence, any action is then justified no matter what the consequences because the future identity of individuals is determined by that action.

These lines of reasoning fail to account for the fact that there can be wrongs to future persons despite indeterminacy concerning their identities and our ignorance of their special needs. Whoever exists in future can reasonably be expected to have the same biological and social needs as those now existing. Along these lines Baier (1984) has concluded that we can identify the interests of future persons and can commit ourselves to protecting these interests. A safe assumption is that the basic human needs for food, shelter, health and security will remain prerequisites for the satisfaction of other desires.[8]

In addition, Richards (1983) has argued that the relevant moral issue is to determine how persons will fare under different policies, irrespective of who exists. Thus, regardless of who exists they will be better off without, for example, cancer. The choice between societies made up of cancer-ridden individuals and cancer-free individuals does not require that the individuals be identified. The identity of the persons under alternative policies is irrelevant.

The third attempted justification is that the human race will at some stage become extinct, so more consumption today prevents potential resource wastage tomorrow. If this extinction is exogenous (for example, due to the cooling of the sun) and the date can be predicted, the intergenerational distribution of world resources could be arranged to ensure nothing was left.[9] Uncertainty concerning the extinction date would be solved by maintaining a reserve as an insurance policy. This is much the same problem as an individual faces in allocating consumption over his/her lifetime. The point is that exogenous extinction can, at least theoretically, be considered without discriminating against the future to the extent of effectively excluding it from current decisions.

Endogenous extinction implies the human race is in control of the factors which determine extinction. For example, assuming the earth has a finite stock of energy and evolution is irrevocable, a high consumption rate today means fewer lives in the future. Yet such control over our own destiny does not imply weighing the importance of the future less than that of the present. The literature concerning such internal determination of extinction varies in solution from Georgescu-Roegen (1981), arguing for intergenerational equity, to the spaceship earth literature (d'Arge, 1971; d'Arge and Kogiku, 1973), emphasizing increases in future consumption to balance environmental degradation.

The fourth and final justification for discounting relies upon the uncertainty of future events. For example, where this uncertainty concerns the demand for a depletable resource, it is assumed to be positively related to the distance in time from the depletion decision. The conventional answer is to reflect such uncertainty in an increase in the discount rate, resulting in a faster rate of depletion. Fisher (1981) has shown how the type of uncertainty under consideration can result in either increased or decreased depletion rates. That is, uncertainty can result in resources being preserved for the future rather than depleted faster. Thus, where assimilative capacity is being depleted, with uncertainty as to the extent of such a capacity, risk aversion would argue in favour of reducing the rate of depletion; for example, reducing the rate at which carbon dioxide is released and atmospheric capacity is mined (see Chapter 13).

Similarly, in public project appraisal the argument is put forward that the appropriate adjustment for risk is made by raising the discount rate used to calculate the present value of the investment (see Appendix 8.1). However, except under special circumstances, there is no well-defined way to adjust the discount rate such that it will make the appropriate adjustment for risk in the present value of uncertain future benefits and costs in each period. This is explained at length, in the context of energy-related projects, by Lind (1982); whilst Hanley (1992) discusses risk-sharing in public investments.

The argument might also be applied to projects which create long-term damages. In this context, there is a probability that no damages will occur, a probability which might increase over time. This is equivalent to arguing that undertaking actions which can harm others is justified because there is a chance they will remain unharmed. My loosening the wheels on your car is acceptable because you might not crash as a result.[10]

8.3 INTERGENERATIONAL TRANSFERS: EQUITY AND ETHICS

Utilitarian economists such as Ramsey and Harrod have criticized discounting as being wrong. Ramsey (1928) referred to it as being "ethically indefensible" whilst Harrod (1948) called it "a polite expression for rapacity". In fact, the process of discounting the future, at almost any positive rate, creates insignificant present values for even catastrophic losses in the further future. Thus, the standard application of cost-benefit analysis to long term environmental damages gives the impression that the distant future is almost valueless. In addition, the distribution of net costs in the future, and net benefits now, makes actions responsible for long-term environmental damages falsely attractive (Spash, 1993).

8.3.1 Ethical Rules in Environmental Economics

The concern over discounting has led environmental economists to experiment with a variety of social welfare functions. Thus, the compatibility of a positive discount rate with other rules, besides the utilitarian, can be analysed. In order to focus attention on the inter-temporal (between generations) resource allocation and distribution of welfare, economists commonly assume consumption to be split equally among the members of any given generation; for example, see Page (1977, p.153) and Solow (1974). This assumption avoids inter-temporal (within a generation) distribution and aggregation issues, and as a result treats generations as if they were individuals. Karl-Goran Maler (1974) has discussed the conditions under which the well-being of members of a generation can be aggregated and treated as a single unit. A similar assumption is to treat each generation as consisting of homogeneous individuals who can be represented as a single agent; see Norgaard and Howarth (1990). Thus, even though economists work with a brand of utilitarianism which is individualistic (that is, all interests and benefits are interests and benefits of individuals), such assumptions effectively treat generations as single agents having utilities. This approach is followed below.

In order to clarify the relationship between generations, environmental economists have reviewed the implications of adopting several ethical rules.[11] In most instances the ethical rules have been defined in terms of individual welfare in a given state, and simplified so as to be expressed in mathematical formulae. Four ethical rules are the classical utilitarian, the egalitarian (Rawlsian), the libertarian (Paretian) and the elitist.

Neo-classical utilitarianism (maximizing total utility) focuses upon gains and losses of personal welfare, without any concern about welfare levels; it requires any generation to sacrifice one unit of utility when another generation can, as a result, be provided with more than one unit of utility. Intergenerational redistributions are made according to the respective marginal utilities of consumption, where utility is dependent upon own consumption alone.[12] A utilitarian ethical system would require intergenerational welfare redistributions if future generations had a marginal utility greater than that of the current generation. (Determining the marginal utility of future generations poses a practical barrier to making this requirement operational.) Compensation for the effects of long-term pollution will occur when the marginal utility of the current generation's loss, from the compensation payment, is less than the future generations' marginal utility gain.

The chief competitors for choice as the ethic to lie behind the social welfare function, if it is not to be a utilitarian one, are the Rawlsian approach and the Paretian approach. Under the former, a fair allocation is defined as one resulting from a decision rule agreed upon by all parties affected by the decision, from a position in which they cannot be sure which way any decision will affect them. This is the "veil of ignorance" procedure, and although Rawls did not intend it to apply to intergenerational allocations, many have used it in this way (Solow, 1974; Grout, 1981; d'Arge et al., 1982). Under this procedure, we imagine all future individuals drawn together before the start of time. No-one knows which generation they will inhabit, or whether they will be rich or poor. What decision rule would such a body seek to impose on the about-to-commence society? If individuals are risk averse, then they will choose a maximin strategy, as this minimizes the worst that can happen to them. In other words, the planner's objective changes from

$$\text{Max} \sum_{t=0}^{\infty} W_t = \text{Max} \sum_{t=0}^{\infty} \lambda_t \left[U(C_t) \right] \qquad (8.7)$$

where λ_t is the social discount factor, $0 \leq \lambda_t \leq 1$, to

$$\text{Max} \left[\text{min} \ (W_t) \right] = \text{Max} \left[\text{min} \ \left(\lambda_t \ U(C_t) \right) \right] \qquad (8.8)$$

where t indexes generations. Using the objective function (8.8), society will always seek the maximum *sustainable* discounted consumption level. What would the discount factor λ_t be under a Rawlsian ethic? The answer is unity, so that the discount rate equals zero. To see why, imagine that our meeting behind the veil of ignorance was considering whether it would support a nuclear power scheme planned for year t_s. This would result in decommissioning expenses of £Y at year t_F, where $(t_F - t_s)$ is the lifetime of the project. There is a finite probability that any individual will be alive during this period, but they do not know when within it. They would thus want all costs and benefits occurring within this period to be equally weighted. This means that a £'s worth of cost in year t should be the same as a £'s worth of cost in year t_F. This is only sustained if the discount rate is zero.

Choosing a Rawlsian social welfare function would thus imply constant consumption through time and a maximin decision rule. Such an egalitarian result requires that the welfare of different generations be equated with each other. This implies a subsistence argument, given an indefinitely large or infinite time horizon, finite life-supporting resources and an atemporal viewpoint. That is, in order to spread a finite amount of resources across infinite generations and maintain equity, all generations would be committed to living at a subsistence level. The fact that moving to such a subsistence level is precluded, because the future would then have lower welfare, means distributional transfers should maintain the level of welfare inherited. Any reduction of that welfare level must be countered by a corresponding increase in utility.

Under the strict egalitarian rule no generation would be allowed to make a sacrifice, however small (that is, take its welfare below the steady-state level) even if investment possibilities with very high returns existed. This, as Rawls himself noted, condemned society to impoverishment if the initial capital stock is low. This is noted by Grout, who also points out that "...acting as if the worst possible outcome will occur is unreasonable if it is only one of an infinite number of possible alternatives all having a positive chance of occurring" (Grout, 1981, p.103). However, one may argue that so long as an investment costing £x and yielding consumption worth £y (y>x) pays off at least £x within the lifetime of the current generation, then the "impoverishment argument" is weakened.

An alternative to the utilitarian and Rawlsian social welfare functions is the libertarian or Paretian one. Under a Paretian ethical rule the status quo is maintained; no redistribution of welfare is allowed unless at least one person is made better off and *none* worse off. The outcome of the rule will depend upon the definition of the starting point. Assuming the next generation can be at least as well off as the welfare level inherited, the Paretian rule requires transfers to maintain at least that level. Causing the welfare of the next generation to fall below that received from the previous generation would make the next generation worse off. Injury must then be fully compensated.

No action that harms any individual is thus to be permitted, unless that individual is willing to be compensated for his/her loss and such compensation actually occurs. The ethic is thus supportive of the strict definition of Pareto-optimality, but not the related Kaldor-Hicks definition. Unfortunately, CBA is based on the latter and not the former. Schulze et al. (1981) argue that a Paretian social welfare function would contain a discount rate equal to that used in the utilitarian equivalent. However, if compensation of losers from a particular project is impossible, then that project is not acceptable. They provide an example of such a situation by considering the decision over whether to undertake a nuclear power programme and thus produce long-lived waste. If financial institutions do not exist whereby monetary compensation can be passed on to losers far in the future (when the waste must still be managed), then under a Paretian social welfare function, the nuclear power programme would be rejected. Lind (1990) identifies this difficulty in arranging for very long-period financial transfers (including the problem of how generation one can commit generation two to maintaining the compensation fund to be paid to some generation T) as a major reason for not discounting impacts that reach across generations.

Modern welfare economics is based upon the principle of "potential compensation". The only use of the potential compensation criterion is, as argued in Chapter 2, to deny the need for compensation. The ethical implications of such a recommended definition of efficiency are hardly acceptable. Hypothetical compensation is consistent with making the poor yet poorer and is reminiscent of elitist rule.

The utilitarian social welfare function is not without its defenders in the matter of intergenerational equity. The most familiar argument is that of Harsanyi (1955). Harsanyi shares with Rawls the view that one can only decide on fair allocation rules from a position of ignorance with regard to what one's place in society will be (rich or poor, future or present). Harsanyi assumes that individuals are rational over their ethical preferences, and that the probability of finding oneself in any given generation is the same across all generations. If this is the case, individuals would choose a utilitarian social welfare function as leading to the best possible outcome given the uncertainty they face behind the veil of ignorance.[13]

Thus, according to Harsanyi, using a utilitarian social welfare function will result in a fair outcome. One may criticise this conclusion on several grounds. First, the utilitarian criterion involves allocating resources where "utility production" is highest: one utility monster, to use Page's terminology, could efficiently be allocated all resources. This seems unfair in terms of justice. Second, the equal probabilities assumption may be challenged as it does not necessarily make sense for individuals to act as if this were the case. Consider a project to fund R&D into a commercially-viable nuclear fusion reactor within five years. There are two possible states of the world. State I is that the project fails (no commercially viable scheme is found); state II is that it succeeds. The suggestion that the probability of either state occurring is 0.5 seems open to question. Third, ethical preferences may be "irrational" in Harsanyi's sense: see Grout (1981) and Heal (1986) for a discussion. Heal notes that Harsanyi's approach can also lead to a max-min decision rule if each generation is infinitely risk averse.

A final deviant from the utilitarian rule is worth mentioning due to its apparent relevance to modern society. The elitist rule requires that the welfare of the best off be improved and sees actions decreasing their welfare as wrong. This is the exact opposite of the egalitarian rule which requires the same for the worst off. Both rules focus entirely upon the relative level of well-being, without any concern for the exact sizes of welfare gains or losses. Elitism considers future generations only in so far as their welfare features in the welfare functions of individuals (selfish altruism) or in so far as the future comprises the elite. Distributional transfers will be made only if this increases the welfare of the best-off generation. Injuries caused to future generations will be uncompensated as long as the welfare of the elite is unaffected. More than this, changes which improve the welfare of the elite at the expense of others will be undertaken.

8.3.2 Limitations of the Ethical Rules

The attempts to vary the ethical basis of economics are somewhat limited from a philosophical viewpoint. Effectively the process of incorporation transforms all the rules into variations on a utilitarian theme. The Paretian ethic is a case of restricted utilitarianism, where total utility is maximised unless this makes somebody worse off.[14] Central facets of utilitarianism also exist in each of the other rules.

Utilitarianism has two main features, the principle of consequentialism and the utility principle (Pojman, 1989). Consequentialism regards the rightness or wrongness of an act as being determined by the results that flow from it. The utility principle holds some specific type of state (for example, pleasure, happiness, welfare) as the only thing that is intrinsically good. The egalitarian and elitist rules (as above) also incorporate the consequentialist principle and the utility principle. The only change from neo-classical utilitarianism is concern over the welfare levels of specific groups, as opposed to the welfare of all groups as if they were one.

This concern for welfare levels is not to be derided but is misleadingly represented as the incorporation of alternative ethical concepts. In fact, the two types of rule can be combined in one criterion. The use of welfare levels is but a variation on a neo-classical utilitarian theme; see Sen (1982) and Page (1983).

The problem which economists are confronting seems to go beyond the utilitarian framework. That is, in an effort to incorporate new philosophical ideas, a challenge is being mounted against utilitarianism, but is then retracted by being subsumed into the utilitarian framework. As is argued below, the confrontation is between a deontological perspective and a teleological one, terms first introduced in Chapter 3.

Teleological ethical theories place the ultimate criterion of morality in some non-moral value (for example, welfare) that results from acts. Such theories see only instrumental value in the acts themselves, but intrinsic value in the consequences of those acts. In contrast, deontological ethical theories attribute intrinsic value to features of the acts themselves. For example, lying is wrong even when it produces better consequences than any other alternative.

8.3.3 Inviolable Rights Versus Compensation

Under the ethical rules considered above, the relative merits of social states depend uniquely on the personal welfare characteristics of the respective states, excluding considerations of rights. If two states generate the same personal welfare values for each person, under welfarism, they must be treated in exactly the same way. Intergenerational efficiency as defined under these ethical rules allows for the violation of human rights. The idea of a right to remain unharmed by others can easily conflict with these rules.

As Sen (1982) has pointed out, even if the future generation may be richer and may enjoy a higher welfare level, and even if its marginal utility from the consumption gain is accepted to be less than the marginal welfare loss of the present generation, this may still not be accepted as decisive for rejecting intergenerational transfers when the alternative implies uncompensated long-term effects of pollution. As far as the Pareto criterion is concerned, the present generation might be well off and future generations starving and cancer-ridden due to the greenhouse effect and stratospheric ozone depletion, yet the future could only be made better off by making the present worse off. That is, a rights-based ethic is incompatible with such welfarism where rules can be defined by circumstances rather than being absolute. Intergenerational transfer under a rights system becomes of secondary importance to the violation of the rule.

The transfer of a set of "goods" may be unacceptable as an attempt to correct for loss or injury due to the violation of the rights of future generations. As Barry (1983) has stated, doing harm is in general not cancelled out by doing good. Conversely compensation does not license society to pollute, provided the damages created are less than the amount of compensation. In this case compensation cannot be used as an excuse to continue actions causing long-term environmental damages. The question is, given that they will exist, do future generations have *inviolable* rights?

The justification for rights of future generations is similar to that for rights of foreigners. For example, consider the export of toxic wastes, say from country A to country B. Country A wants to be rid of toxic wastes and therefore pays country B to accept them. The right of B's citizens to have an environment free of toxic wastes is bought and sold. Yet, should A act in this fashion? If A does not wish to have toxic wastes, neither should they be imposed upon other countries. The rights of A's citizens to a toxic waste-free environment cannot be bought by violating the same rights of B's citizens. The same argument extends to future citizens of B or future citizens of A.

Many economists would object to the above line of argument as well as to a ban on the international trade in toxic wastes because the contracting parties are entering into an agreement of their own free will. Yet, even if asymmetries of information between contracting parties and disparities in their relative wealth are absent, a ban can be justified by appealing to a different philosophy. Contrary to economic philosophy, there are many cases of intrinsic human values which societies protect from violation by contractual agreement. Examples would include the right not to be a slave, to freedom of speech, to freedom from torture, to sue another party. Freely contracting children are protected from working in coal mines despite potential economic gains. The value of such inviolable rights is maintained despite those who would, and do, accept the loss of their rights given enough money (Sagoff, 1988).

The acceptance of the inviolable right of future generations to be free of intergenerational environmental damages would have serious policy implications. Compensation could no longer be used to justify environmental degradation in violation of such rights, although there would still be a role for compensation. Irreversible damages, which cannot be prevented by stopping pollutant emissions or other actions responsible for future damages, would still require compensation. Uncertainty over the consequences of our actions and a persistent drive away from environmentally benign production and consumption processes would ensure a continued need for compensation. That is, due to our ignorance and risk taking, acts will be performed which are (in the context of the rights base system) immoral in that they violate the ruling ethic. Once such acts are realized, just as the world has recognized global warming and ozone depletion, the case for compensation arises.

However, all actions (which are reversible and of which we are not ignorant) causing long-term environmental damages would have to be stopped. The current generation would be obliged to identify all activities causing long-term damages and ban them regardless of the cost. Immediately this raises the problem of conflicting rights across generations: insisting that the actions of the present generation be restricted might be viewed as interfering with its rights.

8.3.4 Compensation and Justice as Opportunity

The discussion of inter-temporal allocations has evolved over time from the idea of splitting a fixed, finite cake to one of productivity and opportunity maintenance. This moves the emphasis from a particular resource stock towards the welfare generated from a given economic and political system given available resources and technology. As Solow (1986, p.142) has stated: "The current generation does not especially owe to its successors a share of this or that particular resource. If it owes anything, it owes generalised productive capacity or, even more generally, access to a certain standard of living or level of consumption".

What can we say about the time path of consumption or utility in the presence of environmental constraints? Working with a utilitarian social welfare function, Dasgupta (1982) and Solow (1974) both show that, if the discount rate is positive, then consumption falls through time as the non-renewable resource essential to output is depleted. Solow's model shows, however, that if population is constant and the elasticity of substitution between the exhaustible resource and capital is greater than or equal to unity, then a constant stream of consumption is possible forever.

Hartwick (1977) gives a possible escape route from the cake-eating dilemma via the rule "invest all rents from non-renewable resource extraction in reproducible capital". Given a Cobb-Douglas production function, this allows for a constant overall capital base to be maintained. Again, the elasticity of substitution in production is crucial. Following the Hartwick rule in this economy allows constant output and consumption per capita through time so long as reproducible capital does not deteriorate. Pezzey's simple cake-eating model finds that, for the optimal path to be a sustainable one, the (exogenous) rate of technical progress must exceed the rate of utility discounting. Allowing for (1) individuals to derive utility directly from the stock of environmental capital and (2) capital accumulation, Pezzey finds that, with positive discounting, the socially optimal path will (a) be sustainable only with certain parameter restrictions, and (b) will not be reproduced by the free market due to property rights problems. Adopting a zero discount rate in such a world, however, would lead to perpetual saving and therefore perpetual impoverishment of the current generation (Pezzey, 1988).

The problem posed by non-renewable resources is that future generations will have fewer options, other things remaining the same, at any positive rate of depletion. That is, for a given technology and capital stock, output will be lower and environmental degradation higher. Barry (1983) suggests that reduced access to easily extractable and conveniently located resources be "compensated" via improved technology and increased capital investment (this is a restatement of Hartwick's rule).

The level of "compensation" being referred to in this literature is restricted to the maintenance of a basic opportunity set, and therefore is appropriately regarded as a basic transfer. However, there is no particular reason to limit compensation for damages to a specified rule in order to determine distributional transfers. The reference point for compensation is the level of damages caused to the individual. The reference point for distributional transfers is the welfare level, difference in welfare or opportunity set of others; for example, the current generation compared to future generations.

Productive opportunity fails to clarify the two strands of moral argument being made here. First, that future generations have the right to a certain welfare or opportunity to obtain that welfare. Second, that actions which harm future generations require that compensation be made or activities be stopped. Reducing the stocks of non-renewable resources affects future generations in a different manner from the creation of long-term environmental damages. The concern in the case of resource depletion is for the maintenance of basic transfers. The concern in the case of environmental damages is for reparations for the violation of the right not to be harmed.

Compensation (defined as making amends for loss or injury) implicitly involves an asymmetry of loss and gain. Long-term environmental damages entail an asymmetric distribution of loss and gain over time. Inter-generational compensation is the counterbalancing of negative transfers by positive transfers. This requires the use of transfer mechanisms, though all transfers need not be compensatory. For example, under an egalitarian ethical system, the welfare level received from the previous generation should be maintained for the next generation. The current generation starts with a set of natural resources, environmental assets, capital, knowledge and capabilities which can be regarded as a means of compensation only in so far as they can be used to increase, not merely maintain, welfare.

An example in the inter-temporal context should help clarify the distinction being made here and also show the usefulness of the definitions. Assume there is an individual who receives government payments because he or she is unemployed and has no means of support. The government provides for him or her a minimal standard of living. Without the government payments the individual's welfare may be assumed to be much lower.

Assume that this individual lives next to a weapons factory run by the government. Unfortunately, there is a toxic waste dump on the site which has been leaking radioactive materials into the local environment. Following discovery of the leak, there is a proven cause-effect relationship between the radioactive releases and the local high incidence of cancer cases. This individual has developed cancer since living in the area.

Can the government now say to this individual that he or she is so much better off already, due to the payments the government makes to provide a minimal standard of living, that they need not be compensated for the cancer? It should not take long to realize that the two payments cannot be morally linked. One is made on the grounds of equity, and the other on grounds of injury.

Yet, a common argument is that the current generation need not be concerned over the loss or injury caused to future generations because they will benefit from advances in technology, investments in capital and direct bequests. These are the transfers society has deemed should be made to provide some minimal standard of living. Thus, on the discovery of the long-term environmental impact of emissions of the greenhouse gases, this generation cannot turn to the future and state that it has simply no obligation for intergenerational compensation, because basic transfers were supplied.

8.4 POLITICAL CHOICE OF THE SOCIAL DISCOUNT RATE

The choice of discount rate, especially in public sector projects impacting on the environment, has become a political issue. This was certainly the case for objections to dam construction programmes in the west and south of the USA during the 1960s and 1970s (Lind, 1982). Page (1977) observes that raising the discount rate used by the Army Corps of Engineers from the 2.5% used to 8% would have "... killed off 80 percent of the dam projects approved in 1962 ...". We shall comment later on whether environmentalists should favour "high" rates over "low" rates, although obviously the opposite choice to that indicated above would be taken by supporters of the oak forest or by objectors to nuclear power programmes.

Surveying the literature, Page (1977) commented that "After a lot of time trying to discover an unassailable definition of the social rate of discount, economists are beginning to decide that a totally satisfactory definition does not exist" (p.155), whilst Heal (1981) states that "The discount rate is not something we measure: it is something we choose". Clearly our choice depends on our view of intergenerational equity and how we characterize the nature of the economy. The discount rate in social project appraisal is, however, a political choice. In the UK, to take an example, the rate of 5% that was used until very recently was a compromise arrived at by civil servants as a value lying somewhere between estimates of the rate of return on private investments and the consumption rate of interest. This rate was, however, lowered to 3% for the benefit of the Forestry Commission as an *ad hoc* adjustment for the external benefits (net of external costs ??) of their activities. In the USA, Lind argues that the Nixon Administration chose a rate near the top of the wide range (3%-12%) previously being publicly used as the standard government rate in an attempt to achieve the

Administration's stated objective of reduced public expenditure. Interestingly, the rate used to evaluate water resource developments, such as new dams and irrigation schemes, has been lower than that used for all other Federal projects. Presumably, such investments were felt to be sufficiently politically sensitive to warrant favouring them with a low rate: echoes of forestry policy in the UK.

As with most other decisions made by governments, decisions over discount rates will be influenced by lobbying from pressure groups. What rate will environmentalists favour? High rates might kill off undesirable afforestation of wilderness areas, dam construction and wetland drainage, but would also deter the development of alternative (greener) energy sources. High rates also speed up non-renewable and renewable resource depletion rates, and might imply extinction of more species being economically efficient. Low rates, however, will increase the volume of investment and thus increase both the level of mineral and energy resource extraction and (by the materials balance principle) the quantity of effluent generated. Perhaps the best option for environmentalists as well as the most sensible option for society, given uncertainty, is to (1) impose a constant environmental capital stock constraint on investment decisions across the public sector; and (2) adopt a maximin strategy to protect choice when there is uncertainty about assimilative capacity, substitution possibilities and damage costs. This is basically similar to Page's recommendation for reconciling the NPV and "conservation criteria" (that is, sustainable use) decision rules; Costanza (1989) also advocates a max-min approach to environmental management in the presence of uncertainty. This theme is taken up in the next chapter.

8.5 CONCLUSIONS

Much debate in the literature on discounting has been concerned with the "correct" rate to choose. Imperfections and distortions in actual markets when compared to their theoretical counterparts mean that no unique rate exists. In practice the rate used for CBA will be legislated by government departments. Whether environmental factors should result in a lower discount rate, for example because some natural capital is unproductive and irreplaceable, has still to be determined. These questions about specific rates have distracted attention from intergenerational issues and from the way in which long-term environmental damages are encouraged.

Economics has failed by and large to confront the ethical implications of discounting. As a result, intergenerational damages are accepted without much concern. Where long-term environmental damages are acknowledged and taken into account, they are weighted to be less important than present benefits. If, after weighting, damages are still significant enough to warrant compensation, this concern can be dispelled by either the potential compensation criteria or the existence of basic transfers. Two fundamental steps forward would be to recognize the need for actual compensation and to start considering the existence of the intrinsic rights of future generations.

APPENDIX 8.1 RISK AND THE DISCOUNT RATE

The link between risk and the discount rate has been long debated, a debate which has special features with respect to the environment. Here, we run quickly over the general debate, but spend more time on these "special features". It seems reasonable to suggest that one reason for positive time preference is uncertainty about future outcomes: the further into the future cost/benefit flows occur, then the more uncertain they are. Therefore, it might be argued, one should add a "risk premium" to the consumption rate of interest i, which varies positively with the degree of risk for a risk-averse individual. Such a procedure is open to question, as (1) it assumes a particular time path for risk; and (2) the riskiness of the particular investment at hand is not the main parameter of interest: rather, it is the covariance between expected returns from the project and the overall expected returns from the portfolio of investments held by the investor. If these two expected returns are negatively correlated, then the investment provides insurance and should be discounted at a rate below the risk-free rate. If the expected returns are positively correlated, then a risk premium should be added to the risk-free rate.

Even if a positive correlation is expected, however, Arrow and Lind (1970) have argued that the risk-adjusted discount rate for public sector projects should be lower than that for private sector projects. This is due to risk pooling (the public sector can undertake a larger number of investments than the private sector, and so better diversify its portfolio) and risk spreading. The risk-pooling argument can be rejected on the grounds that (1) private firms can be large enough to hold portfolios as wide as those held by some governments and that, in any case, (2) the number of securities necessary to hold in order to reduce most specific risk is relatively low. The risk-spreading argument seems more attractive. As the number of risk-bearers rises to infinity, the risk borne by each reduces to zero. One might object that the number of taxpayers in any country is not infinite, and that for very large projects the cost to each might be significant. However, the general thrust of the argument is that governments should normally use a risk-free rate.

However, where projects impact on environmental quality, there are complications. Fisher (1973) points out that the risk-spreading argument does not work for public "bads", as they are non-rival in consumption. For example, my consumption of radioactive fall-out from an accident at a nuclear power plant does not reduce the amount of fall-out available for you to consume. Brown (1983) goes further and argues that, for public bads, the risk-adjusted discount rate lies below the risk-free rate. The implication of this would be, for instance, that the expected present value of leakages from the nuclear power plant would be increased, compared to the expected value under Arrow-Lind. Whilst this is a valid point for discounting future external costs, Price (1985) demonstrates that for future expected external benefits, the risk-adjusted discount rate for risk-averse individuals is greater than the risk-free rate; i.e., the risk premium is positive, not negative. In general, uncertainty over environmental damages will result in the optimal level of environmental quality in all life-preserving mediums being higher than in the absence of such uncertainty. This result is also reached by Siebert (1987). Finally, a recent discussion of the implications for the discount rate of uncertainty over future costs and benefits in inherently-unstable environmental systems is given by Drepper and Maisson (1993).

REFERENCES

Arrow K and Lind R (1970) "Uncertainty and the evaluation of public investment decisions" *American Economic Review* 60: 364-378.

Baier A (1984) "For the Sake of Future Generations" in *Tom Regan (editor) Earthbound: New Introductory Essays in Environmental Ethics* Philadelphia: Temple University Press.

Barry B (1983) "Intergenerational justice in energy policy" in D Maclean and P G Brown (editors) *Energy and the Future* Totowa, NJ: Rowan and Allanheld.

Brown S P (1983) "A note on environmental risk and the rate of discount" *Journal of Environmental Economics and Management* 6 (10): 282-286.

Costanza R (1989) "What is ecological economics?" *Ecological Economics* 1 (1): 1-8.

Culyer A J (1973) *The Economics of Social Policy* New York: Dunellen Company.

d'Arge R C (1971) "Essay on economic growth and environmental quality" *The Swedish Journal of Economics* 73 (1) March.

d'Arge R C (1989) "Ethical and economic systems for managing the global commons" in D B Botkin et al (editors) *Changing the Global Environment: Perspectives on Human Involvement* Orlando: Academic Press.

d'Arge R C and Kogiku K C (1973) "Economic growth and the environment" *Review of Economic Studies* 40: 61-78.

d'Arge R, Schulze W and Brookshire D (1982) "CO_2 and intergenerational choice" *American Economic Review* 72 (2): 251-256.

Dasgupta P (1982) "Resource depletion, research and development and the social rate of discount" in R C Lind (editor) *Discounting for Time and Risk in Energy Policy* Baltimore: Johns Hopkins Press.

Dower N (1983) "Ethics and environmental futures" *International Journal of Environmental Studies* 21: 29-44.

Drepper F and Maisson B (1993) "Intertemporal valuation in an unpredictable environment" *Ecological Economics* 7 (1), 43-68.

Feldstein M (1977) "Does the U.S. save too little?" *Review of Economic Studies* 116-125.

Fisher A C (1973) "Environmental externalities and the Arrow-Lind public investment theorem" *American Economic Review* 63: 722-725.

Fisher A C (1981) *Resource and Environmental Economics* Cambridge University Press.

Freeman A M (1986) "The ethical basis of the economic view of the environment" in D Van De Veer and C Pierce (editors) *People, Penguins, and Plastic Trees: Basic Issues in Environmental Ethics* Belmont, CA: Wadsworth Publishing Company, 218-227.

Georgescu-Roegen N (1971) *The Entropy Law and the Economic Process* Cambridge MA:

Harvard University Press.

Grout P (1981) "Social welfare and exhaustible resources" in J A Butlin (editor) *Economics of the Environment and Natural Resource Policy* Boulder, CO: Westview Press.

Hanley N (1992) "Are there environmental limits to cost-benefit analysis?" *Environmental and Resource Economics* 2: 33-59.

Harrod R (1948) *Towards a Dynamic Economy* London: St. Martin's Press.

Harsanyi J (1955) "Cardinal welfare, individualistic ethics and interpersonal comparisons of utility" *Journal of Political Economy* 63.

Hartman R W (1990) "One thousand points of light seeking a number: a case study of CBO's search for a discount rate policy" *Journal of Environmental Economics and Management* 18: 53-57.

Hartwick J A (1977) "Intergenerational equity and investing rents from exhaustible resources" *American Economic Review* 972-976.

Heal G M (1981) "Economics and Resources" in R Butlin (editor) *Economics of the Environmental and Natural Resource Policy* Boulder, CO: Westview Press.

Heal G M (1986) "The intertemporal problem" in D Bromley (editor) *Natural Resource Economics* Boston: Kluwer-Nijhoff.

Kneese A V, Ben-David S, and Schulze W D (1983) "The ethical foundations of Benefit-Cost Analysis" in D Maclean and P G Brown (editors) *Energy and the Future* Totowa, NJ: Rowan and Allanheld.

Kneese A V, Ben-David S, Brookshire D S, Schulze W D and Boldt D (1983) "Economic issues in the legacy problem" in R E Kasperson (editor) *Equity Issues in Radioactive Waste Management* Cambridge, MA: Oelgeschlager, Gunn and Hain 203-226.

Kneese A V and Schulze W D (1985) "Ethics and environmental economics" in A V Kneese and J L Sweeney (editors) *Handbook of Natural Resource and Energy Economics, Vol.1* Amsterdam: North Holland 191-220.

Kula E (1988) "Future generations: The modified discounting method" *Project Appraisal* 3 (2): 85-88.

Lemons J (1983) "Atmospheric carbon dioxide: environmental ethics and environmental facts" *Environmental Ethics* 5 (1).

Lind R C (1990) "Reassessing the government's discount rate policy in light of new theory and data in a world economy with a high degree of capital mobility" *Journal of Environmental Economics and Management* 18: 58-528.

Lind R C (1982) "A Primer on the Major Issues Relating to the Discount Rate for Evaluating National Energy Options" in *Discounting for Time and Risk in Energy Policy* R C Lind (Editor) Baltimore: Johns Hopkins.

Maler K (1974) *Environmental Economics: A Theoretical Inquiry* Baltimore: Resource for the Future, Johns Hopkins Press.

Marglin S (1963) "The social rate of discount and the optimal rate of investment" *Quarterly Journal of Economics* 77: 95-111.

Norgaard R B and Howarth R B (1990) "Sustainability and discounting the future" Paper to Conference on Ecological Economics of Sustainability, Washington D C, May.

Norton B G (1982) "Environmental ethics and the rights of future generations" *Environmental Ethics* 4: 319-337.

Olson M and Bailey M (1981) "Positive Time Preference" *Journal of Political Economy* 89 (1): 1-25.

Page T (1977) *Conservation and Economic Efficiency* Baltimore: Johns Hopkins University Press.

Page T (1983) "Intergenerational justice as opportunity" in D MacLean and P Brown (editors) *Energy and the Future* Totowa NJ: Rowan and Allanheld.

Page T (1988) "Intergenerational Equity and the Social Rate of Discount" in *V K Smith (editor) Environmental Resources and Applied Welfare Economics: Essays in Honour of John V Krutilla* Baltimore: Resources for the Future, Johns Hopkins Press 71-89.

Parfit D (1983) "Energy policy and the further future: The identity problem" in D Maclean and P G Brown (editors) *Energy and the Future* Totowa, NJ: Rowan and Allanheld.

Pearce D (1983) "Ethics, irreversibility, future generations and the social rate of discount" *International Journal of Environmental Studies* 21: 67-86.

Pezzey J (1988) "Economic analysis of sustainable growth and sustainable development" World Bank Paper.

Pigou A C (1932) *The Economics of Welfare* London: Macmillan.

Pojman L P (1989) *Ethical Theory: Classical and Contemporary Readings* Belmont Ca: Wadsworth Publishing Company.

Pope C and Perry G (1989) "Individual versus social discount rates in allocating depletable resources over time" *Economic Letters* 29: 257-64.

Price C (1989) "Equity, consistency, efficiency and new rules for discounting" *Project Appraisal* 4 (3): 58-65.

Price R (1985) "A note on environmental risk and the rate of discount: A comment" *Journal of Environmental Economics and Management* 12: 179-80.

Quirk J and Terasawa K (1991) "Choosing a government discount rate: an alternative approach" *Journal of Environmental Economics and Management* 20: 16-28.

Ramsey F (1928) "A mathematical theory of saving" *Economic Journal* 38 December.

Richards D A J (1983) "Contractarian theory, intergenerational justice, and energy policy" in D Maclean and P G Brown (editors) *Energy and the Future* Totowa, NJ: Rowan and Allanheld.

Routley R and Routley V (1980) "Nuclear energy and obligations to the future" in E Partridge (editor) *Responsibilities to Future Generations* New York: Prometheus Books.

Sagoff M (1988) *The Economy of the Earth* Cambridge University Press.

Schulze W D and Brookshire D S (1982) "Intergenerational ethics and the depletion of fossil fuels" in J Quirk, K Terasawa and D Whipple (editors) *Coal Models and Their Use in Government Planning* New York: Praeger.

Schulze W D, Brookshire D and Saddler T (1981) "The social rate of discount for nuclear waste storage" *Natural Resources Journal* 21 (4): 811-832.

Sen A (1982) "Approaches to the choice of discount rate for social Cost-Benefit Analysis" in R C Lind (editor) *Discounting for Time and Risk in Energy Policy* Baltimore: Johns Hopkins Press.

Siebert H (1987) *Economics of the Environment* Berlin: Springer Verlag.

Solow R (1974a) "Intergenerational equity and exhaustible resources" *Review of Economic Studies* 41: 29-45.

Solow R (1974b) "The economics of resources or the resources of economics" *American Economic Review* 64 (2): 1-14.

Solow R (1986) "On the Intergenerational Allocation of Natural Resources" *Scandinavian Journal of Economics* 88 (1): 141-156.

Spash C L (1993) "Economics, ethics, and long-term environmental damage" *Environmental Ethics* 15 (2): 117-132.

Spash C L and d'Arge R C (1989) "The greenhouse effect and intergenerational transfers" *Energy Policy* 17 (2): 88-96.

Thomson K (1988) "Future generations: The modified discounting method: A reply" *Project Appraisal* 3 (3): 171-172.

ENDNOTES

1.   The standard method of discounting has been questioned by Kula (1988) who proposes an alternative known as "modified discounting". Here, the average life expectancy of individuals is incorporated into the discount rate, to derive a set of discount factors that mean that an individual's benefit from consuming a welfare increasing good is only discounted over the number of years that individual actually waits for consumption to become possible. The effect is to reduce discount rates especially over the long term. However, the method has been subject to much criticism; see Thomson (1988) and Price (1987) for examples.

2.   Positive time preference means that individuals prefer benefits now rather than later.

3.   The expression $e^{-\delta t}$ is the continuous equivalent of the discount factor $(1+\delta)^{-t}$ introduced in Chapter 1.

4.   Namely, that raising funds for public investments reduces the amount of private investment.

5.   This fourth category is a realistic scenario. Consider for example the extreme sacrifices made by Russians after the revolution in order that their descendants might be better off. There is also experimental evidence of negative time preferences.

6.   The first three arguments occur in several sources, some of which are given in Spash (1993).

7.   Discounting assumes no dividing line because benefits and costs are reduced towards an asymptotic limit. However, the future effectively becomes insignificant as future values tend to zero.

8.   The Sumerians, living more than five millennia ago, enjoyed poetry, music, elaborately decorated pottery, art, and cuneiform writing, as well as having the same basic needs we have today.

9.   Such an argument has been made by Heal (1986). The comment, by Cummings and Pearse, following that article is also directly relevant to the discussion here.

10.   This same point has been made in an application to nuclear waste; see Routley and Routley (1980).

11.   For example, see Schulze et al. (1981) 811-832; Schulze and Brookshire (1982); Kneese et al. (1983a); Kneese et al. (1983b) 203-226; Pearce (1983) 67-86; Kneese and Schulze (1985) 191-220; d'Arge (1989).

12.   An egalitarian argument can be made to follow from the utilitarian approach. This requires an appreciation of the law of diminishing marginal utility (additional income yields less than previous additions, though the total continues to rise), and assumes that all individuals are fundamentally alike in their preferences and capabilities for enjoying goods. In the strict form, the utilitarian argument for egalitarianism depends crucially upon the identity of the utility of income across generations. At the opposite extreme, an elitist argument can be made, if the marginal utility of income of the rich generation is higher than that of the poor generation. On these points and their discussion in an intratemporal context, see Culyer (1973) 64-90.

13.   If there are n generations and the probability of occurring in any one is the same for all, this probability is $1/n$. Individuals are "ethically rational" if they seek to maximize $1/n\ U_1\ (C_1) + 1/n\ U_2\ (C_2) \ldots + 1/n\ U_n\ (C_n)$ which is always maximized when the utilitarian social welfare function $W = \Sigma\ U_t\ (C_t)$ is maximized (Grout, 1981 p.98).

14.   The Pareto criterion is commonly applied in the intergenerational context in the same fashion as in the intragenerational context. That is, an initial endowment is allocated to each generation and then redistributions are allowed if they are Pareto improvements.

9 IRREVERSIBILITY, ECOSYSTEM COMPLEXITY, INSTITUTIONAL CAPTURE AND SUSTAINABILITY

9.1 INTRODUCTION

In this chapter, completing Part I of the book, four important methodological issues are considered in the context of applying CBA to the environment. The four issues are:

(i) *Irreversibility.* Many projects impacting on the environment have irreversible effects. In section 9.2 the special techniques which have been proposed for looking at such projects are described. These proposals will affect the outcome of CBA and emphasize the value of information.

(ii) *Ecosystem complexity.* The static interrelationships and the processes of change in almost all ecosystems are extremely complex. The difficulties entailed in establishing cause and effect relationships can pose major problems for CBA. Some of the approaches to uncertainty over ecosystem impacts suggested by economists are discussed in section 9.3.

(iii) *Institutional capture.* Public bodies responsible for undertaking CBA of projects can do so in such a way as to best serve their own interests rather than the "public interest". Where CBA allows an element of discretion, agencies may have a vested interest in influencing the outcome in their favour, thus bringing CBA into disrepute. Section 9.4 addresses this issue.

(iv) *Sustainability constraints.* Some analysts have suggested that CBA is a decision-making mechanism that directs the economy towards a sustainable development path. The success with which CBA can achieve this role will depend upon the definition of "sustainable development". In section 9.5, and again in Chapter 14, the economic view of sustainability is considered.

9.2 IRREVERSIBILITY

Many projects that impact on the environment have effects that are, for all intents and purposes, irreversible. The most extreme examples concern projects which lead to the extinction of a species (by, for example, destroying its last remaining habitat). Equally, the conversion of wetland, the quarrying of a national park or the clear-felling of rainforest can also have irreversible impacts, as soil and water chemistry are changed, landscape is altered and soil is washed away.

The crucial point for economists regarding irreversible developments is that the *benefits of preservation* are foregone forever if development of a wilderness goes ahead. Consider a project to build a large hydroelectric dam in the Amazon. The action of clear-felling, the consequent loss of soil through erosion, the siltation of downstream areas and the loss of wildlife constitute an irreversible loss of preservation benefits. A further irreversible effect might be changes in regional climate. Due to the loss of the latent heat energy transfer from the rainforest, there could be a rise in surface temperature and a decrease in annual precipitation for Amazonia (Shukla et al., 1990).[1] Assume that these preservation benefits could be estimated for the current year, both in physical and monetary terms, using the methods described earlier in this book. This would enable the preservation benefits foregone, if development occurs, to be estimated; that is P_t (where t indexes time periods). If these foregone benefits are assumed to remain constant in real terms, the future value of preserving the site can be known.

In this example, the *benefits of development* are principally comprised of power generation. Such benefits are usually calculated by considering the savings in electric power generation costs due to the use of hydro rather than the next cheapest source, say small-scale gas fired units. In order to carry out the CBA the benefits of development, net of variable costs incurred in generating and distributing the hydropower, must be estimated; that is D_t. As with the preservation benefits, these costs are, for now, assumed to be constant over time. Both these benefits and costs of development are to be discounted at some non-zero rate i, which is the social rate of time preference. In Chapter 1, the present value of an infinite, constant series of returns X, was given by:

$$PV\ (X) = X/(i).$$

If development benefits are assumed to be a perpetual flow, the NPV of the development scheme is:

$$NPV_d = [D_t/(i)] - C_o - [P_t/(i)] \qquad (9.1)$$

where $(i>0)$, C_0 is the year zero construction cost, and P_t and D_t are assumed constant in real terms. The cost-benefit rule is, as normal, to proceed if the NPV>0.

Development benefits will not be perpetual in this case, since hydro schemes have a fixed life span. However, this assumption is maintained to simplify the analysis though, due to the effects of discounting, it is unimportant as far as the argument being put forward is concerned. In contrast, the assumption that D_t will remain constant in real terms for all t needs to be challenged. Krutilla and Fisher (1975) have argued that development benefits will fall over time, especially for projects where such benefits are in terms of cost savings over alternative technologies (as is the case in most energy project appraisal). In the case of a hydro scheme, technology is "frozen in" to the dam and turbines while technology outside the scheme continues to advance. This technological progress will reduce the costs of generating electricity by alternative sources and thus erode the cost savings of the dam, i.e., the development benefits. Let us call this annual rate of decline in real development benefits g.[2]

Preservation benefits are also likely to be unstable over time. There are several reasons to expect preservation benefits to grow at a positive annual rate, r. First, because of increasing relative scarcity. As the area of tropical rain forest declines, each remaining hectare becomes more valuable and WTP increases due to the law of diminishing marginal utility. Second, because information on the importance of ecosystems' structure and diversity is increasing and being more widely dispersed over time, people become better informed; thus aggregate global WTP to preserve natural resources, such as rain forests, is likely to increase. Finally, as real incomes rise, demand for environmental goods and services may also increase (Hanley and Craig, 1991). This means both an increase in the WTP to preserve ecosystems (such as rain forests or wetlands) amongst non-users, and an increased rate of visitation by users, pushing up use value.

Thus, assuming r is positive and taking g to be negative (i.e., a rate of decline in real development benefits) equation (9.1) becomes (9.2)

$$NPV_d = [D_t/(i-g)] - C_o - [P_t/(i-r)] \qquad (9.2)$$

where $g<0$ and $r>0$. This equation is a statement (in infinite time) of the Krutilla-Fisher model of irreversible development. The effect of the g parameter is to reinforce the discounting process (since g is a negative number), whilst the effect of r is to offset this. As Porter (1982) shows in his excellent summary paper on the Krutilla-Fisher model, for given values of P, D, g and r, the sign of NPV depends on which discount rate, i, is used. Two possible outcomes are shown in Figures 9.1(a) and 9.1 (b).

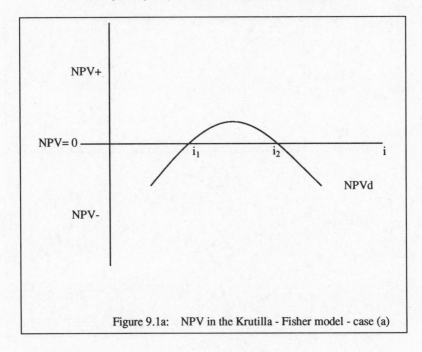

NPV+

NPV= 0

i_1 i_2 i

NPVd

NPV-

Figure 9.1a: NPV in the Krutilla - Fisher model - case (a)

In Figure 9.1(a), NPV_d is only positive within the range i_1 to i_2. Below i_1, the discount rate is so low that the exponentially growing preservation benefits dominate. Above i_2, the development benefits are discounted so much that the project fails to recover its initial cost, net of preservation benefits foregone. However, a development project with negative g and positive r may never be socially profitable if C or P are high enough, or D is low enough, a situation pictured in Figure 9.1(b).

The Krutilla-Fisher model is an interesting approach to irreversible developments, since it explicitly recognizes asymmetric growth rates in development and preservation benefits. It has been applied to downhill ski developments, mineral extraction and hydro schemes in North America (Krutilla and Fisher, 1985) and to wetland losses (Hanley and Craig, 1991). However, there are a number of problems with the approach:

(i)   The growth rates g and r can be difficult to estimate and may be unstable over time.

(ii)   The initial values for P and D can be difficult to measure.

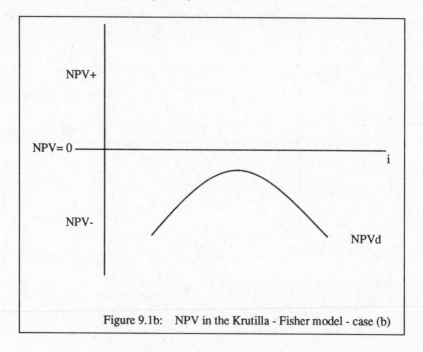

Figure 9.1b: NPV in the Krutilla - Fisher model - case (b)

(iii)   Future preservation benefits foregone are measured using the preferences of current individuals, which may conflict with future preferences.

Arrow and Fisher (1974) were jointly responsible for pursuing another line of economic thinking on irreversible changes. They advanced the concept of a "quasi-option value" when making a decision to prevent an irreversible development. The concept is also associated with Henry (1974). Quasi-option value is an insurance premium (cost). The value of clearing and re-using a site is no longer the discounted net benefits, but rather the *expected* future net benefits, where the probabilities are unknown. Citizens may be willing to pay an insurance premium in order to maintain access to alternative states of the world, i.e., to keep their options open.

Quasi-option value is most easily understood in a two-period model, where in period one a decision is taken either to develop a wilderness area entirely or else leave it untouched.[3] If new information is received at the start of period two about preservation benefits, then this information has value only if the area has been preserved in period one. Based on the new information, a decision is then taken in period two over how much (if any) of the wilderness to develop. Such information might be, for example, that the area contains the last remnants of some rare species or is home to a plant with important medicinal properties. So long as there is a non-zero probability of such information becoming available, then a positive quasi-option value arises for the alternative of avoiding an irreversible development. This raises the opportunity costs of development. Development is therefore less likely to be preferred, *ceteris paribus*, when the existence of quasi-option value is admitted. However, while this is a helpful caution, the concept may be of little empirical use in CBA because of the difficulty of actually estimating quasi-option value.

Pethig (1991) has argued that quasi-option value is an inseparable element of preservation benefits. As Pethig states, "... good decisions about irreversibilities cannot be reached unless the best possible use of *all* available information is made". This includes the information that more information will become available in the future with a non-zero probability. Thus, the optimal procedure may be a strategy of sequential postponing of the decision to destroy a resource until new information becomes available (Pethig, p.94). Clearly, this argument can be carried to the point where society would never undertake irreversible actions, since additional "crucial" information may always be imminent. This would be similar to accepting the need for protecting natural capital from development as a response to the realization that humans are fundamentally ignorant in a way that denies reduction to probabilistic states of the world (Spash and Clayton, 1992).

9.3 ECOSYSTEM COMPLEXITY

CBA is a system of appraisal which needs figures for all relevant impacts of a project. As an example, take the benefits of reducing pesticide levels in ground water. A model is needed which relates reductions in pesticide use in certain areas to pesticide levels in ground water, which are in turn related to biological and chemical effects on aquatic ecosystems, and finally to economic welfare: the effect on the human welfare of farmer A applying pesticide X in quantity Q under conditions Y. This model will contain predictive errors if important variables are omitted, if the relationships between included variables are incorrectly specified, or if stochastic features (such as rainfall) have been inadequately represented. Building such models without these errors is thwarted due to the sheer complexity of ecosystems, the reactions between them, and between the economy and a group of ecosystems.

There are many instances where applying CBA to environmental management forces the analyst to deal with very complex phenomena. For instance, the action of cutting down rain-forest in Borneo, through its impact on latent heat exchange, may affect the El Nino-Southern Oscillation, which is responsible for climate regulation in many areas of the world. One impact of this action might be warm winters on the Prairies or droughts in Africa. Economic systems themselves are complex, combining economic with ecosystem effects increases the complexity of the problem many-fold.

As an illustration, consider an analyst seeking to estimate the costs of supporting grain prices for European farmers through the Common Agricultural Policy (CAP). By holding grain prices high, the CAP encouraged European livestock producers to seek cheaper feedstuffs for their animals. Cassava was imported from countries such as Thailand to partially meet this need. But land on which to grow cassava was obtained by felling rain forest, whilst the expansion, especially in the Dutch pig herd, lead to a big increase in manure production. This resulted in increased acid levels, both directly via ammonia release, and indirectly through eutrophication leading to an increase in sulphur-producing algae in the North Sea (Nisbet, 1991). These effects were unlikely to be predictable or predicted at the time when the support regime for grain in the CAP was being designed.

A substantial research effort has and is being targeted at modelling the complex interactions of economic policy and the environment. Examples include the International Institute for Applied Systems Analysis (IIASA) model of acid deposition in Europe; and the Centre for Agricultural and Rural Development (CARD) model of pesticide use and transport in the Mid West corn belt of the USA (Shogren et al., 1991). However, some economists have suggested that the methodology of economics and the nature of environmental systems are largely incompatible. Norgaard (1989) points to two features of economic methodology (more strictly, neo-classical economics) which weaken it as a useful approach. These are: (i) methodological monism and (ii) the atomistic-mechanistic approach.

Methodological monism means that neo-classical economics seeks single answers, searching for "the truth" or "true values". For example, economists attempt to determine the NPV of projects; the correct explanation of inflation; what rational agents will do when faced with a particular set of constraints and a particular objective. Norgaard argues that a pluralistic approach is more likely to be of use to environmental management. The atomistic-mechanistic emphasis in neo-classical economics relates to such fundamentals as the sovereignty of individual preferences over collective preferences which are more than the sum of the parts; as well as the desire to produce theories that give deterministic predictions. This atomistic-mechanistic approach is misleading where concern is for ecosystems which show synergism, antagonism and cumulative effects.

Yet, ultimately, CBA reduces to one number which represents the outcome of this process. This number may be an expected value (specifying a probability distribution for possible outcomes and deriving a mathematical expectation for the outcome), or it may be alternative values which are run through a sensitivity analysis. This reductionist feature of CBA has excited much criticism. For example, Soderbaum (1987, p.151) has commented:

For those who consider evolutionary processes and the paths that ecosystems take over time, the idea that non-monetary impacts at different points in time can somehow be pressed together ... is absurd.

The emergent paradigm of ecological economics seeks to address these problems, whilst retaining many of the useful features of neo-classical economics, such as the clarity with which arguments can be made, the emphasis on opportunity costs and price/profit signals, and the rent-seeking literature. However, ecological economics is very much an infant paradigm, and many methodological problems remain to be solved. The main features of this new approach, according to Klaasen and Opschoor (1991), are as follows:

(i)   Co-evolution. This concept, discussed by Norgaard (1984), refers to the tendency of economic and environmental systems to evolve together, linked by many feedback mechanisms which are themselves changing over time.[4] This implies that a growing economy is never in equilibrium, since the very process of growth alters the natural environment in which it must operate; these alterations in turn demand adjustments in economic activity (Perrings, 1987). Reductions in diversity reduce the resilience of ecosystems, which makes sudden shocks or "surprises" the rule rather than the exception (Timmerman, 1986).

(ii)   An emphasis on physical limits to recycling and technological improvements, which derive from the first and second laws of thermodynamics (Daly 1987; Christensen 1989).

(iii)   Community values that count for more than individual preferences. This point relates both to the lack of information on environmental impacts on the part of individuals, and to the environmental side-effects of individual actions. Values are judged to be different from wants (individual preferences), with the most important value being the continuity of life. This limits the importance given to individual wants, by placing environmental constraints on the set of possible behaviour. As Klaasen and Opschoor (1991, p.110) note:

... the value society attaches to natural resources and the environment is not merely the sum of all individual values. Environment is a "merit good", not merely to be determined by the aggregation of individual ... willingness to pay at any point in time.

9.4 INSTITUTIONAL CAPTURE

In any CBA, the analyst has considerable degrees of freedom in how she or he conducts the analysis. For example, what procedure should be used to forecast future benefits and costs? Which environmental impacts should be considered as significant, and how should they be measured? What discount rate should be used? What assumptions should be made regarding the "without" in a with-and-without type of appraisal? What is the relevant population over which to aggregate gainers and losers?

Often, CBA exercises are performed by government agencies and departments to decide on project and policy selection. Whilst, in many cases, certain aspects of the CBA process will be laid down by other arms of government (in the UK, for example, by the Treasury), in other parts of the analysis there is frequently considerable room for discretion and unilateral decisions. This sets up a potential problem if government agencies and departments are regarded as biased, self-interested and self-serving institutions. Public agencies could be regarded as revenue-maximizing monopolists, intent on maximizing their budgets since this brings power and influence. Whilst competition for a finite total of public spending will restrict this tendency, at least some public agencies can be expected to conduct CBAs in such a way as to maximize the probability of producing outcomes which are in their interest (and/or those of their senior managers).

There is some evidence to support this suggestion. Bowers (1988) has argued that water authorities in England carried out appraisals of large-scale land drainage schemes to maximize the probability that such projects passed the cost-benefit test. These projects were typically designed to allow farmers to change their production activities, switching from, for example, low-intensity livestock grazing on areas flooded in winter, to more profitable enterprises such as the growing of winter wheat. Bowers (1988) cites the following practices as examples of this:

● Assuming that the productivity levels of farms, after drainage had occurred, would replicate those on experimental farms.

● Ignoring the running costs of pumps operated by the water authority, either by itself or via Internal Drainage Boards (IDBs).

● Ignoring the capital costs to farmers of connecting their land to new channels and widened rivers provided by the IDBs.

● Using farm gate prices to value outputs, even though such prices are distorted by support payments to the extent that the marginal social benefits of additional farm outputs are, in most cases, below the farm gate equivalents.

In the case of the USA, Sagoff (1988) has argued that CBA was "captured" by the incoming Reagan administration in 1981 to help forestall new regulatory policies and to aid in the deregulation of the market economy. This related in particular to environmental regulations passed by the EPA and to health and safety regulations (Smith, 1984). The Reagan administration passed Executive Order 12291 requiring all major new regulatory proposals to be subject to a CBA. This lead Sagoff (1988, p.22) to observe:

> The Reagan administration reasoned correctly that hundreds of economists happily whacking away at their CBAs would constitute a layer of bureaucracy impervious to any effort line agencies might make to fulfil their legislative mandate.

The time dimension of projects offers another avenue for rent-seeking. Governmental agencies may choose to exclude long-term future costs implied by project/policy choices (such as the decommissioning of nuclear reactors in the UK). If the types of projects an agency typically promotes are particularly sensitive to the choice of discount rate, then the agency may lobby for the right to use a rate which favours acceptance of the type of project it promotes. Two obvious examples as mentioned in the preceding chapter are publicly-funded dam construction and irrigation schemes in the USA, where lower rates of discount were permitted relative to the rate on other public-funded projects; and forestry in the UK, where for a long time the Forestry Commission argued for, and was allowed to use, a lower discount rate than the rest of the public sector. This latter example is perhaps the clearest instance of an agency with an incentive to bid for low rates, since forestry returns are far removed in time from the bulk of expenditures. This low rate was, interestingly, justified by appealing to the non-market benefits of forestry (such as recreation), but not the non-market costs. Finally, Lind (1982) argues that the Nixon administration in the US chose a high discount rate for most federally-funded projects to help achieve its stated aim of reducing public expenditure. These problems over discount rate selection clearly result from the point made in Chapter 8 that there is no universally appropriate rate of discount for the government to use.

In order to illustrate how CBA results can be presented in a manner likely to be advantageous to proponents (or opponents) of a development, we will use the case of Cardiff Bay, an estuarine area which divides South Wales from South-West England. A development plan proposed the construction of a barrage across Cardiff Bay. This would convert the bay from a tidal saltwater area into a freshwater lake. The bay is a winter roosting site for about 5,000 to 6,000 wildfowl and waders, who return to Greenland, Russia and Scandinavia in summer, and resident birds, giving a peak population of about 88,000 birds (Nugent, 1989). If the barrage went ahead, the feeding grounds (the inter-tidal mud flats) would be permanently flooded. Most of the birds would have to move elsewhere - which is apparently unlikely - or would simply die (EAU, 1989). In addition, since the natural flushing process in estuaries would be hindered by the barrage, pollutants flowing in from the Rivers Taff and Ely would accumulate in the freshwater lagoon. Statutory and voluntary nature conservation bodies have opposed the scheme.

The project has been promoted by an arm of regional government, the Cardiff Bay Development Corporation (CBDC), encouraged by the Welsh Office. The CBDC has claimed that the barrage would create new recreational developments, such as leisure boating marinas made possible as the barrage stabilizes water levels. As the project would use public funds, the CBDC presented CBAs of the project, prepared by consultants, to support its case for development. Initially, these compared development effects in the entire Cardiff Bay area under two scenarios: with the barrage and without the barrage.[5] Neither of these appraisals contained allowance for environmental impacts. Later, a third alternative was added, that of a mini-barrage, as proposed by a confederation of environmental groups opposing the development. This mini-barrage would cut off a much smaller part of the Bay.

As can be seen from the (unadjusted) NPV results shown in Table 9.1, the CBA appears to favour the full barrage scheme. However, many criticisms can be levelled at the CBAs carried out for the CBDC; see Bowers (1989) and Hanley et al. (1991). For example, given a barrage go - ahead, unrealistic growth rates for commercial property values were used, whilst no allowance was made for the higher environmental damages of the full barrage option. CBDC also listed the benefits attached to a new road link as being relevant to the barrage alternative. This road project will go ahead despite the barrage project and should therefore be excluded from the benefits calculated for the barrage project relative to the other two alternatives.

Another area where choices can be crucial to the outcome of a CBA is the selection of the population over which benefits are aggregated. If the Cardiff area only is taken as relevant, then all development benefits of the project are incremental or additional, to use the term from Chapter 1. However, for the UK as a whole, some of the new housing and commercial investments made possible by the barrage are unlikely to be additional, due to displaced investment elsewhere in the country. This is irrelevant to CBDC, since its remit is simply to further prosperity in the Cardiff Bay area. However, given that UK taxpayers would be funding much of the bill for the project, the UK government should take a broader view than that proposed by the CBDC.

Including some of the criticisms in the CBA of the barrage project, while continuing to exclude the environmental damages, makes the full barrage option much less attractive. As may be seen in the last line of Table 9.1, NPV adjusted, by allowing for 50% displacement in development benefits, by omitting the road project and by assuming lower growth rates for commercial rents and land values, a very different picture emerges. Even excluding the environmental cost, the barrage is now no longer the preferred alternative and neither of the development projects appears attractive.

Table 9.1 CBA of Cardiff Bay Barrage (£million, 1989/90)

	Alternative Project Options		
	Barrage	Mini-Barrage	No Barrage
Costs:			
Barrage	121.55	28.38	0.00
Shadow Project[1]	4.00	4.00	0.00
Site Preparation	147.25	90.29	86.36
Access Costs[2]	152.80	143.44	140.65
Landscaping	95.89	53.29	18.22
Others	25.00	25.00	25.00
TOTAL COST	433.00	267.00	203.00
Benefits:			
Land Value	490.00	120.00	26.00
Property Appreciation	244.00	62.00	11.00
TOTAL BENEFITS	734.00	182.00	37.00
NPV	301.00	-85.00	-166.00
NPV Adjusted	-206.00	-139.00	-100.00

[1]Creation of a bird reserve.
[2]Includes a link road and light transit scheme.
NPV is rounded. Costs and benefits discounted at 8%.
Source: adapted from Hanley et al. (1991).

9.5 CBA AND SUSTAINABLE DEVELOPMENT

Since the publication of the report of the World Commission on Environment and Development in 1987 ("Our Common Future"), sustainable development has been a buzz-word much in use. Economists have tried to formalize the concept, and to see how traditional and new models of economic development fit in with it. In particular, economists have been concerned to try and work out the necessary conditions for an economy's development to be sustainable. Does undertaking CBAs of all projects having environmental impacts make an economy's development path more or less sustainable?

In order to answer this question, a definition of sustainable development is needed. Following Pezzey (1989), four alternative definitions may be considered:

(i)   Non-declining consumption through time.
(ii)   Non-declining utility through time.
(iii)   A non-declining stock of total capital (man-made and natural) through time.
(iv)   A non-declining stock of natural capital through time.

Definition (i), which is the focus of neo-classical optimal growth models such as that of Hartwick (1977), is clearly restrictive since individuals only derive happiness from the consumption of produced goods and services. Definition (ii) deals with an unmeasurable concept (utility), and has proved intractable when the many influences on utility and their interdependence are considered. Also, approach (ii) forces the definition of utility functions for the unborn. Definitions (iii) and (iv) are concerned with the maintenance of opportunity, that is, allowing future generations the opportunity to derive such utility as they choose, by guaranteeing them a no less effective set of building blocks than is possessed at present. If these building blocks consist of a combination of man-made capital assets (such as machines) and natural capital assets (such as fossil fuels and the ozone layer), then so long as there is a sufficient degree of substitutability between the two types, society need only worry about holding constant the aggregate of the two.

However, there are clearly many elements of the natural capital stock which cannot easily be substituted for by man-made capital. Outside of a technocentric dream world, mankind is unable to replace the stratospheric ozone layer. Similarly, a film featuring blue whales is a poor substitute for a viable population. The very term "natural capital" may be misleading since the ability of mankind to substitute and reproduce capital is implied (Victor, 1991). In addition, natural capital is required to produce man-made capital. If natural and man-made capital are poor substitutes and if some elements of the natural capital stock are viewed as essential to future generations, then a sub-set of the natural capital stock must be maintained intact.[6]

This view seems an attractive safety-first option. Yet, there are considerable problems concerning the way in which natural capital is defined, which will affect the strategies adopted for the maintenance and the success with which they are regarded (see Spash and Clayton, 1992). For example, should natural capital be measured in physical or monetary units? Physical units confound addition since an oak forest cannot be added to a blue whale. Only if the two types of natural assets are expressed in a common metric can they be aggregated, the most obvious unit being money. However, this may be seen as objectionable, since one whale worth £10 million is then equivalent to 1000 whales worth £10,000 each. However, if natural assets are held constant in physical terms, the level at which the category is defined will become all-important. Consider the maintenance of woodlands in Britain by constant total area. This woodland stock definition might raise the objection that a hectare of sitka spruce is less valuable than a hectare of native Scots pine or of ancient oak. The category could be disaggregated to hold constant the stock of deciduous trees and the stock of conifers. However, some might wish to go further and adopt the Nature Conservancy Council's definition of 25 different types of woodland. Van Pelt (1993) identifies another problem with the constant-natural capital stock concept. This is the problem of spatial aggregation: within which geographic area should we hold stocks constant?

If the natural capital stock cannot be fully aggregated, then it may be necessary to compartmentalise it, and keep each compartment constant. Van Pelt (op cit) suggests pollution, renewable resources, biodiversity, pollution assimilation capacity and non-renewable resources as possible categories. However, non-renewable resources, such as oil, are by definition fixed finite stocks which must decline with use.[7] The only way to maintain a constant economic reserve is for new discoveries to equal extraction; also for cost-savings per unit extracted to decrease with technological progress as quickly as they rise due to cumulative extraction. More strictly, given a finite total crustal abundance of each non-renewable resource, only a zero extraction rate is consistent with a constant natural capital stock unless tradeoffs are permitted between renewable and non-renewable resources. This tradeoff approach is favoured by Daly (1991) who advises that (i) extraction be minimised, and (ii) enough of the returns from extraction be reinvested in renewable alternatives, such as biomass for oil, so that when the non-renewable resource is exhausted, the renewable replacement is available. This requires that the renewable should be a perfect substitute for the non-renewable resource it replaces in terms of maintaining potential consumption.

If the constant stock of natural capital definition of sustainable development is adopted in monetary terms, can CBA be regarded as consistent with this rule? According to Pearce et al. (1990), the answer is a qualified "yes". Consider a project with net environmental costs e_c^1. This magnitude might measure the loss, in money terms, of air quality due to increased carbon dioxide emissions. One rule for holding the natural capital stock constant would be to prohibit any project i for which $e_c^i > 0$. However, this would be very restrictive. An alternative is to insist on some other project (a "shadow project") being undertaken which has a net environmental benefit e_b^2 which is equal to or greater than e_c^1. More generally, society could insist that, across a portfolio of projects, the sum of net environmental damages should be no greater than the sum of net environmental benefits, so that:

$$\sum_i e_c^i \leq \sum_i e_b^i \quad (i = 1 \ldots n) \qquad (9.3)$$

Equation (9.3) can be interpreted as a sustainability constraint on CBA. The portfolio in question could be the capital spending programme for one financial year of a government agency, or total investment spending by the public sector, or even total investment spending by the private sector. Pearce et al. define a strong and a weak sustainability constraint. The strong form is where, in each time period over which an investment portfolio runs, equation (9.3) holds. In other words, in every year, net environmental damages are less than or equal to zero. The weak form of the constraint is where, across the time-span of the portfolio, the discounted sums of environmental gains should be at least as great as the discounted sums of environmental losses. This means that equation (9.3) would be interpreted in present value terms. As Van den Bergh and Nijkamp (1991, p.15) note, shadow projects try to replace lost environmental values or, preferably, avoid the environmental degradation and disturbance caused by the original project. However, they go on to point out that natural resources fulfil many functions, and the future consequences of shadow projects may be many, uncertain and also negative. Four further difficulties exist with the above approach. First, it assumes perfect substitutability between types of natural assets. In other words, a $1 million loss in redwood forest is equivalent to a $1 million gain in urban air quality. Second, all environmental impacts of all investment projects must be assessed in monetary terms. Third, if the weak form of the constraint is used, this sets up the possibility of a small quantity of current environmental improvements being used to offset a very large quantity of environmental losses in the future. Suppose society knows that emissions of mercury into the sea will cause a sudden collapse of the dolphin population in 40 years time, which in real terms has a value (estimated say from a recent CVM survey) of £3 million. At a 10% real rate of discount, a year one environmental benefit of £66,285 is sufficient to offset this. That is commensurate, perhaps, with staffing a small countryside park for a year. Fourth, the issue as to who will pay for the shadow projects is unresolved.

The definition of shadow projects considered so far denominates both the impacts of such projects and the effects they are designed to offset, in money terms. A dollar's worth of environmental gain is to offset a dollar's worth of environmental loss. Alternatively, shadow projects can be conceived of in physical terms. Here, the goal changes from being a constant money value of the natural capital stock to constant physical amounts of different types of natural assets. This is the form in which such shadow projects have been used (to a very limited extent) in reality. Examples of such physical compensation include planting trees to absorb the carbon dioxide equivalent to the emissions from a new thermal power station, and physically relocating part of a heath in Eastern England (Hanley et al., 1991). Some proposed shadow projects have not stood up to close scrutiny. For example, the Cardiff Bay development discussed in section 9.4 contains a proposal to replace the lost feeding and roosting grounds by creating a replacement mud flats site. One hundred and sixty-five hectares of Cardiff Bay are designated as a Site of Special Scientific Interest (SSSI). The development corporation proposed creating a shadow project at Wentloodge, a nearby site of twenty-three hectares. Such a small site is an imperfect substitute for the loss of the Cardiff Bay SSSI, resulting in a net decline in both mud flats area and wildfowl numbers. Furthermore, Wentloodge itself is due for notification as an SSSI, due to its current status as a regionally-rare wet pasture. So even if the decline in mud flats and feeding grounds was at least offset, the regional stock of wet pastures would fall. More generally, if a physical, type-specific definition of the natural capital stock is used, only ecologically worthless elements of the stock are available to act as substitutes. Otherwise, a loss in one asset type will accompany an offsetting increase in another type.

In a review of strategies for natural capital maintenance Spash and Clayton (1992) argue that both the economic CBA approach and physical compensation schemes suffer from the same problems. By definition both methods allow for tradeoffs which the very concept of natural capital maintenance is trying to refute. The proposition that a core or critical natural capital stock is all that society need preserve only relaxes the constraint on trade-offs for the current generation. The recognition that humanity is ignorant of the outcomes of some actions and cannot reduce the world to a set of probabilistic events argues for extreme caution, which maintenance of natural capital supports. An alternative to the previously mentioned methods is to adopt a systems approach, where economic values and indicators such as CBA are but one class of inputs to judging the success which society is achieving in terms of sustainability.

9.6 CONCLUSIONS

In this chapter, four problem areas for CBA have been identified and discussed: irreversibility, ecosystem complexity, institutional capture and sustainability considerations. Some progress is being made on improving practice with regard to irreversibility as new research is conducted on quasi-option value. Economists realizing the importance of ecosystem complexity have moved towards a closer union with ecologists and have high hopes for developments in ecological economics. Institutional capture emphasizes the political nature of decision-making. CBA is increasingly being used as a tool of argument and/or litigation between opposing agents, such as between the environmental lobby and Exxon over the Exxon Valdez disaster, over the construction of nuclear power stations (e.g., Sizewell B), and over visibility in the Grand Canyon. The best approach is to recognize that there are many problem areas in applying CBA to environmental management, and that analysts should proceed with great caution in both conducting and appraising CBA studies.

The concept of sustainability and the constraints it implies on economic activity have proved difficult to operationalize. Work is beginning to emerge on improving our conceptualization of the natural capital stock approach (Perrings, 1991). The complexity of the issues involved favours an approach which allows information to be maintained rather than reduced to a single metric. However, the process of conducting a CBA and the monetary values it estimates are both sources of new information in themselves. There are no obvious replacements for the information CBA provides on environmental problems, and we would therefore argue that it is a useful input to the decision-making process.

REFERENCES

Arrow K and Fisher A (1974) "Environmental preservation, uncertainty and irreversibility" *Quarterly Journal of Economics* 88: 312-319.

Bowers J (1988) "Cost-benefit analysis in theory and practice: agricultural land drainage projects" in R K Turner (editor) *Sustainable Environmental Management* London: Bellhaven Press.

Bowers J (1989) "The economic evaluation of the Cardiff Bay barrage scheme" University of Leeds, Leeds Public Sector Policy Unit.

Christensen P (1989) "Historical roots for ecological economics: biophysical versus allocative approaches" *Ecological Economics* 1: 17-36.

Costanza R (1991) *Ecological Economics: The Science and Management of Sustainability* Irvington, NY: Columbia University Press.

Daly H (1987) "The economic growth debate: what some economists may have learnt but many have not" *Journal of Environmental Economics and Management* 14: 323-336.

Daly H (1992) "Allocation, distribution, and scale: towards an economics that is efficient, just, and sustainable" *Ecological Economics* 6(3): 185-194.

Environmental Advisory Unit (1989) "Cardiff Bay barrage: environmental assessment" University of Liverpool, EAU.

Hanley N and Craig S (1991) "The economic value of wilderness areas: an application of the Krutilla-Fisher model to Scotland's flow country" in Dietz, van der Ploeg and van der Straaten (editors) *Environmental Policy and the Economy* Amsterdam: Elsevier.

Hanley N, Munro A and Jamieson D (1991) "Environmental economics, nature conservation and sustainable development" Report to Nature Conservancy Council, Peterborough, England.

Hartwick J (1977) "Intergenerational equity and investing rents from non-renewable resources" *American Economic Review* 972-976.

Hanemann W (1989) "Information and the concept of option value" *Journal of Environmental Economics and Management* 16: 23-37.

Henry C (1974) "Option values in the economics of irreplaceable assets" Review of Economic Studies (symposium on the economics of exhaustible resources) 89-104.

Klaasen G and Opschoor J (1991) "Economics of sustainability or the sustainability of economics" *Ecological Economics* 4: 93-116.

Krutilla J and Fisher A (1975, 1985) *The Economics of Natural Environments* Baltimore: Johns Hopkins Press for Resources for the Future.

Lind R (1982) *Discounting for Time and Risk in Energy Policy* Baltimore: Johns Hopkins Press for Resources for the Future.

Nisbet E (1991) *Leaving Eden: To Protect and Manage the Earth* Cambridge University Press.

Norgaard R (1984) "Co-evolutionary development potential" *Land Economics* 60: 160-173.

Norgaard R (1989) "The case for methodological pluralism" *Ecological Economics* 1: 37-58.

Nugent M J (1989) Evidence to House of Lords Hearing on the Cardiff Bay Barrage Bill.

Pearce D, Markandya A and Barbier E (1990) *Sustainable Development* Cheltenham: Edward Elgar.

Perrings C (1987) *Economy and Environment* Cambridge University Press.

Perrings C (1991) "The preservation of natural capital and environmental control" Mimeo, The Beijer Institute, Stockholm.

Pethig R (1991) "Problems of irreversibility in the control of persistent micro-pollutants" in H Opschoor and D W Pearce (editors) *Persistent Pollutants: Economics and Policy* Dordrecht: Kluwer.

Pezzey J (1989) Economic analysis of sustainable development and sustainable growth. Discussion Paper 15, Washington DC, World Bank.

Porter R (1982) "The new approach to wilderness appraisal through cost-benefit analysis" *Journal of Environmental Economics and Management* 9: 59-80.

Sagoff M (1988) *The Economy of the Earth* Cambridge University Press.

Shogren J, Bouzaher A, Johnson S and Manale A (1991) "CEEPES: an evolving framework for agri-ecological economic analysis" Mimeo, Center for Agricultural and Rural Development, Iowa State University.

Shukla J, Nobre C and Sellers P (1990) "Amazon deforestation and climate change" *Science* 247: 1322-5.

Smith V (1984) *Environmental Policy under Reagan's Executive Order* Chapel Hill: University of North Carolina Press.

Soderbaum P (1987) "Environmental management" *Journal of Economic Issues* 21: 139-165.

Spash C L and Clayton A M D (1992) Strategies for the Maintenance of Natural Capital. Paper to the International Society for Ecological Economics, Stockholm, August.

Timmerman P (1986) "Mythology and surprise in the sustainable development of the biosphere" in W C Clark and R E Munn (editors) *Sustainable Development in the Biosphere* Cambridge University Press.

Van den Bergh J and Nijkamp P (1991) "Operationalizing sustainable development: dynamic ecological economic models" *Ecological Economics* 4(1): 11-34.
Victor P A (1991) "Indicators of sustainable development: some lessons from capital theory" *Ecological Economics* 4(3): 191-214.

ENDNOTES

1. Latent energy transfer from tropical forests also transfers heat from the equator to the poles, making the heat distribution on earth less unequal than it would otherwise be (Nisbet, 1991).

2. This parameter might, for other development projects, show the rate of *increase* in real development benefits. For example, in the case of a forestry project g would be the real rate of growth in the price of timber.

3. Hanemann (1989) considers the case of intermediate levels of development, but admitting this possibility complicates the analysis.

4. An example from ecology is the co-evolution of the shapes of hummingbirds' beaks and the shapes of the flowers they feed from (Christensen, 1989).

5. Some development has and will occur without the barrage: improved road links, for example, to make the area more attractive for further development.

6. As Victor has pointed out, this involves placing a further restriction on the relative elasticities of output with respect to man-made and to natural capital (Victor, 1991).

7. Renewable resources, such as North Sea herring, can be maintained by constraining harvesting to less than the sustainable annual yield at the current population level.

PART II

Case Studies

10 TROPOSPHERIC OZONE DAMAGE TO AGRICULTURAL CROPS

10.1 INTRODUCTION

The topic of this chapter is ozone smog or tropospheric ozone pollution and the assessment of one aspect of this problem: impacts on agricultural crops. However, the techniques and their problems are applicable to a wide range of impacts from materials damages to human health effects. In addition, the methods explained have been applied to agricultural damages related to both acid deposition (see section 10.4 and Adams et al., 1985) and global climate change (Adams et al., 1988). We concentrate on the estimation of the tangible benefits from policies to reduce tropospheric ozone concentrations.

10.2 TROPOSPHERIC OZONE POLLUTION

Ozone at the tropospheric level (the lowest 10-15 kilometres of the atmosphere) is a separate issue from ozone holes in the upper atmosphere (the stratosphere). All references to ozone here are to tropospheric ozone, unless otherwise stated. While perhaps a less dramatic issue, tropospheric ozone is a well-documented cause of a range of environmental impacts, and is commonly associated with the urban pollution problems of cities such as Los Angeles, Tokyo and Athens. Photochemical oxidants, of which ozone is the most prevalent, are capable of causing plant damage, affecting human health, disrupting ecosystem structures and stability, and reacting with a number of non-biological materials (e.g., rubber), as well as forming a visibility-reducing blue haze. As the most prevalent photochemical oxidant, ozone has been studied extensively and is commonly used as the basis for photochemical oxidant air quality standards.

Injury to plants from photochemical smog was first noted in 1944 when stippling and glazing or bronzing of the leaves of vegetables were discovered in the Los Angeles basin, California. Tropospheric ozone concentrations alone or in combination with sulphur dioxide and nitrogen dioxide have since been identified as the major source of crop losses caused by air pollution in the United States (Heck et al., 1982). The scientific evidence is growing that both ozone and acid deposition are causing extensive damage to vegetation in both Europe and the U.S. (see MacKenzie and El-Ashry, 1989).

Sources of Ozone

Ozone is formed in the atmosphere from "precursor emissions". Non-methane hydrocarbons, nitrogen dioxide and nitric oxide are the main precursor emissions causing oxidant formation. Naturally occurring, background tropospheric ozone varies seasonally and with latitude, but is normally assumed constant, e.g., 0.025 ppm (parts per million) measured over seven hours of daylight during the growing season (i.e., 7 hours/day seasonal) in U.S. experiments on plant response (Heck et al., 1984). Recognition of the existence of a background level implies a base concentration which policies designed to control anthropogenic sources will leave unaffected.

The basic process of ozone formation is a part of the nitrogen dioxide photolytic cycle. Oxygen atoms (O) are derived principally from the dissociation of nitrogen dioxide (NO_2) by solar radiation: NO_2 + ultra-violet radiation = NO + O. This atomic oxygen reacts rapidly with molecular oxygen (O_2) to form ozone (O_3): $O + O_2 = O_3$. Ozone in turn reacts with nitrogen oxide (NO) to form nitrogen dioxide again: $NO + O_3 = NO_2 + O_2$.

The transportation sector is normally the primary source of anthropogenic ozone precursors. Hydrocarbons released from vehicle exhausts unbalance the naturally occurring nitrogen dioxide cycle by converting nitrogen oxide to nitrogen dioxide without consuming an equivalent amount of ozone. The resulting concentration of ozone varies with temporal variations in precursor emissions (e.g., rush-hour traffic), atmospheric dispersion capacity, and the intensity of solar radiation. The multiple input of pollutants (cumulative loading) as a parcel of air moves across a region can cause downwind (e.g., rural) areas to receive high ozone concentrations absent from upwind (e.g., urban) monitoring stations. For example, there is clear evidence of the effects of such cumulative loading on areas downwind of the London plume (Varey et al., 1980).

Primary and Secondary Standards

The approach to ozone regulation taken by the United States consists of a primary standard designed to protect human health, and a secondary standard to protect other aspects of human welfare (e.g., materials, crops, visibility). The primary standard aims to protect the health of even the most sensitive members of the public with a safety margin. The initial U.S. national ambient air quality standard for ozone was set in 1971 at 0.8 ppm for both standards, not to be exceeded more than one hour per year. Review of the standards in 1979 relaxed both to 0.12 ppm, with the standard not to be exceeded on an average of three days over three consecutive years. While economic information has no role in setting these standards, economists have attempted to measure the social costs of pollution to assess whether a particular standard should be supported. In this respect the relaxation of the ozone standard from 0.08 ppm to 0.12 ppm led to several studies of the economic implications for crop production. In addition, there is good reason to have different primary and secondary standards and to adopt alternative measures of concentration for each, given the different damages society is trying to prevent in each case.

In Europe ozone itself is uncontrolled. This might imply that ozone is either below levels at which damages occur or that current controls of precursor emissions are sufficient. However, the persistence of ozone smogs in cities such as Athens suggests otherwise. The trend towards hot dry summers implied by global warming will increase the concentration of tropospheric ozone from available precursors. In addition, precursor emissions will increase with the volume of traffic, which is rising with both population and car ownership per capita, as well as with sales to the previously unexploited market of the former Eastern bloc. Thus, ozone control is likely to be a policy issue across Europe in the near future.

10.3 DEFINING DOSE

The effects of air pollution on vegetation are influenced by biotic, climatic and edaphic (i.e., soil) variables. Inherent genetic resistance has been cited as probably the most important factor influencing plant response to air pollutants. Plant response to ozone varies among species of a given genus (e.g., potato) and varieties or cultivars within a given species (Linzon, et al., 1984).

Ozone, as with other air pollutants, damages a plant after entering the stomatal leaf opening (Holdgate, 1979). Thus, factors affecting stomatal size and opening determine pollutant uptake and the potential for damage. For example, reduced moisture or increased temperature can cause reduced stomatal apertures and higher resistance to air pollution. Plants under no such stresses, growing under favourable conditions, may therefore be more susceptible to damage. In general, plants are better able to cope with exposure to ozone at night (because stomata are closed), and at lower temperatures and relative humidity; they are more susceptible to ozone damage when the leaves are mature, due to the increase in cell gaps (Medeiros and Moscowitz, 1983).

Farm practices may also alter plant response to air pollution. For example, attempts to improve growing conditions (e.g., irrigation) and reduce plant stress could increase ozone susceptibility. The mixture of production inputs is a factor often ignored in the derivation of dose-response functions under experimental conditions (Adams and Crocker, 1984). Cultural and input variations between regions make dose-response functions which have been derived in one area inappropriate for use in another area. Even when the same inputs and cultivars are used in two different regions, all the other factors would have to concur before a dose-response function derived in one region could be used accurately to predict the yield loss in the second region. This problem is an important criticism of current dose-response methods.

The ambient ozone concentration, the length of time a particular concentration persists and the frequency of occurrences combine to form a measure of the dose of an air pollutant to which a plant is exposed: the "exposure dose". Other characteristics of plant exposure may also be important determinants of the nature and magnitude of the effects of ozone on plants: the length of time between exposures, the time of day of exposure, their sequence and pattern, and the total flux of ozone to the plant as it is affected by canopy characteristics and leaf boundary layers. However, as Table 10.1 shows, ozone studies into crop productivity have largely defined exposure dose in terms of concentration, duration and frequency to the exclusion of other factors.

Table 10.1 Details of Ozone Exposure in 23 Studies of Crop Loss

Details Provided	Number of Publications
Concentration	23
Duration	18
Frequency	16
Time between exposures	13
Time of day	6
Fluctuation of concentrations	3
Patterns (sequence)	0
Flux	0

Source: Jacobson (1982) p.298, Table 14.2.

Several types of exposure dose measures have been employed in ozone studies. An extensive project on crop damage due to ozone was conducted by the National Crop Loss Assessment Network (NCLAN) of the United States Environmental Protection Agency (EPA) in the 1980s. NCLAN employed a seasonal seven hour/day mean ozone concentration exposure statistic in all its published dose-response functions. This mean is calculated upon the seven hours judged to be the most susceptible for plants; that is, between 0900 and 1600 hours. The daily means for the seven-hour period are then averaged over the entire growing season, i.e., the period of pollution concentrations relevant to the object being damaged.

The seasonal seven-hour mean statistic combines a large number of ozone concentration observations. However, as Heck et al. (1984) state:

> There is no consensus on an exposure statistic(s) that will best relate to the potential response of plants to varying O_3 concentrations over a growing season. It is generally accepted that the degree of plant response is affected more by differences in concentration than by differences in duration of exposure. Thus a given seasonal mean concentration that includes many high O_3 concentrations could cause greater effects than would the same mean that includes few high O_3 concentrations. This hypothesis is untested for O_3. Possibly no single exposure statistic will be adequate for all crops under all environmental conditions.

The implication is that high ozone concentrations may be lost in the statistic but could be an important explanation of crop loss and therefore need to be taken into account. Thus, NCLAN discussed the use of alternative exposure statistics such as the peak (maximum) daily seven-hour mean ozone concentration occurring during the growing season; the seasonal mean of the daily maximum one-hour mean ozone concentrations; and the peak (maximum) one-hour mean ozone concentration occurring during the season.

The measure of dose used must be compatible with ambient air quality data to enable the development of useful predictive models (Heck et al., 1980). Typically, ozone standards are set where the primary concern is with the threshold for acute damage to human health, and may therefore be inappropriate for dose-response studies. In order to use a different exposure statistic for a standard and a response model, the distribution of ozone in the ambient air needs to provide a basis for using one statistic as a surrogate for another. For example, assume that a seasonal average concentration is discovered at which there is no crop loss, and that this seasonal average is *never* exceeded when a certain hourly peak ozone concentration is not exceeded. Under these circumstances the analyst can reasonably assume that crops are protected when the hourly peak is not exceeded. Unfortunately, the seasonal mean can vary widely, while the peak value remains constant and is unlikely to *always* remain at or below a certain value. The implication for ozone standards is that they should employ concentration measures which relate to chronic, as well as acute, damage.

10.4 DERIVING DOSE-RESPONSE FUNCTIONS FOR CROPS

Three main approaches have been employed to derive dose-response relationships for ozone: (a) foliar injury models, (b) secondary response data and (c) experimentation.

(a) Foliar Injury Models

Early studies assumed a threshold below which no damage was presumed to occur and related this to visible, normally foliar, injury. These foliar injury models can be misleading as signs of yield loss because tubers, roots and dry weight, among other factors, can be affected without visible damage. Conversely foliar injury may overestimate damage because some plants can suffer severe leaf damage without loss of photosynthetic ability, and recovery from visible injury can be quick (Leung, et al., 1978). Generally, three types of response to air pollution can be defined; visible injury symptoms, growth responses and quality changes. Foliar injury models ignore "hidden injury" which may occur with the latter two responses. Medeiros and Moscowitz (1983, p.506) note that:

> Hidden injury may include: (1) reduced photosynthetic activity, (2) accumulation of a pollutant or its byproducts within a leaf, (3) an overall unhealthy appearance without necrotic lesions, (4) reduced growth or yield, and (5) increased susceptibility to disease, particularly insect invasion.

Studies with soybeans, tomatoes, annual rye grass, spinach, wheat, lettuce and potatoes have demonstrated that foliar-symptom production is an unreliable index of ozone effects on plant growth or yield (Jacobson, 1982).

(b) Secondary Response Data

Cross-sectional analysis of crop yield data is used to obtain dose-response functions via regression techniques. Information is required on the existing outdoor variations in air pollution, actual crop yields and other environmental factors. Such an approach can save time and money compared to the use of chamber studies under the experimental approach, discussed below.

Leung et al. (1982) obtained statistically significant results for nine crops using this technique; however, the results were sometimes inconsistent when compared to experimental chamber studies, and ozone levels in the study region were high. Rowe and Chestnut (1985) attempted to derive dose-response functions for 10 crops but could only obtain significant results for four of these. They found that the success of the approach was generally dependent upon the effort made to measure and incorporate non-air pollution variables in the yield functions. Generally, their results suggested that ozone was causing yield losses, but the secondary data regression approach captured the effects for only the most sensitive crops, i.e., those which experienced high rates of damage at low ozone levels such as dry beans, cotton, grapes and potatoes.

(c) Experimentation

Several experimental approaches have been developed in studies of ozone effects on crops; these include the use of greenhouses, field chambers (open-top or close-top), unenclosed field plots and the pollution gradient approach. Each approach varies in design or exposure system but, for use in economic assessments, the environmental and exposure conditions occurring on actual farms should be replicated, with only air pollution concentration being modified (Unsworth, 1982). While general responses to ozone of plants grown in different environments may be similar, the quantitative relationships between dose and response are clearly affected by environmental conditions.

10.5 RESPONSE FUNCTIONS IN ECONOMIC ASSESSMENTS

Response functions derived from a variety of methodologies have been applied in economic assessments of air pollution damage to agricultural crops. Early work in this area depended upon trained field observers using their judgement to estimate crop damage from visible symptoms (US EPA, 1974). These subjective estimates (often arbitrarily converted into monetary values) were replaced by foliar injury models. In turn, foliar injury models have been found deficient in several aspects, and response functions derived from scientific field experimentation are now commonly applied in economic assessments.

As Table 10.2 shows for the U.S., 10 out of 15 studies since 1982 have relied upon NCLAN response data, derived from field experiments, as their main source. Of the six studies recently carried out at the national level (for the U.S.), all used the NCLAN data. At the regional level a mixture of data sources is often used. For example, the two studies using secondary data, discussed above, also made use of experimental data for some crops. NCLAN data is a primary source of response information but has so far been restricted to major U.S. agricultural crops. Thus the research of other scientists is employed for important regional crops.

While the derivation of response functions used in economic assessments has improved, the application of the functions has sometimes been both technically and economically deficient. Serious errors can arise from extrapolating from a limited data base. For example, the Organization for Economic Cooperation and Development (OECD, 1981) performed a cost-benefit analysis of sulphur oxide which included the benefits expected from

Table 10.2: Main Source(s) of Response Functions Used in 15 Recent Economic Studies of Ozone Effects on Agriculture

Source of Dose-Response Data		Number of Publications
Experimentation:	NCLAN	10
	Other	3
Secondary		2
Foliar injury		1
Field observation		0

Source: Spash (1987), Table 11.

crop loss reductions under various scenarios. A dose-yield relationship was developed from information on the response to sulphur dioxide of rye grass (Lolium perenne) and applied to all crops throughout Europe. Barnes et al. (1983) have made the following major criticisms of this study:

(i)   It ignored crop and cultivar sensitivities: rye grass is one of the crops most sensitive to sulphur dioxide, resulting in over-estimation of damages.

(ii)   It ignored differences in soil sulphur content: the rye grass studies used gave the plant nutritionally adequate supplies, again leading to over-estimation of damage because nutrient-deficient soils actually benefit from sulphur deposition.

(iii) Over-estimation was created by extended extrapolation beyond plant threshold and background pollutant levels, thus creating the illusion of damages when they would be absent or irrelevant to the control of anthropogenic sources.

(iv)   The research into rye grass used was mostly from laboratory or greenhouse experiments. This can give results varying widely from plant response to sulphur oxide under field conditions.

This kind of extrapolation and use of response functions ignore the limits of the data base. The application of one set of results to other crops, cultivars, regions or countries abstracts from variations in plant sensitivity and environmental conditions. However, a certain amount of extrapolation can be justified. In the case of ozone, data are unavailable for many regionally important crops and cultivars; so far, experimental results are largely derived for the major crop-growing regions of the U.S. In the absence of alternative data, "surrogate" response functions have been used for crops judged to be of similar sensitivity. For example, Howitt et al. (1984) studied the economic effects of ozone on 13 crops. They used NCLAN data for 7 crops and derived 5 "surrogate" response functions. Such use of response data relies upon the judgement of researchers and implicitly involves the subjective estimation of uncertainty. This type of probabilistic estimation requires explicit explanation of the areas of uncertainty so that the accuracy of, and possible bias in, the final results are clear.

10.6 REGIONAL ECONOMIC ASSESSMENTS OF CROP LOSS

In this section studies using the methods explained in Chapter 6 are described. The majority of recent economic assessments of ozone damage to crops have been at the regional level, and these have employed most of the economic modelling techniques outlined in Chapter 6 (Adams et al., 1984b gives a review of some national level studies). The work done in this area before circa 1982 was scientifically orientated and concentrated upon the accuracy of physical estimates of ozone damage to crops. Where monetary values of damages were given, the traditional model was employed without regard for the over-estimation this technique can cause. Published studies have concentrated on two main regions of the U.S.; namely, the Corn Belt (Illinois, Indiana, Iowa, Ohio and Missouri) and California. These areas have a good supply of data on crop response and air quality, and are nationally important crop-growing regions.

A Traditional Study
Linzon et al. (1984) analysed 15 crops grown in two regions of Ontario, Canada. Yield reductions were estimated for each crop using the experimental results of other researchers. No damage was assumed to occur at ozone levels of 0.03 ppm or lower (seven hour seasonal average). The traditional model was used to calculate monetary equivalents of the approximated crop losses. Increased yields, due to pollutant reduction, were multiplied by the current market price to give a producer benefit estimate equal to total revenue; extra production costs were deemed too small for subtraction. The constancy of price assumption was justified (a) by the small magnitude of crop production from the region relative to total market production, and (b) by the existence of supply management and Marketing Boards.

In Figure 10.1 the implicit assumptions of the traditional model are shown. A constant price level is assumed to exist at p_0. The aggregate demand curve D_0 is perfectly elastic (i.e., horizontal) because the quantity of the crop produced, before and after ozone concentrations are altered, is assumed

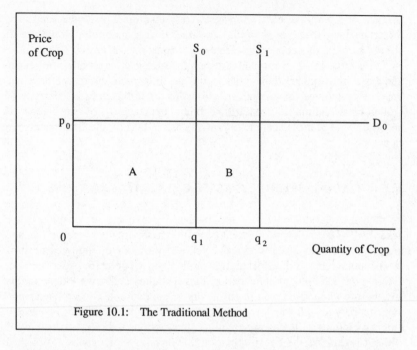

Figure 10.1:   The Traditional Method

to sell at the same price. The original quantity supplied is q_1 at high ozone concentrations, and shifts to q_2 when concentrations are reduced; the respective aggregate supply curves are S_0 and S_1. Instead of the normal upward sloping supply curve equal to marginal cost (under perfect competition), the model assumes that marginal cost is zero up to the quantity being produced and infinite thereafter; that is, supply is perfectly elastic up to q_2 and then price inelastic.

The fact that aggregate supply curves are normally positively sloped was ignored by Linzon et al.; thus the disjointed function of the traditional model was implicitly accepted. As has been discussed, the traditional model seems certain grossly to over-estimate the gain to producers from ozone reductions. This study estimated the average gain to producers of reducing ozone from current levels (the highest regional category being 0.05 ppm, 7hr seasonal mean) to 0.03 ppm as $15 million per annum, with a range of $9 to $23 million (1980 dollars). Five crops accounted for over 80% of the estimate due to their sensitivity to ozone - namely, potatoes, soybeans, tobacco, wheat and white beans.

Quadratic Programming Approaches

Four economic regional studies of ozone crop losses published since 1982 have used the price endogenous QP approach. Three of these were based on the agricultural crop-growing regions of California and employed similar models. The fourth study generated welfare estimates via a micro-macro model, using farm models to derive the effects of regional production changes on national markets.

Adams et al. (1982) studied 14 field crops in four regions of southern California. The dose-response functions are a major weakness of the study, being calculated from foliar injury models which have been converted to reflect yield loss. This approach showed broccoli, cantaloupes, carrots, cauliflower and lettuce to be ozone resistant, with little or no damage occurring. Lettuce in particular seems to be incorrectly classified, with evidence existing which states it to be an ozone sensitive crop. The optimal crop mix after ozone concentrations were reduced showed a very significant decrease in the production of these air pollution tolerant crops, due to their substantially reduced profitability relative to crops that were more sensitive to ozone.

Linear inverse demand functions were assumed for each crop, i.e., price as a function of quantities. The supply functions for all production inputs were assumed to be perfectly price elastic. The Willig approximation conditions were invoked so that any differences between ordinary and compensated consumers' surplus were assumed to be trivial. This invocation was justified because neither income elasticities nor expenditures as a percentage of income seemed likely to be large for the crops being studied.

The model (calibrated to 1976) was set up to maximize the sum of producers' and consumers' surpluses. Reducing ozone levels to 0.08 ppm, the state standard, would have increased 1976 producer quasi-rents by $35.1 million and consumers' surplus by $10.1 million. Production changes induced by altering ozone concentrations were assumed to leave the input mix constant. Changes in ozone concentrations from 1976 levels were reflected by changes in the optimal mix of outputs. Due to the variety of demand price elasticities across crops, the distribution of benefits was a function of the mix of demand curves and resultant crop proportions in the solution. For example, the removal of cotton from the study caused the balance between consumers' and producers' surpluses to be reversed. Cotton has an elastic demand curve, so that the benefits from ozone reduction were largely in terms of a producers' surplus. The exclusion of cotton reduced the producers' gain to $9 million and left the consumers' gain almost unchanged at $10 million.

Although mitigation was allowed for by cross-crop substitution, the authors felt that the use of fixed 1976 production coefficients and resource levels potentially constrained the possible producer mitigative adjustments on the input side. Thus, they warned that the subsequent programming results and welfare effects might be over-estimated. They also suggested, among other things, that improvements could be made by allowing for non zero cross-price elasticities, widening the scope to include effects in other regions and markets and studying a greater variety of crops.

Howitt et al. (1984) studied 13 crops, also in the state of California. They employed the NCLAN experimental results to derive dose-response functions for seven of the crops and other experimental results for one other crop. The remaining five crops were given "surrogate" response functions. The California Agriculture Resources Model (CARM) was used to calculate consumers' and producers' surpluses. This QP model allowed for constrained cross-crop substitution and included 27 other crops which were assumed unaffected by ozone concentrations. The model was similar to that used by Adams et al. (1982) above but was calibrated to 1978 instead of 1976.

Three ozone scenarios were compared with a base case for 1978. The total welfare gain from a reduction in ambient ozone of approximately 25 per cent (to 0.04 ppm, seasonal seven-hour average) was $35.8 million per annum, and the welfare loss from an increase in ozone levels by approximately 33% (to 0.08 ppm, seasonal seven-hour average) was $157.3 million. (These percentage estimates are given in Adams et al., 1984, p.10.) Reductions in ozone concentrations cause a "downward shift" of the supply function, which is shown graphically as a rotation, i.e., the price intercept remains the same.

Rowe and Chestnut (1985) used the CARM, as utilised by Howitt et al. (1984), to study 16 crops in the San Joaquin Valley, California. Although 33 crops were included in the economic model, only 16 were judged to be affected by ozone or could be supplied with dose-response functions. The study analysed the use of field data regression to derive dose-response functions, but obtained statistically significant results for only four crops: dry beans, cotton, grapes and potatoes. As a result, NCLAN functions were used for six other crops, while a further six were derived from other sources and by the use of "surrogate" functions. Three ozone scenarios were studied (0.12, 0.10 and 0.08 ppm seasonal hourly maximum) and results were given for both consumers and producers. Sulphur dioxide was also included in the study, but over 98% of the economic value of the agricultural damages was attributed to ozone. If an ozone standard at which little or no crop damage was expected (defined as 0.08 ppm seasonal hourly maximum) had been met in 1978, the estimated gain to consumers would have been $30.3 million and the gain to producers $87.1 million.

Adams and McCarl (1985) studied three crops in the Corn Belt region of the U.S. with a QP model calibrated to 1980. The dose-response functions were taken from NCLAN results for 1980-1982 and were Illinois specific. The model analysed the changes occurring throughout the agricultural sector at the national level as a result of the adjustments in Corn Belt output, *ceteris paribus*. This was achieved by characterizing regional agricultural production using 12 representative farm models. These representative farms were then used to generate supply adjustments in the national level model. Consumers' and producers' surpluses were calculated under two scenarios.

An improvement in air quality of 25% (a reduction of ozone from 0.12 ppm to 0.08 ppm one hour seasonal average) gave total benefits of $688 million (1980), a loss to producers of $1,411 million and a gain to consumers of $2,079 million. The other scenario took a 50% degradation in air quality (an increase in ozone from 0.12 ppm to 0.16 ppm one hour seasonal average) and gave a total loss of benefits of $2,225 million, a reduction of consumers' surplus by $4,986 million and an increase of producers' surplus by $2,761 million. Increases in crop supply were found to favour consumers while reductions in crop supply favoured producers. These distributional consequences are a result of supply shifts in the face of a price inelastic demand curve. That is, output increases but farmers lose out as the price falls by a relatively large amount.

Econometric Approaches

Several econometric approaches have been applied to the assessment of crop damage due to ozone pollution, including a dual model which is reviewed in the next section. In this section we discuss a model which analyses producers' surplus changes. Published research shows variation between models, for example concerning assumptions about the nature of agricultural crop supply curves and production responses (see Leung et al., 1982; Page et al., 1982; and Spash, 1987).

Benson et al. (1982) studied four crops in Minnesota. Originally, six crops were to have been studied but since dose-response functions could not be calculated for soybeans and oats, they were dropped. Dose-response for the four remaining crops was calculated using experimental data reported by other researchers. The dose-response functions allowed for episodic (as opposed to chronic or acute) exposure by breaking the exposure into multiple time periods over the growing season. The functions were applied to Minnesota using actual or simulated county-level ozone data. This was used to derive a range of yield losses under different ozone concentrations.

The economic analysis, using a comprehensive econometric model of U.S. agriculture, was carried out under two separate conditions: (a) crop loss was restricted to Minnesota alone, and Minnesota and U.S. production levels were estimated; (b) the same rate of loss as occurred in Minnesota was assumed to occur over the entire U.S., and again Minnesota and national production levels were estimated. A range of producer welfare estimates was derived, with the worst case ozone level (0.12 ppm hourly concentration with ten occurrences per week) causing a *loss* of $30,366,409 under assumption (a) compared to 1980 production. The worst case estimate under assumption (b) gave a *gain* to producers of $67,540,745 compared to 1980 production.

The explanation for the gain under (b) is that price rises as output is restricted and the "price effect" dominates, whereas under (a) the "production effect" dominates. The increase in the total value of production as ozone increases is due to the price inelastic nature of demand for the commodities studied. This "gain" to producers is in fact misleading in that: (1) costs have risen due to ozone pollution, and so a loss of comparative advantage is suffered by all affected farmers (the gain is at best a short-run phenomenon as competition from other sources would drive high-cost producers out of the industry; as the authors note, scenario (a) is more likely in the long run). (2) focusing on the "gain" to producers ignores the dynamics of consumer and producer welfare. Benson et al. do not calculate consumers' surplus; therefore the net change in societal welfare and the distribution of welfare changes, are unknown. In addition, scenario (b) is highly dubious because of the assumption that regional dose-response/ozone estimates can be extrapolated to the national level.

Although a detailed national-level model was used, Benson's economic analysis is similar to that of the traditional model. A comprehensive econometric model of the U.S. agricultural sector (calibrated to 1980) was used to capture crop supply and demand across multiple domestic and foreign markets. Despite accounting for national-level changes, the regional model remains simplistic in that quantity is being multiplied by price in order to estimate the "value" of production (namely producer quasi-rents). Also, cross-crop substitution is ignored as a mitigative strategy.

A Duality Study

Mjelde et al. (1984) employed the neo-classical econometric model with a profit function. Duality models are not dependent on an explicit dose-response function to estimate the welfare changes from a change in crop yield. However, experimental data are required to frame the initial hypothesis and to cross-check the resulting estimates. The profit function, which includes ordinary economic variables and environmental variables (as fixed inputs), shows the effects of varying ozone concentrations on farm profits.

Pollution, which is deleterious to the production process, will exert an exogenous force upon producer decisions. Producers may respond by varying input mixes, even if they are unaware of the phenomenon causing the observed effects. As Dixon et al. (1985, p.404) state:

> A profit function that has air quality as an input can be used directly to determine the producer's loss in profit and how other inputs are adjusted in response to a change in air quality. A dose-response function, while useful in establishing cause and effect relationships, does not provide this latter type of information. Furthermore, the change in the supply of a crop can be computed directly and this response is the net effect in agricultural output, i.e., the response incorporates producer adjustments triggered by price yield effects.

Part of this theoretical advantage may be lost in the case of ozone as producer adjustments should exclude a change of input mix. In order to compare the results of a dual study with experimental results, such as those of NCLAN, the mix of variable inputs is assumed constant. However, producers may adjust their output mix, but are prevented from doing so in this study.

The study analysed three crops in Illinois. Detailed farm level cost and production information was made available by the Illinois Association of Farm Business Farm Management which provided a rich source of individual farmer data unavailable in many other states. The study found that increased ozone levels depressed output and reduced the marginal productivity of variable inputs so that less were used. Ozone resulted in an aggregate loss in profits to Illinois farmers of approximately $50 million (1980). The assumption of a constant price ignores consumers' surplus and may be unjustified because Illinois is a major grain producer. Also, if ozone reduction improved crop yields throughout the Corn Belt, both consumers and producers would be expected to benefit. As the study states (Mjelde et al., 1984, p.361):

> These loss figures should be interpreted with extreme caution. They are computed under the assumption that price remains constant. Such an assumption is not valid if ambient ozone levels increased in other grain producing regions. If this latter case occurs then the supply curve of feed grains would shift to the left. Given an inelastic demand curve (which is typical of demand in the short run), the corresponding price rise may leave producers better off than before the ozone increase. However, consumers would be worse off than before. This illustrates the importance of analyzing both producer and consumer interactions in drawing conclusions about the impact of any pervasive environmental change.

10.7 ECONOMICALLY IMPORTANT ASPECTS OF RESPONSE FUNCTIONS

In performing an economic assessment of crop loss, the response changes of interest are those related to both the costs of production and the marketability of a product (Adams et al., 1985). That is, there are two routes via which pollution-induced crop damage can influence the welfare of consumers and producers. First, a reduction in crop damage, expressed as an increase in yield, will reduce costs and therefore reduce the minimum price the producer must receive to supply a given quantity. Secondly, altered levels of air pollution may affect the attributes of a crop, thus changing the consumer's willingness to pay and the welfare derived from the consumption of a given quantity of a crop. The change in cost implies a supply response, while the change in quality a demand response.

Studies conducted on ozone crop damage have tended to concentrate upon yield, and therefore are only relevant to the supply response. Research into potential crop quality changes has received little emphasis. Yet there is evidence that such quality changes do result from ozone pollution. Examples of quality changes which have been found are shrivelling in kernels of corn, reduction in the size of tomatoes, and alterations in chemical composition that affect cooking quality of potatoes and nutritional values of alfalfa (Jacobson, 1982). Table 10.3 clearly shows that there is a wide range of possible crop responses to ozone. Research is required to estimate the importance of these responses. This may be a difficult problem to resolve where consumer tastes are concerned, requiring objective characteristics to be associated with economic values in order to allow the derivation of dose-response functions appropriate for economic benefit assessments. However, without work in this area, economic assessments cannot be made of the full range of possible economic impacts.

Table 10.3: Processes and Characteristics of Crop Plants that may be Affected by Ozone

Growth	Development	Yield	Quality
Rate	Fruit set & development	Number	Appearance: size, shape, colour
Pattern	Branching	Mass	Storage life
	Flowering		Texture/cooking quality
			Nutrient content
			Viability of seeds

Source: Jacobson (1982), p.296, Table 14.1.

10.8 CONCLUSIONS

In this chapter we have concentrated on benefit estimation without comparison with the costs. Costs will vary depending upon the policy approach and are over-estimated by the inevitable reduction of other intangible damages and other forms of pollution due to ozone precursors, such as acid deposition. A particularly efficient way of controlling ozone for threshold damages could be to avoid high concentrations by enforcing episodic controls e.g., restrictions on vehicle use associated with ozone levels. In the case of Chicago episode regulation has been estimated at $12.9 million (in 1978 dollars; Cohen and Macal, 1981). Four stages of episode are defined: advisory 0.07 ppm, yellow alert 0.17 ppm, red alert 0.30 ppm and emergency 0.5 ppm. The frequencies of occurrence were 60, 4, 0.5 and 0.056 days per year respectively. The temptation to transfer such estimates to other regions should be avoided as the cost of control varies with specific concentrations, e.g., 1hr/day annual (to prevent human health effects) versus 7hr/day seasonal mean (to prevent crop damages); it is also highly region specific due to meteorological conditions.

The dose which a particular crop will receive in a given growing season is a function of precursor emission levels, as well as of meteorological, climatological and topographical factors. When certain meterological conditions prevail, high ozone concentrations may result. The highest ozone levels occur during the spring and summer months coinciding with the growing season for many agricultural crops.

Crop damage is a function of the ozone dose, crop species and cultivar, and biological, climatic, edaphic, production and other factors. The interaction of these variables makes accurate crop loss assessment, especially over large areas, an error prone task. Results from field experiments, especially those of NCLAN, have increased the accuracy with which the economic consequences of plant damage caused by ozone can be estimated. Where crop or region specific information is lacking, qualified approximations to actual responses can be made using surrogate functions. Current economic assessments of crop loss from ozone are restricted by a lack of information as to the importance of crop quality responses and must therefore concentrate upon supply response alone.

Several methodologies are available for crop loss assessment and have been applied to the analysis of welfare changes due to alterations in ozone pollution levels. Among these the microtheoretic econometric models provide a theoretically rigorous structure and have become a common approach to studying the agricultural sector. In conceptualizing agricultural crop production changes, neutral factor productivity enhancement is unanimously accepted (i.e. no input is favoured or harmed more than any other by ozone concentrations), while output substitution will depend upon particular circumstances. Demand functions must be estimated if credible welfare measures are to be obtained. Finally, the supply function characteristics used in recent studies have not been fully explained and may cause unjustified bias in benefit estimates.

REFERENCES

Adams R M (1983) "Issues in assessing the economic benefits of ambient ozone control: some examples from agriculture" *Environment International* 9: 539-548.

Adams R M, Callaway J M and McCarl B A (1984a) "Pollution, agriculture and social welfare: The case of acid deposition" *Canadian Journal of Agricultural Economics* 34 (March): 3-19.

Adams R M and Crocker T D (1984) "Economically relevant response estimation and the value of information: Acid deposition" in T D Crocker (editor) *Economic Perspectives of Acid Deposition Control* London: Butterworth.

Adams R M and Crocker T D (1980) "Analytical issues in economic assessments of vegetation damages" in P S Teng and S V Krupa (editors) *Assessment of Losses which Constrain Production and Crop Improvement in Agriculture and Forestry*. Proceedings of E C Stakman Commemorative Symposium, Misc Publication No.7, Agricultural Experimentation Station, University of Minnesota.

Adams R M, Crocker T D and Katz R W (1985) "Yield response data in benefit-cost analyses of pollution-induced vegetation damage" in W E Winner, H A Mooney and R A Goldstein (editors) *Sulphur Dioxide and Vegetation: Physiology, Ecology and Policy Issues* Stanford, California: Stanford University Press.

Adams R M, Crocker T D and Thanavibulchai N (1982) "An economic assessment of air pollution damages to selected annual crops in Southern California" *Journal of Environmental Economics and Management* 9: 42-58.

Adams R M, Hamilton S A and McCarl B A (1984b) "The economic effects of ozone on agriculture" Corvallis, Oregon: Environmental Research Laboratory, US Environmental Protection Agency.

Adams R M and McCarl B A (1985) "The effects of acid deposition on agriculture: Summary and recommendations" Corvallis: Department of Agricultural and Resource Economics, Oregon State University.

Adams R M, McCarl B A, Dudek D J and Glyer J D (1988) "Implications of global climate change for western agriculture" *Western Journal of Agricultural Economics* 13 (2): 348-356.

Barnes R A, Parkinson G S and Smith A E (1983) "The costs and benefits of sulphur oxide control" *Journal of Air Pollution Control Association* 33: 737-741.

Benson E J, Krupa S, Teng P S and Welsch P E (1982) "Economic assessment of air pollution damages to agricultural and silvicultural crops" Final report to Minnesota Pollution Control Agency.

Cohen A S and Macal C M (1981) "Cost effectiveness of a photochemical oxidant episode regulation" *Journal of Air Pollution Control Association* 31(6): 651-660.

Dixon B L, Garcia P, Mjelde J W and Adams R M (1984) Estimation of the Cost of Ozone on Illinois Cash Grain Farms: An Application of Duality. Urbanna: Agricultural Economics Staff Paper No.84 E-276, University of Illinois.

Dixon B L, Garcia P and Mjelde J W (1985) "Primal versus dual methods measuring the impacts of ozone on cash grain farms" *American Journal of Agricultural Economics* 67(2): 402-406.

Hamilton S A, McCarl B A and Adams R M (1984) "The effect of aggregate response assumptions on environmental impact analysis" Corvallis: Department of Agricultural and Resource Economics, Oregon State University.

Heck W W, Cure W W, Rawlings J O, Zaragoza L J, Heagle A S, Heggestad H E, R J Kohut, Kress L W and Temple P J (1984) "Assessing impacts of ozone on agricultural crops: I" *Journal of Air Pollution Control Association* 34(7).

Heck W W, Taylor O C, Adams R, Bingham G, Miller J, Preston E and Weinstein L (1982) "Assessment of Crop Loss from Ozone" *Journal of Air Pollution Control Association* 32(4).

Heck W W, Larsen R I and Heagle A S (1980) "Measuring the acute dose-response of plants to ozone" Presented at E C Stakman Commemorative Symposium, University of Minnesota, Minneapolis.

Holdgate M W (1979) *A Perspective of Environmental Pollution* Cambridge: CUP.

Howitt R E, Gossard T E and Adams R M (1984) "Effects of alternative ozone levels and response data on economic assessments: The case of California crops" *Journal of Air Pollution Control Association* 34: 1122-1127.

Howitt R E, Gossard T E and Adams R M (1985) "The economic effects of air pollution on annual crops" *California Agriculture* March/April: 22-24.

Jacobson J S (1982) "Ozone and the growth and productivity of agricultural crops" in M H Unsworth and D P Ormond (editors) *Effects of Gaseous Air Pollutants in Agriculture and Horticulture* London: Butterworths.

Just R E, Hueth D L and Schmitz A (1982) *Applied Welfare Economics and Public Policy* London: Prentice-Hall International Inc.

Leung S K, Reed W, Cauchois S and Howitt R (1978) "Methodologies for valuation of agricultural crop yield changes: A review" Sacramento, California: Eureka Laboratories; Corvallis, Oregon: US, EPA, EPA/600/5-78/018, NTIS/PB-288.

Leung S K, Reed W and Geng S (1982) "Estimation of ozone damage to selected crops grown in Southern California" *Journal of Air Pollution Control Association* 32: 160-164.

Linzon S N, Pearson R G, Donnan J A and Durham F N (1984) "Ozone effects on crops in Ontario and related monetary values" Ontario: Ministry of Environment.

MacKenzie J J and El-Ashry M T (1989) *Air Pollution's Toll on Forests & Crops* New Haven: Yale University Press.

Medeiros W H and Moscowitz P D (1983) "Quantifying effects of oxidant air pollutants on agricultural crops" *Environment International* 9.

Mjelde J W, Adams R M, Dixon B L and Garcia P (1984) "Using farmers' actions to measure crop loss due to air pollution" *Journal of Air Pollution Control Association* 31: 360-364.

Organization for Economic Cooperation and Development (1981) *The Costs and Benefits of Sulphur Oxide Control* Paris, France: OECD.

Page W P, Arbogast G, Fabian R G and Ciecka J (1982) "Estimation of economic losses to the agricultural sector from airborne residuals in the Ohio River Basin region" *Journal of Air Pollution Control Association* 32: 151-154.

Rowe R D and Chestnut L G (1985) "Economic assessment of the effects of air pollution on agricultural crops in the San Joaquin Valley" *Journal of Air Pollution Control Association* 35: 728-734.

Smith M and Brown D (1982) "Crop production benefits from ozone reduction: An economic analysis" Indiana: Agricultural Experimentation Station, Purdue University, Station Bulletin No.388.

Spash C L (1987) Measuring the Tangible Benefits of Environmental Improvement: An Economic Appraisal of Regional Crop Damages due to Ozone. Unpublished M.Sc. dissertation, University of British Columbia, Canada.

United States, Environmental Protection Agency (1985) "Air quality criteria for ozone and other photochemical oxidants: Draft" Research Triangle Park, North Carolina 7-190.

United States, Environmental Research Centre, Environmental Protection Agency (1974) "The economic damages of air pollution" EPA-600/5-74-012.

Unsworth M H (1982) "Exposure to gaseous pollutants and uptake by plants" in M H Unsworth and D P Ormond (editors) *Effects of Gaseous Air Pollutants in Agriculture and Horticulture* London: Butterworths.

Varey R H, Ball D J, Crane A J, Laxen P H and Sandalls F J (1988) "Ozone formation in the London Plume" *Atmospheric Environment* 22(7): 1335-1346.

Willig R D (1976) "Consumer's surplus without apology" *The American Economic Review* 66(4): 589-597.

11 COSTS AND BENEFITS OF CONTROLLING NITRATE POLLUTION

11.1 WHAT IS NITRATE POLLUTION?

Nitrogen is essential to plant growth because it is a key component of amino acids and proteins. Plants absorb nitrogen either as ammonium (NH_4) or as nitrate (NO_3) compounds which are formed by the process of mineralization and nitrification respectively. Nitrogen, in its related forms, enters soil in a number of ways: through fixation by some plants; in rain; through the application of inorganic and organic fertilizers; and through plant and animal residues. Plants take up some of this nitrogen from the soil whilst they are growing. Other nitrogen is lost to the atmosphere by volatilization (as NH_3) and by denitrification (as N_2 and N_2O). A portion of the nitrogen, as NO_3, is also leached from soil by the action of water; the ultimate destination of this nitrate is either rivers and streams, or groundwater. In addition to these processes which remove nitrogen from the soil, some of the nitrogen remains in the soil in either organic or inorganic forms. Table 11.1 shows nitrogen inputs into and outputs from agricultural land in kilo-tonnes, for 1978.

The increasing use of nitrogen fertilizers in agriculture has been well documented; for example, see Association of Agriculture (1985). Table 11.2 shows that nitrates from fertilizers applied to agricultural land in England and Wales accounted for an increasing share of total available nitrogen, while this total itself was rising during the period from 1931 to 1981. Since then, during the mid to late 1980s, UK use rates seem to have stabilized at around 1.6 million tonnes per annum. As Table 11.2 also shows, of the three sources of nitrates in water (agricultural run-off, sewage effluent and atmospheric deposition), agricultural run-off is by far the most important.

Nitrate losses from the soil through leaching (i.e., nitrate flows into groundwater and surface water) vary with the type of vegetation coverage, across crops and seasonally. Nitrate leaching is lowest under forest cover according to evidence cited by Croll and Hayes (1988) and Conrad (1988). Permanent grassland also has low leaching rates, around 10 kilograms of

193

Table 11.1 Nitrogen Balance for Agricultural Land (1978)

Inputs	N (kt)	Outputs	N (kt)
Rain	275	Crop and grass uptake	1367
Seeds	14	Leaching	326
Fertilizer	1150	Ammonia Volatilization:	
Sewage	26	Livestock wastes	536
Livestock wastes	1020	Crop wastes	50
Silage effluent	9	Sewage	9
Straw	15	Balancing figure[1]	380
Feed waste	9		
Biological fixation	150		
TOTAL	2668	TOTAL	2668

[1]Lost through denitrification and immobilization into organic nitrogen.
Source: Royal Society (1983).

nitrogen per hectare (kg N/ha). Although, as stocking rates and/or nitrogen applications rise, leaching increases up to the level associated with arable crops, around 40 to 80 kg N/ha (Ryden et al., 1984). Root crops such as potatoes can give still higher leaching rates, whilst the highest rates (280 kg N/ha) are associated with the ploughing of grasslands. This is unsurprising given that soil under grassland can contain up to 9,000 kg N/ha, compared with an equivalent figure of 3,000 to 6,000 kg N/ha in arable soils (Deptartment of Environment, 1986).

The seasonal pattern of nitrate leaching is particularly crucial. Leaching risks are highest when (i) rainfall is high, (ii) evaporation is low and (iii) crop demands are low. For autumn sown crops, nitrate applied at that time of year is particularly vulnerable to leaching as factors (i) to (iii) all hold. The level of nitrate in the crop rises from sowing through to harvest, as the plants take up more and more nitrate from the soil. In the spring, rainfall may be high enough to remove up to 30% of fertilizer nitrate (from the soil solution to watercourses and/or groundwater) although, according to Addiscott (1988), 15% is a more normal figure; in spring nitrate is also more

Table 11.2 Sources of Nitrogen in Soil for England and Wales (1938-81)

Time Period	Sources of Nitrogen (000s tonnes per annum)				
	Fixation	Rain	Animal Waste	Human Waste	Fertilizer
1938 - 1939	1180	260	610	170	50
1940 - 1949	1200	240	540	180	90
1950 - 1959	1290	260	670	200	180
1960 - 1969	1270	260	780	220	490
1970 - 1972	1230	240	810	230	730
1980 - 1981	NA	NA	600	NA	1150

Source: Croll and Hayes (1988).

likely to be lost through denitrification (i.e., to the atmosphere). Crop uptake also rises through the spring.

The popular link between increasing nitrogen fertilizer applications and the resulting nitrate levels in watercourses and groundwater has arisen because they have increased simultaneously during the 20th century, in both the UK and other European countries, such as Germany. In terms of the UK, nitrate levels in both rivers and groundwater have been rising. This has been particularly true in the South and East of England where arable agriculture is dominant and rainfall is lower than in the North and West. Croll and Hayes (1988) provide evidence on rising nitrate levels in aquifers underlying chalk and triassic sandstone. Lincolnshire limestone aquifers have recorded nitrate levels in excess of 100 miligrams per litre (mg/l). Time series data on nitrate levels in the River Stour (Eastern England) show an increase from 22 mg/l in 1940 to over 100 mg/l in 1980. This compares with an upper limit of 50 mg/l, suggested by the World Health Organization (WHO) and set by the EEC.

Upper limits have been recommended for nitrate in drinking water because of the potential health effects. Excessive nitrate levels have been linked to two health problems. The first of these, methaemoglobinaemia, is caused by oxygen starvation in bottle-fed infants. Reported instances of the illness have numbered 14 in the UK in the last 35 years. The UK's Department of Health has, however, drawn the conclusion that methaemoglobinaemia is unlikely to occur so long as nitrate levels are kept below 100 mg/l, as opposed to the EC upper limit of 50 mg/l. This latter figure nevertheless remains the UK's official target (House of Lords, 1989). The second associated health problem is stomach cancer, which is far more controversial. Bacteria in the human body convert nitrates into nitrites and N-nitroso compounds, including N-nitrosomines, which are believed to be carcinogenic. The UK's Chief Medical Officer reported in 1986 (cited in Dudley, 1986) that mixed medical evidence existed on this link, he concluded that on balance the links were unproven. Dudley cites American evidence that indicates close correlations between nitrate intake and stomach cancer incidence. However, Conrad (1988) points out that it is unclear whether intakes in excess of 200 or 300 mg/litre are a relevant health hazard; humans also consume nitrates from other sources. However, the public perception may be that excessive nitrates are undesirable; see Hanley (1989) for survey evidence to this effect. In addition, as Conrad notes, some individuals who have already high intakes of nitrogen (e.g., vegetarians) may be particularly at risk.

The other principal environmental side-effect of rising nitrate levels in water bodies relates to the phenomenon of eutrophication. Nitrates are nutrients, and as nutrient levels rise in certain waters, algal growth can reach such a level that the decaying of this algal matter severely depletes dissolved oxygen levels. Algal blooms are thus associated with oxygen starvation in, for example, pelagic fish. Nitrate related eutrophication problems have been noted in, amongst other areas, the Baltic, Skagerak and Kattegat seas off the coast of Sweden, and in shallow coastal waters off the Dutch and German coasts. Eutrophication in the UK's Norfolk Broads has been linked to increased nitrate and phosphate inflows from agricultural sources, although non-agricultural sources (such as sewage) are more important with respect to rising phosphate levels. Eutrophication in coastal and estuarine waters in the UK has, until recently, been confined to sheltered sites such as Langstone harbour and Cardigan Bay, though inland lochs, such as Loch Leven in Fife, have also become eutrophied.

Eutrophication incidents in the UK have recently become both more frequent and more widespread. During the summers of 1989 and 1990, greatly increased levels of blue-green algae (cyanobacteria) were recorded in marine and freshwaters. Several fatalities to dogs and sheep were attributed to their coming into contact with water containing these blue-green algae, leading to bans on recreational use of popular areas such as Rutland Water. In 1989, the National Rivers Authority (NRA) identified 22 waters containing these toxic algae, mainly in the Midlands and East Anglia. In 1990, 32 inland waters were identified by the NRA as being affected. At the same time, shellfish caught off the North-East coast, from the Humber to Montrose, were found to be contaminated with toxins from blue-green algae, leading to a government ban on catching shellfish in the affected areas.

11.2 COSTS OF CONTROLLING NITRATE POLLUTION

Undesirable environmental side-effects due to nitrate leaching have led to several policy options for mitigating these side-effects. These options can be divided into two categories: (a) those that attempt to reduce the amount of nitrates entering the environment and (b) those that attempt to remove nitrates once they are present in watercourses.

(a) Preventing Nitrates from Entering Watercourses
In the following discussion we restrict our attention to nitrates originating from agricultural sources. The control options here are:

(i)   A reduction in inorganic nitrogen fertilizer applications. Choosing this policy entails forcing farmers, by means either of price incentives (such as a nitrogen tax) or by command-and-control strategies, to reduce nitrate applications in this form. As the marginal cost of nitrogen is increased by such schemes, changes in cropping patterns are likely.

(ii)   A reduction in animal manure applications. This could be achieved by a headage tax on livestock or direct restrictions on stocking rates. Restrictions may also be placed on the storage or disposal of animal manures, as is currently the case in The Netherlands.

(iii)   Better management of nitrate applications. By changing their management practices, farmers can reduce the amount of nitrates leached from their holdings. The move to winter sown cereals has helped, as ground is no longer bare over the winter. Nitrate losses can also be reduced by avoiding autumn nitrogen applications and sowing catch crops. Finally, the avoidance of large-scale ploughing of pastures and of animal manure application at times of high rainfall and/or low crop growth will also reduce nitrate leaching.

(iv)   The pattern of land use may itself become an instrument of policy. Government can enforce "protection zones" in sensitive areas (e.g., around boreholes). Thus, farmers are forced or encouraged to avoid certain cropping or management schemes and/or to undertake others (such as replacing arable crops with grass). Set-aside programmes could be used for this end, with legislation encouraging the planting of woodlands in sensitive areas. However, Croll and Hayes (1988) argue that, to reduce nitrate concentrations to no more than 50 mg/l in groundwater supplies in Lincolnshire limestone, the maximum permissible nitrate leaching rate from associated agricultural land 20 kg/hectare. Such a low emission rate would be, as mentioned earlier, associated with low-intensity grassland and forest cover only. Catchment areas for boreholes are large; typically around 10 km for boreholes with an average daily output of 4000m. This implies that to safeguard all the boreholes in Anglia Water's area of jurisdiction, using protection zones would entail the creation of a total grassland area of 4000 km^2. This would constitute a very large change in the land use pattern of the area, which is principally an arable one.

In addition to the above policy options, reductions in nitrate emissions may come about as an indirect result of policies aimed at other objectives. For example, the Conservation Reserve Program (CRP) in the USA is aimed primarily at reducing soil erosion. However, as sediment run-off is reduced, this also reduces the amount of nutrients transported away with the soil. Achieving the CRP's target of 45 million acres of enrolled land has been estimated to reduce total organic nitrogen run-off by 700,000 tonnes, which is a fall of 9-10% over current run-off (USDA, 1989).

Any analysis of nitrate policy is complicated by the dynamic nature of the problem. Nitrates may take up to 40 years to travel from the soil to groundwater, depending on the nature of intervening rock layers. Thus nitrates first appearing in groundwater supplies in 1989 may be the result of agricultural activity in 1949. Indeed, the major cause of increased nitrate levels in boreholes in many parts of Southern England was the ploughing-up of permanent pasture during the Second World War to facilitate increased home cereal production. This means that policies aimed at reducing nitrate applications in 1990 will have no direct impact on water quality in some boreholes until 2030. Also, in order to arrive at an optimal target for nitrate pollution control, the external costs imposed on citizens at some time in the future must be predicted (in addition to control costs)[1]. Given the serious conceptual and methodological problems associated with estimating contemporaneous external costs, this is, for all practical purposes, an impossible task. Optimality is therefore not a policy option. For nitrate pollution control, as with most other forms of pollution problems, our attention thus switches to ways of efficiently achieving given "arbitrary" standards of water quality and/or nitrate input limits at lowest cost.

Incentive-based control systems have been recognized as being able to achieve arbitrary targets at a lower resource cost than uniform regulation, at least since the work of Baumol and Oates (1971) and Montgomery (1972). This is because, when pollution control (abatement) costs vary across the sources of discharge, a policy instrument which permits flexibility in the amount of pollution reduction achieved by each source allows low-cost-of-control discharges to reduce emissions relatively more than high-cost-of-control discharges.[2] As nitrate pollution is an example of non-point pollution, taxes or permits specified in terms of inputs (nitrogen) rather than pollution emissions (nitrates) are relevant here. However, the complexity of the linkage between nitrogen fertilizer applications and nitrate emissions may create difficulty in achieving given reductions in nitrate concentrations in receiving waters.

We now consider some empirical estimates of the control costs associated with the use of such instruments, together with other exercises aimed at estimating control costs and treatment costs from other policy instruments. Much work has been done on estimating the costs to farmers of various policies aimed at reducing nitrate leaching; a full account is given in Hanley (1991). Typically, these studies have compared the costs of achieving a given reduction in nitrate application (or, more rarely, given reductions in NO_3 levels in specified waters) under nitrate taxes, tradeable nitrogen quotas and uniform restrictions on applications. The principal methodology used has been linear programming (LP).

A summary of the conclusions from these studies can be made in four points. (i) Nitrate taxes have to be set at relatively high levels to motivate farmers to reduce applications, due to the low price elasticity of demand for nitrogen (typically around -0.6). For example, Dubgaard (1989) found that a tax rate of 150% was needed to produce a 30% reduction in nitrate use on a sample of Danish farms. (ii) Marginal abatement costs have been found to increase with cumulative reductions in nitrate use. (iii) Mechanisms which permit flexibility, such as taxes and tradeable permits, have lower resource costs than uniform restrictions, with permit systems also having lower costs in terms of reductions in farm income. (iv) Finally, the income effects of taxes on farmers can be large. Most studies unfortunately fail to distinguish between effects on farmers' income and real resource costs.

A recent example of such work is that of Andreasson (1990). She considers three policies for reducing nitrate use on the Swedish island of Gotland, and compares them on efficiency and income redistribution criteria. Gotland, with its limestone bedrock, suffers nitrate (NO_3) levels in drinking water supplies of up to 100 mg/l. This contrasts with the Swedish government's upper limit target of 30 mg/l. Agriculture is by far the largest source of NO_3, due to the spreading of both nitrogenous fertilizers and livestock wastes. A hydrological model was used to predict the necessary reduction in nitrate applications and leaching in order to attain the 30 mg/l target. This produced a target reduction of 5100 tonnes/year (t/yr). Of this, up to 2185 t/yr could be met through improved management of livestock wastes; for instance, by increasing the area of grassland and by changing the spreading time from autumn to spring. This left a residual target of about a 50% reduction in nitrogenous fertilizer application. However, there is some uncertainty over the actual rate at which nitrate leaches from both manure and fertilizer. A second estimate is that manure leaching is more important, implying a smaller desired reduction (14%) in fertilizer applications. Policy implications are calculated under both scenarios.

Andreasson distinguishes between the resource costs and the income effects

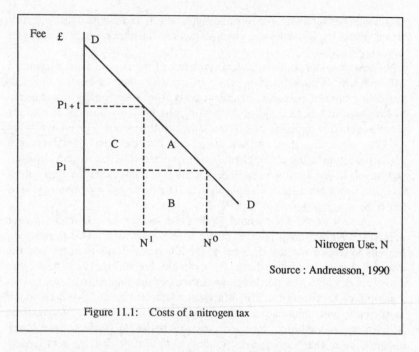

Figure 11.1:   Costs of a nitrogen tax

of each policy. A tax on nitrogenous fertilizer, N, will have two effects which are illustrated in Figure 11.1. First, farmers reduce use, moving back up the demand curve DD, as the price of nitrogen fertilizer rises from P_1 to (P_1+t). This demand curve is calculated as the marginal product of nitrogen (i.e., marginal crop yield) valued at the marginal revenue from selling output. For most farmers, this marginal revenue will be the market price, p^q, which for now is assumed to be a good indicator of marginal social benefit. DD slopes downward due to the law of diminishing returns. Since DD shows the marginal value of increasing N use to the farmer, the area under it shows the total value of lost yields. For a reduction in N use from N^0 to N^1, this is the area (A+B) above. However, smaller quantities of valuable inputs are now being used up, resulting in a fall in input costs: this is shown as area B, giving a net resource cost of A. Second, under the tax scheme, farmers also pay a higher price for N used: an amount (t multiplied by N^1) is paid in tax revenue to the government, where N^1 is the amount of N purchased after the tax is imposed (N^0 shows the pre-tax purchase of N). This amount, shown by the area C above, is a real effect on farmers' incomes but not a resource cost to society, as it represents a transfer of income from farmers to government. As a transfer payment, it would be excluded from a CBA, given the "equal weighting" assumption discussed in Chapter 1.

Under a tradeable permit system, each farm would initially be allocated fertilizer permits, whereby the maximum desired kilos to be applied in Gotland were divided up on the basis of applications from each farm in the previous year. Permits would then be tradeable; if the permit market is competitive, a price equal to t will emerge in equilibrium. Those farmers who desire greater allocations than they initially receive will buy permits from those for whom the reverse holds. The former will make windfall losses; the latter windfall gains. However, assuming transactions costs are zero, the net effect in terms of transfer payments will be zero.[3] Under a non-tradeable quota scheme, transfer payments are also zero, but here this holds both for individual farmers and in aggregate.

Note that the resource cost, identified above as A, is at a minimum amount. If there are many producers (there are 2400 farmers on Gotland) and abatement costs vary across producers, only a policy which allows marginal abatement costs to be equalized across polluters will be efficient (that is, will minimize the resource costs of meeting a target). Both tax and tradeable quota schemes can do this, since all producers adjust their input use (in this case) until their marginal abatement costs (identical to the demand curves for that input) are equal to the tax rate (tax policy) or the market clearing permit price (tradeable permit policy). Uniform regulation, which in this instance might give each farm a non-tradeable quota of N equal to N^1 on average, cannot do this. The control authority would have to know the marginal abatement costs for each farm, compute the least-cost allocation of quotas, and then issue quotas on this basis. Andreasson's analysis is considerably simplified because, due to the nature of the limestone bedrock, the amount of leaching from a given quantity of nitrogen applied does not vary significantly with the physical location of a farm. If this were not the case, then both the tax and tradeable permit systems would have to be spatially differentiated to be efficient.

Having set up the policy options, Andreasson is able to simulate the impacts of each. Instead of the more customary mathematical programming approach (e.g., Hartley, 1986), an econometric approach is used. This involves estimating nitrogen demand equations for six types of farms on Gotland using time series data over the period 1948-1984. Price elasticities of demand varied between -0.15 and -1.09. Across all farms, the value was -0.5. Losses to farmers are calculated as the area, A, under the demand curve, plus transfer payments under the tax scheme. For the tax and tradeable permit schemes, the overall demand curve is used. For the non-tradeable quota policy, separate demand curves for each farm type are used. To calculate resource costs, farm-gate prices must be adjusted for any price supports (see Chapter 1). Andreasson does this by valuing output at world market, rather than Swedish farm-gate, prices. This gives the results in Table 11.3.

Table 11.3 Costs of Reducing Nitrate Pollution in Gotland, Sweden

	Resource Costs (Krona millions)		Farm Income (% of total income)	
	Scenario A	Scenario B	Scenario A	Scenario B
Quotas	24.1	34.2	-10.0	-15.4
Tax	18.7	21.2	-13.9	-12.4
Tradeable permits	18.7	21.2	- 7.6	- 9.0

Scenario A: leaching higher from manure; planting of cover crops becomes cost effective when combined with reductions in fertilizer applications.
Scenario B: equal leaching rates: cover crops not cost effective.
Source: adapted from Andreasson (1990), p.295.

By definition, the tax and tradeable permit schemes give the same resource costs as each other; both are more efficient than non-tradeable quotas. But taxes reduce income by a greater amount, with tradeable permits the least damaging in this respect (assuming zero transactions costs and a perfectly competitive permit market). In reality, the relative attractions of the permit scheme would be less, since farmers might be unable to find out who is offering permits and who wants to buy them: potential gains from trade may thus go unrealized. This study reveals two lessons. First, the costs of alternative policies for achieving a given target can be assessed. This is, in fact, cost-effectiveness analysis (CEA): no attempt is made to justify the 50 mg/l target in terms of economic benefits, although this is a feasible undertaking for nitrate pollution (see below). Second, although CBA (or CEA, for that matter) is only concerned with resource costs (unless a non-equal weighting of costs/benefits is used), the income effects of a policy are still important. This is because they provide some guidance as to which policy option will actually be selected. The government decision-making process consists of more than a CBA since other criteria are judged important. These include the redistributional effects of a policy; that is, who gains and who loses and by how much. If losers are politically powerful, then the policy option generating these losses stands little chance of adoption. This is especially true of pollution taxes. Although, in most settings, taxes are more efficient than regulation, the transfer payments involved in a tax scheme militate against its acceptance; see Hanley et al. (1991). Thus, while transfer payments are strictly irrelevant to CBA under the equal weighting assumption, they are an important part of the decision-making process.

(b) Removing Nitrates in Watercourses

If nitrate pollution is defined as an excessive level of nitrates in drinking water, then one option is to do nothing about farming activity, but merely to treat water before it is supplied to customers. Several methods exist for removing nitrates from water, such as blending, ion exchange and reverse osmosis. However, treatment alone is of no use where eutrophication, rather than drinking water, is the policy target, when non-point emissions from farmland predominate.

Treatment could, therefore, be combined with agricultural intervention. Several studies have attempted to find the least-cost mix of such strategies (for a more complete account see Hanley, 1991). Two examples can be briefly cited here. In the UK, the Department of the Environment and Severn-Trent Water produced a joint study of methods of reducing nitrate levels to 45 mg/l in the Hatton Catchment in the English Midlands. The least-cost option was found to be blending with low-nitrate water, with no restrictions on agriculture, combined with ion exchange treatment. However, this policy was argued to be impractical. Bringing in fairly strict localized agricultural restrictions on nitrate use increased the present value of costs by 7%; this was less expensive than imposing less restrictive regulations concerning nitrate use over a wider area. A combined approach was therefore cost effective. This was also the conclusion of a study by Andreasson (1989) of the Laholm Bay area in Sweden. Andreasson found a combination of agricultural restrictions, sewage sludge treatment and wetlands establishment around the Bay to be the least-cost option.

11.3 THE BENEFITS OF REDUCING NITRATE POLLUTION

As was discussed in section 11.1, excess nitrate levels in receiving waters are associated with two principal problems: eutrophication leading to fish kills, and health risks associated with human consumption of high-nitrate drinking waters. Reductions in the level of nitrate yield economic benefits in that either or both of these problems are reduced (N.B., for groundwater, the time interval between action and effect can be long).

Eutrophication

In the case of eutrophication, lower nitrate levels can yield benefits both to commercial and to recreational fishing activities. For the former, the size of benefits could be measured by looking at increased economic rents over time, whilst for the latter, changes in consumers' surplus might be considered.

Silvander and Drake (1991) report the results of investigations into the benefits of reducing eutrophication damages due to nitrate leaching in Sweden. They consider effects on both commercial and recreational fisheries. In order to grow most plants, including algae, carbon, nitrate and phosphate in the approximate proportions of 40:10:1 are needed. In the southern Baltic and off the west coast of Sweden in the Skagerrak and Kattegat seas, nitrates are the limiting nutrient. Increased inputs of nitrates from a number of sources, including agriculture, have net environmental effects which depend on the species of fish affected, the geographic area and cumulative nitrate input. Silvander and Drake show this using the diagram reproduced as Figure 11.2.

From point A up to point B, nitrate inputs cause fish to breed more rapidly and support a higher population. Eventually, however, these positive effects on the population and growth rate are outweighed by the deleterious effects of eutrophication (the burning up of oxygen as algae decompose, the lower oxygen production by plants due to the lack of sunlight filtering through the algal blooms and the toxic content of algae). Net marginal environmental costs become positive, so that previous good effects start to be cancelled out (all points to the right of B). Once point C is reached, net cumulative effects are nil, but after C net cumulative effects are negative. If eutrophication continues to increase, the population crashes at point D.

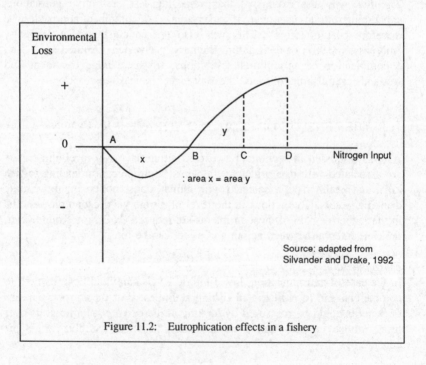

Figure 11.2:   Eutrophication effects in a fishery

Curves such as the one shown in Figure 11.2 will be specific to individual species and also specific to the area of sea being analysed (for example, there are differences between effects in coastal and deep-sea areas). For many economically important species in the Baltic and Skagerrat/Kattegat, point C has already been passed, one example being cod in the Baltic.

For commercial fisheries, Silvander and Drake compute the effects of a total collapse. This is given as (π-w), where π is the total industry profit, exclusive of labour costs, and w are labour costs calculated at a shadow wage. This is estimated at one-third of the market wage, due to low alternative employment opportunities in areas dependent on fishing. This gives a figure of 65 million Swedish Krona (SK) per year which is an estimate of reductions in economic rent in the worst possible case (total loss of the fishery). Aquaculture operations are also adversely affected by eutrophication, in particular where shellfish farming operations are involved. This is because of the way in which shellfish feed: filtration leads to a concentration of toxins from the algae in the shellfish. Using the same method as that described for commercial fishing gives a figure of 41 million SK per year for the total loss of aquaculture operations.

Silvander and Drake also estimate welfare losses to recreational fishermen as a result of the disappearance of popular species such as cod, mackerel and plaice. This might reduce the number of "angler days" available for fishing, if there are no substitute species available. A CVM study asked how much anglers would be WTP for a management programme that preserved fish populations at current levels. Of a sample of 162 anglers, 95 were WTP a positive sum. After excluding protest bids, a mean WTP of 332 SK per person per year was calculated. A WTA compensation question was also asked; answers to this gave some very high amounts (the highest being 5 million SK). Mean WTA compensation was 4,912 SK, showing once again that WTA>>WTP.

The use of CVM allowed the investigation of whether those who do not go fishing in the study area were WTP to preserve fish populations. Of this sample, 52% were WTP some positive amount to preserve existing populations, with a mean bid of 296 SK (less than the mean bid for fishermen). This figure can be seen either as a pure existence value or, if some of this sample were intending to fish in the future, a combination of option value and existence value. Bid curves were estimated for both anglers and non-anglers: adjusted R^2 values of 13% and 18% respectively were obtained. Aggregating the CVM figures for both users and non-users, and combining these with the previously described figures for commercial fishing losses and losses to aquaculture, gave the annual amounts shown in Table 11.4. Whilst one can level several criticisms at Silvander and Drake's figures (for example, that the commercial fishing losses are evaluated at maximum sustainable yield rather than economically optimal yields; and that a total loss of the fishery does not describe the current situation), they do show how economic analysis can be applied to such a complex environmental phenomenon.[4]

Table 11.4 Total Costs of Eutrophication in a Swedish Fishery

Activity	Annual Cost (millions SK)
Commercial fishing	65
Aquaculture	41
Recreational fishing (users plus non-users)	1321 to 1547

Source: adapted from Silvander and Drake (1991), p.173.

Effects on Human Health

The second problem associated with excess nitrate levels is that of risks to human health from excess nitrate levels in drinking water. In principle, a reduction in these risks could be valued using avoided resource expenditure from reduced health care costs (the averting expenditure approach of Chapter 6). A more direct approach is to discover individuals' WTP to benefit from a reduction in the nitrate level of their drinking water supplies, using CVM. This approach was used by Hanley (1989) to estimate the value to householders of a water supply with a nitrate level guaranteed to be below 50 mg/l, in the area supplied by Anglia Water in Eastern England. Anglia Water supplies one of the major excess nitrate problem areas in the UK.[5] Questionnaires were sent to a stratified systematic sample of 400 householders in the area. Households were asked to state their maximum WTP per annum for water supplies below the EEC/WHO limit of 50 mg/l. In the questionnaire, information was given about both the reason for payment (that Anglia Water might have to incur treatment costs in reducing nitrate levels) and of the then-existing situation (that water supplies occasionally exceeded the 50 mg/l limit). Households were told that if the policy was implemented, all households would pay the mean bid.

Protest bids were omitted, giving a mean bid of £12.97 per household per year. Bids were found to be positively related to disposable income. The bid curve was also used to test for anchoring bias: two figures were used for the initial positive value in the payment card (£2.50 and £5.00 per annum), resulting in two subsamples which were then analysed using a dummy variable in the bid curve. As the coefficient on this dummy was insignificant, the study concluded that no anchoring bias was present.

Aggregation of the mean bid to a WTP for the population of households which would benefit was made difficult by uncertainty over the size of this population. However, using a preferred figure of 835,212 households gave an aggregate benefit of £10,832,707 per annum. Using Anglia Water's own figure of £70 million for the capital costs of installing sufficient treatment equipment to meet the standard, and £5 million for associated annual running costs, gives a positive Net Present Value for the treatment option (given a 30-year lifetime for the capital). Whilst there are clearly problems associated with the small sampling fraction in the above study (0.05%) and the low response rate (34%), the results are at least indicative that households place significant value on a reduction in the nitrate level of drinking water.

Edwards (1988) has also attempted to place a value on the benefits to householders of lower levels of nitrate in drinking water. Edwards looked at the Cape Cod area of the Eastern USA and used CVM to estimate the benefit of preventing the one existing aquifer from being polluted by nitrates from sewage disposal. Here, pollution is defined as a nitrate concentration is excess of 10 parts per million (ppm). Using this definition, the aquifer was unpolluted at the time of the study. A CVM study of 1000 householders was attempted, yielding a response of 585 usable replies. Householders were given a range of possible costs of control from $10 per annum to $2000 per annum, using a closed-ended version of the CVM approach. The average annual WTP for supplies guaranteed to remain below 10 ppm and for those households certain to remain in the area was $1650. Interestingly, householders intending to move out of the area had positive WTP values. Bids were related positively and significantly to income levels.

Finally, Silvander (reported in Silvander and Drake, 1991) has also used CVM to estimate the benefits of reduced nitrate levels in drinking water. His sample was divided up according to whether respondents were aware of excess nitrate levels in their drinking water supplies (here, groundwater). For those who were aware of the situation, their mean WTP to have groundwater nitrate levels reduced to the 50mg/l level was 244 SK/person/year. Giving this group additional information that high nitrate levels led to a greater risk of cancer increased the mean bid to 347 SK/person/year. No significance tests are reported. For those who were unaware that their water contained high nitrate levels, mean WTP to have them reduced to the 50 mg/l limit was 593 SK/person/year. Additional information on the related risk of cancer raised this bid by 340 SK[6]. These results are difficult to explain (although, whether the mean bids across the two groups are significantly different is unknown). Some of those who knew of high nitrate levels might have already taken averting action (e.g., installing water filters) and so bid lower. Alternatively, if this were not the case, those who were aware of high nitrate levels may have researched the problem and come to the conclusion that nitrates in drinking water pose low health risks, whereas those who were unaware bid high due to fear. Yet if this were true, the bid of the well-informed should have remained constant when told about cancer links, since presumably they would already know this and have incorporated it into their first bid. Aggregating CVM bids gave a national benefits figure for preventing nitrate levels from rising above the 50mg/l limit of 2,304 million SK per year.

11.4 CONCLUSIONS

The issue of nitrate pollution is one where economists have made considerable progress in estimating the costs of pollution controls. The important distinction between resource costs and transfer payments has been highlighted. Regarding the benefits of pollution control, less work has been done, but such studies as exist show that (i) households place significant value on reductions in nitrate pollution, and (ii) such value can be estimated using the techniques described in Part I.

REFERENCES

Addiscott T (1988) "Farmers, fertilisers and the nitrate flood" *New Scientist* 8/10/88: 50-54.
Andreasson I-M (1990) "A cost-efficient reduction of the nitrogen load to Laholm Bay" in A Dubgaard and A Nielsen (editors) *Economic Aspects of Environmental Regulations in Agriculture* Kiel: Wissenschaftsverlag Vauk Kiel.
Andreasson I-M (1990) "Costs for reducing farmers' use of nitrogen in Gotland, Sweden" *Ecological Economics* 2(4): 287-300.
Association of Agriculture (1985) *The Role of Fertilisers in Modern Agriculture* London: Association of Agriculture.
Baumol W and Oates W (1971) "The use of standards and prices for the protection of the environment" *Swedish Journal of Economics* 73: 42-54.
Baumol W and Oates W (1988) *The Theory of Environmental Policy* Cambridge University Press.
Conrad J (1988) "Nitrate debate and nitrate policy in FR Germany" *Land Use Policy* April: 207-218.
Croll B and Hayes C (1988) "Nitrate and water supplies in the United Kingdom" *Environmental Pollution* 50: 163-187.
Department of the Environment (1986) *Nitrate in Water* Pollution paper no.26 London: HMSO.
Dubgaard A (1989) "Input levies as a means of controlling the intensities of nitrogenous fertiliser and pesticides" in A Dubgaard & A Nielsen (editors) *Economic Aspects of Environmental Regulations in Agriculture* Kiel: Wissenschaftsverlag Vauk Kiel.
Dudley N (1986) *Nitrates in Food and Water* London: London Food Commission.
Edwards S F (1988) "Option prices for groundwater protection" *Journal of Environmental Economics and Management* 15: 475-487.
Hanley N (1989) "Problems in valuing environmental improvements resulting from

agricultural policy changes: the case of nitrate pollution" in A Dubgaard and A Nielsen (editors) *Economic Aspects of Environmental Regulations in Agriculture* Kiel: Wissenschaftsverlag Vauk Kiel.

Hanley N (1991) "The economics of nitrate pollution control in the UK" in N Hanley (editor) *Farming and the Countryside: an Economic Analysis of External Costs and Benefits* Oxford: CAB International.

Hanley N, Moffatt I and Hallett S (1991) "Why is more notice not taken of economist's prescriptions for the control of pollution?" *Environment and Planning A* 22: 1421-1439.

Hartley A (1986) "Controlling Nitrogen Fertiliser Use: An Analysis of the Impact of Selected Policies on Farm Income and Output" Bulletin No. 205, Department of Agricultural Economics, University of Manchester.

House of Lords (1989) *Nitrate in Water*. Select Committee on the European Communities, 16th Report London: HMSO.

Kahn J (1991) "Atrazine pollution and the Chesapeake fisheries" in N Hanley (editor) *Farming and the Countryside: an Economic Analysis of External Costs and Benefits* Oxford: CAB International.

Montgomery W (1972) "Markets in licences and efficient pollution control programmes" *Journal of Economic Theory* 5: 395-418.

Royal Society (1983) *The Nitrogen Cycle of the UK* London: Royal Society.

Ryden J, Ball P and Garwood E (1984) "Nitrate leaching from grassland" *Nature* 311: 50-53.

Severn Trent Water (1988) The Hatton Catchment Nitrate Study, Birmingham: Severn Trent Water.

Silvander U and Drake L (1991) "Nitrate pollution and fisheries protection in Sweden" in Hanley N (editor) *Farming and the Countryside: an Economic Analysis of External Costs and Benefits* Oxford: CAB International.

Tietenberg T (1992) *Environmental and Natural Resource Economics* 3rd edition New York: Harper Collins.

USDA (1989) "Agricultural resources: cropland, water and conservation" Situation and Outlook Report, September, 16-18.

ENDNOTES

1. Formally, the entire schedule of discounted present and future damage costs must be known.

2. Those wishing to review the relevant literature might like to look at Tietenberg (1992), for an introductory treatment, or Baumol and Oates (1988) for a more advanced treatment.

3. Unless, of course, permits are initially auctioned.

4. Silvander and Drake also give figures for losses to the fish processing industry, which are excluded from the discussion here. Readers interested in appraising the economic value of environmental damages to commercial fisheries might like to look at Kahn (1991).

5. Since 1990, Anglia Water has become a private company rather than a public utility, under the privatization programme.

6.   These numbers are difficult to compare with those obtained by Hanley (1991) since income levels will differ across the two samples. At face value, Silvander's figures are higher, given an exchange rate of £1=10 SK.

12 VALUING HABITAT PROTECTION

12.1 INTRODUCTION[1]

In this chapter case studies will be considered which are concerned with the CBA of development projects and how different types of natural and semi-natural habitat might be protected from development. The three examples presented are: (i) the protection of lowland heaths in Southern England, (ii) the protection of ancient woodlands and (iii) development threats to wetlands in Northern Scotland and Louisiana. In each case, the methods described in Part I of the book are used to estimate the non-market values of preserving environmental quality in the face of development threats. These preservation benefits are compared to the foregone benefits of development.

12.2 LOWLAND HEATHS[2]

12.2.1 A Description of Lowland Heaths

Lowland heaths are semi-natural habitats, dependent on particular forms of agricultural activity and geology for their existence. A regime of low-intensity grazing on soils overlying sand and gravel deposits produces an open landscape characterized by low-growing shrubs, especially those of the heather family, with occasional trees and taller shrubs. Gorse (Ulex europeaus), bell heather (Erica cinerea) and ling (Calluna vulgaris) are especially prevalent on the type of heath considered here, namely lowland dry heath.

Lowland heaths are one of the world's rarest habitat types, being confined to Western Europe. Within this area, large losses have occurred since the beginning of the 19th century. Britain's existing 57,222 hectares (ha) represent only 28% of the area in the early 1800s, whilst the Netherland's 42,000 ha is a mere 5% of its mid-1800's stock. Lowland heaths are regarded as important by ecologists for both the plant and animal species they support. Some of England's rarest vertebrates are confined to lowland heaths: examples include the smooth snake and sand lizard. Several notable bird species are also dependent on the existence of the habitat, especially the Dartford warbler, hobby and red-backed shrike although, due to the poor levels of nutrients and lack of habitat diversity in heathlands, both bird species and numbers are small relative to other habitat types. However, heaths provide a home to a rich variety of insects, including dragonflies and butterflies.

12.2.2 Threats to Lowland Heaths

Many of the areas now covered by heathland were once woodland, but were converted to heath by animal grazing. Heathland has undergone cycles of being cleared for arable land during periods of high cereal prices, then reverting back to heathland (colonized from neighbouring areas) when cereal prices have fallen back. A complete absence of grazing would allow heathland to revert to scrub and then woodland. In fact, some UK heathland has deliberately been converted to woodland by planting, especially with Corsican pine.

Recent threats to lowland heaths in Southern England include agricultural conversion, especially during the 1970s; commercial extraction of sand and gravel; and house and road construction. Road construction has become particularly contentious due to the proposed expansion of the system and continued pressures for bypasses due to increasing congestion (Department of Transport, 1989). Private owners are likely to face financial incentives to allow the development of heathland, and little or no financial incentive to preserve it, since most preservation benefits are not marketed (wildlife and landscape conservation, giving rise to public existence and use values). Thus, a heathland owner in Dorset could expect to receive around £3,000/ha if the land is converted to arable cultivation, or £1.3 million/ha if planning permission is available for construction of housing on the land (Hanley, Munro and Jamieson, 1991). This contrasts with around £1,500/ha for heathland subject to a conservation order. The result has been a gradual reduction in the area of heathland; for example, Canford Heath (the largest) in Dorset has shrunk from 30,000 ha in the early 19th century to 320 ha in 1991.

Also damaging to the wildlife interest of heaths is the process of habitat fragmentation. As heathlands become increasingly isolated, with greater distances between heaths, the effects of the occasional fires, to which heaths are vulnerable, can result in total loss. For example, the loss of resident flora and fauna cannot easily be replaced, because the probability of re-colonization from neighbouring heaths is lower the greater are the distances separating fragments (Kent, 1989). Conservation authorities have responded to heathland loss by either purchasing heathland or offering management agreements. Under the 1981 Wildlife and Countryside Act, private landowners are compensated for avoiding development. However, given the very large differentials in the values of developed and non-developed heathland, this has proved an expensive process. There are also incentives for landowners to extract rent from the regulatory authorities by threatening to undertake potentially damaging operations in areas which have been designated for protection (Spash and Simpson, 1992). In addition, statutory authorities such as the Department of Transport or Ministry of Defence can over-ride the provisions of the Act, as can the Secretary of State.

12.2.3 Non-Market Benefits of Heathland Conservation

In 1990, a research team from the University of Stirling carried out a study of the benefits of preserving a particular heathland site: Avon Forest Park in Dorset. Avon Forest (which is not a forest, but a heath!) provides a good example of the ecological characteristics of lowland heath, containing many of the plant and animal species associated with this habitat. All six species of reptile native to the UK are found on the site, as well as birds such as the nightjar and woodlark. The site attracts a large number of visitors each year, and is managed by Dorset County Council as a recreational, amenity and nature conservation resource. In particular, the researchers sought to estimate the recreational or user-benefits associated with maintaining the heath. Secondary objectives of the study (both of which are discussed below) were to consider the impact of different information sets on individuals' responses to CVM questions, and carry out a convergent validity experiment, comparing CVM with TCM.

Willingness to Pay
Weekend and week-day visitors were sampled during the autumn of 1990, where possible after respondents had "used" the recreational facilities (e.g., after returning from a walk). A question ranking familiarity with heathland loss problems resulted in a mean score of 3.23 (the scale used was 1, "totally unfamiliar" to 5, "totally familiar"). Thus, respondents were judged to be reasonably well-informed about the issue of heathland conservation.

CVM was used to estimate the option price for this sample of users. Each respondent was asked three CVM questions, a payment card bid collection mechanism being used in each case. The first two of these were:

1.   Avon Forest Park is currently owned and managed by Dorset County Council. Managing the site costs money: money to pay for wardening services, information displays, and monitoring the heathland. Suppose that the council, due to financial pressures, was faced with the decision of either introducing an entrance charge to

the area, or else selling the site to developers. In such a situation, visitors such as yourselves could only retain the opportunity to visit the site by agreeing to pay such a charge. Clearly, the higher the charge that could be collected, the more likely it would be that the heathland would enjoy permanent protection. What is the most that you would be willing to pay as an entrance fee to save this heathland from development? If you would not be willing to pay anything as an entrance fee, please write your reason here.

2.   As (1) above, except that the daily entrance fee bid vehicle is replaced by an annual visitor permit.

The following four features of this application can be noted: (i) WTP, rather than WTA, measures were sought; (ii) a reason for payment was given; (iii) an alternative bid vehicle was offered; (iv) option price was to be estimated (i.e., user benefits under supply and demand uncertainty). In addition, those persons tendering a zero bid in either question were asked to give the reasons for this bid, thus enabling protest bids to be identified. The results are shown in Table 12.1.

Table 12.1 Willingness to Pay for Lowland Heath

	Mean WTP (£)	Range (£)	Std. Dev. (£)	N[1]	Protests[2] (%)
WTP$_a$ Daily Fee	0.74	0 - 3.5	0.56	177	19
WTP$_b$ Annual Permit	9.73	0 - 60.0	10.47	203	10
WTP$_c$ Trust Fund	25.57	0 - 200.0	32.43	211	7

Notes: [1]After removing protests
        [2]As a percentage of total responses

Comparing the results from the two questions requires an assumption concerning respondents' intended future annual visits. Using the median annual visit rate of 24, WTP can be converted into a per visit price of £0.40. In an attempt to explain the willingness to pay amounts, bid curves were estimated for both WTP_a and WTP_b. Results for WTP_b alone are given here since the WTP_a equation had a very low adjusted R^2 of 5.4%.

$$WTP_b = 10.097 + 0.023 \ V + 0.005 \ Others + 0.00015 \ Y - 0.125 \ Age$$
$$\quad (3.62) \quad (7.89) \quad\quad (0.75) \quad\quad\quad (2.43) \quad\quad (-2.89)$$

The figures in parentheses are t-statistics. The R^2 (adjusted for degrees of freedom) was 29%, whilst the F-statistic of 20.48 rejects the null hypothesis that the regression coefficients are insignificantly different from zero. WTP is positively and significantly related to visits per annum (V) and income (Y). The sign on the Age variable indicates that younger people, on average, valued preservation more highly. The variable "Others" indicates the number of trips made by the respondent to other heathland sites. As can be seen, this factor is positive (that is, this heath is complementary to other heaths), but insignificant.

Respondents were also questioned about their WTP for heathland preservation in general. A third CVM question was put to all respondents, as follows:

3. We would now like you to think about a different issue. Suppose a trust fund was being set up to safeguard heathlands *in general*. The trust would buy or lease heaths in Dorset, Hampshire and all other parts of the country where such areas are found, and manage them to retain their wildlife, landscape and recreational interest. Imagine that the fund was financed entirely by voluntary donations. Clearly, the more people who were willing to contribute, the greater the area of heathland that could be protected from housing, roads and other developments. What is the most you as an individual would be willing to contribute to such a fund? Imagine that your payment would be "once and for all".

Again, reasons for zero bids were sought, and a payment card used. Other points to note are that: (i) the bid vehicle has been changed to a trust fund; (ii) people are again given a reason for payment; and (iii) existence values as well as use values are now being estimated. The trust fund bid vehicle was thought to be realistic, since people in the UK are accustomed to conservation bodies acquiring funds for land purchase through the establishment of trusts.[3] Protest bids constituted only 7% of responses under this scenario; however, two bids of £1,000 were excluded from the data set as being greater than 10 standard deviations from the mean.

The descriptive statistics derived for the new scenario, which was termed WTP_c, are shown as the last row of Table 12.1. WTP_c bids were used to estimate a bid curve. This had to be done in log-log form to avoid heteroscedasticity problems, and showed WTP to be related positively and significantly both to income and to total visits to heathland sites over the previous 12 months (which might be seen as both a preference indicator and an indicator of knowledge of threats to heathlands).

Protest Bids

Reasons given for protest bids in CVM surveys are often revealing with regard to the success with which the CVM survey has been designed. For example, did respondents find a bid vehicle particularly controversial, or a hypothetical market particularly unrealistic? Table 12.2 gives the major reasons which respondents gave for their protest bids under the three CVM questions. There is little evidence that any of the CVM scenarios were perceived to be unrealistic. A common objection in all three scenarios was that heathlands protection should be provided by the state at zero cost; in other words, some individuals believe that, as citizens, they have collective property rights over heaths. Several respondents stated that they would be unwilling to pay anything as they could not afford to do so (17 under WTP_a, 3 under WTP_b and 4 under WTP_c). These responses should not be treated as protests. Whilst such individuals may care about heathland preservation, economic value is associated only with demand that is backed up by ability to pay (i.e., effective demand). Income distribution is taken as given when conducting CBA; see Chapter 2.

Information Impacts

In order to test for the impact of information on CVM bids, the respondents were divided into four groups, as follows:

Group 1: received no information additional to that presented in the questionnaire itself.

Group 2: were shown a graph and two further maps indicating the decline in the area of heathlands in the UK, and two maps showing the reduction in heathland in the local area between 1810 and 1978. This was termed "relative scarcity information".

Group 3: were shown a set of colour pictures of some of the kinds of animals and plants that could be found at Avon Forest: Dartford warblers, silver studded blue butterflies, sand lizards, dwarf gorse, heather and dorset heath, together with a brief description (for example, for sand lizard: "80-90% of the remaining British population lives on the Dorset heathlands"). This was termed "habitat specific information".

Group 4: were given both kinds of additional information.

Table 12.2 Protest Bids in the Avon Forest Study

	Rank	Major Reasons for Protest Bids
WTP$_a$ (46 protests)	1	Heaths are common land, which should provide open and free access.
	2	Site should be maintained by existing contributions to local authority funds.
WTP$_b$ (23 protests)	1	Heaths are common land, which should provide open and free access.
	2	Prefer to pay a daily fee.
	3	Site should be maintained by existing contributions to local authority funds.
WTP$_c$ (17 protests)	1	Heaths should be protected by law.
	2	Scheme is impractical.
	3	Prefer to pay a annual or daily fee for access to individual heaths.

Note: Motives described exclude those with less than 3 votes.

The results shown in Table 12.3 were obtained. Increasing the information individuals have on the characteristics of heathland, and its relative scarcity, both increase preservation values for Avon Forest. Relative scarcity information has a bigger impact than habitat specific information, though combining both types of information also increases WTP. For heathlands in general (WTP$_c$), only the unification of both types of information increases bids. Hanley and Munro (1992) report that habitat specific information raises mean bids by a statistically significant amount (at the 95% level of significance) for WTP$_b$, whilst relative scarcity information significantly increases mean bids for WTP$_a$ and WTP$_b$. Combining the two additional information sets produces significant increases in all three cases.

Table 12.3 Information Effects on Mean Bids

	Mean Bids (£)		
	WTP_a	WTP_b	WTP_c
Group 1	0.59	6.77	21.54
Group 2	0.81	11.49	20.64
Group 3	0.76	10.39	21.52
Group 4	0.79	10.32	38.49

Aggregating Bids

In order to aggregate bids for Avon Forest the following procedure was followed. Protest bids and outliers were excluded, and the sample was assumed to be representative of the population of users. Next, total annual visits to the site were estimated. In September, 235 party visits were sampled, which constituted many of those visiting the site. Assuming 400 party visits actually made in total during the sampling period, with an average party size at 2.5 persons implies 1,000 visitors that week. On average, visits will be higher during the summer and lower during the winter, so the September figure probably over-estimates annual average weekly visits. If the over-estimate is in the order of +20%, then an estimate of annual visit days is 41,600. This implies annual consumers' surplus from recreation benefits of £30,784 (41,600 x £0.74) using WTP_a. This figure is very low relative to the development benefits from housing, discussed above.

Under the WTP_c scenario, where general heathland is considered, two problems arise. First, the relevant population needs to be determined. That is, who benefits from conserving heathlands in Southern England? Second, the sample is probably unrepresentative of this population since most individuals do not visit heaths. For these two reasons, no aggregation was performed with regard to WTP_c. However, given the very large potential population of beneficiaries[4] and the mean present value bid under the WTP_c scenario, existence benefits for lowland heath could be very large.

Convergent Validity

As was mentioned earlier, an objective of this study was to conduct a convergent validity experiment. A travel cost analysis was thus performed, using data gathered in the same survey. As will have become clear from Chapter 5, many decisions are made in the course of a TCM analysis which can have a big effect on the value for consumers' surplus per visit generated, comparable here to the recreational use value from the CVM survey. Such decisions involve functional form choice, the value of time, and the treatment of multi-purpose trips. In this analysis, travel time was allocated a zero value, whilst "meanderers" were excluded from the data set. A semi-log (dependent) functional form was used for the trip-generating function. Resource constraints prevented the calculation of travel costs to substitute sites, so these were excluded. As Smith and Kaoru (1990) note, this will bias benefit estimates upwards. After dropping insignificant terms, the following simple travel cost model was estimated:

$$\ln (V_i/P_i) = -8.0733 - 0.307 \, C_i \qquad (12.2)$$

where V_i/P_i are visits per capita from zone i, and C are travel costs. The adjusted R^2 was 49%; the F statistic 51.47. This gives a consumers' surplus per visit of £2.89, implying user benefits of £317,900, which is significantly greater than the CVM estimates. Using a positive value for travelling time increases this TCM estimate.[5]

12.2.4 Conclusions

The heathland study illustrates a number of difficulties in applying the methods discussed in Part I. These include the amount of information which it is appropriate to provide respondents with in CVM studies, and the problem of deciding on the size and nature of the relevant population over which to aggregate bids. It also shows that including environmental impacts of development in CBA is no guarantee that the outcome will favour preservation.

12.3 THE PROTECTION OF ANCIENT WOODLANDS

12.3.1 Introduction

Ancient woodlands are one of the most valuable habitat types in the UK in ecological terms, due to the great diversity of flora and fauna which they support. They are also of great landscape and cultural value. Ancient woodlands are typically considered to be semi-natural habitats in that their current condition is due to human intervention in the form of woodland management. In this case study, the application of CBA to a proposal to drive a new road through an ancient woodland is considered. As is discussed below, CBA is relatively well-developed in the assessment of road improvements. The "COBA" manual produced by the UK's Department of Transport provides detailed guidelines on how such CBAs should be carried out. Until recently, environmental effects were excluded from the COBA procedure. Today, whilst they are still excluded in monetary terms, they do at least enter the decision-making process on a case-by-case basis, through the Manual of Environmental Assessment. This sets out a listing procedure for environmental impacts in the form of an Environmental Impact Assessment (EIA).

12.3.2 Ancient Woodland and Birkham Wood

Ancient woodlands are woodland sites which have existed in a given location since at least 1600-1700. They are distinct from other forms of woodland in the British Isles in that they are largely composed of native species, such as oak and beech. There are about 340,000 ha of such woodland remaining in Britain, a reduction of 40% since 1940 (Whitby, 1991). Ancient woods containing a high percentage of oak species are particularly valuable, due to the very large numbers of insects (and thus birds) which such woods support.

Birkham Wood is located close to Knaresborough in North Yorkshire and is notably rich in species, with 140 plant species having been recorded there (the NCC considers any number in excess of 100 to constitute "species richness" in absolute terms). There is a rare transition zone between acid soils in the southern portion of the wood and alkaline soils in the northern part (an "ecotone"). Thus the wood is classified as a Site of Special Scientific Interest (SSSI). It is also relatively large as fragments of ancient woodland go, with an area of 29.5 hectares. In England and Wales, 90% of ancient woodlands are less than 20 ha, whilst only 12 out of the 360 sites exceed Birkham in size. The wood's proximity to Knaresborough means that it also offers recreational opportunities.

Unfortunately, Birkham Wood stands in the way of the preferred route of a new bypass, which is aimed at reducing congestion in Knaresborough and nearby Harrogate. The focus of the case study was to assess the viability, in cost-benefit terms, of a number of alternative routes to that proposed by the County Council, and to try to estimate the non-market preservation value of the wood. Before looking at the actual study, a brief analysis of the COBA procedure is given because of its relevance to what follows.

12.3.3 Environmental Impacts of New Roads

In 1989, the UK government announced a major expansion in its road-building programme (Department of Transport, 1989), threatening to damage 161 SSSIs (NCC, 1990). New roads have many direct and indirect environmental impacts.[6] Land take is much greater than the area of road itself, with about 6.2 ha of land being required for the construction of each kilometre of 3-lane motorway. Habitat fragmentation occurs similar to that mentioned in the previous section on heathlands. Industrial parks and new housing schemes are wont to spring up around new road schemes, as access is improved (mitigating bypass benefits). Increased noise levels can directly reduce breeding successes of some species (Zande et al., 1980), and animal fatalities will rise, especially where new roads cross regularly used routes. Badgers, amphibians and barn owls have all been affected in this way. Harris (1989) estimated that 47,500 badgers are killed annually by vehicles in the UK. Reh and Seitz (1990) have shown that the breeding success of frog populations has been significantly disrupted as roads cut off migration routes. All these effects constitute potential external costs of road construction, which ideally should be included in any comprehensive CBA.

The COBA procedure itself begins once a local authority or central agency has decided that there is a need for a new road in a given area. If the road is in a city, then rail and bus alternatives may be considered, but this is not done in "out of town" settings such as the Harrogate-Knaresborough bypass, or a new motorway. The principal benefits considered under COBA are time savings and the value of reduced accidents.[7] Reductions in fatalities are valued using a figure of £565,900 per life (1988 £s), estimated from a combination of CVM and hedonic wage studies (see Chapter 6). Costs of construction and maintenance are added to additional running costs to produce a cost stream. Both costs and benefits are computed using traffic forecasts produced by the Department of Transport (many of which have been proved to be under-estimates, e.g., the M25). Alternative designs of roads (e.g., single versus double carriageway) are compared to produce a ranking of cost-benefit ratios, which identifies the preferred design. However, even projects with cost-benefit ratios greater than one are not guaranteed funding, since total public spending on roads is limited by the Treasury.

Once a road scheme has passed the COBA test, it is entered into the roads programme and a favoured route selected. A public enquiry may then be held, at the end of which process a "preferred route" emerges. However, as was mentioned above, the current COBA procedure excludes environmental effects from the cost flows; instead they are merely physically described using procedures laid out in the Manual of Environmental Assessment.[8] These environmental assessments may be carried out at each of the several planning stages and will certainly be undertaken for the preferred route.

The planning enquiry will either approve a particular scheme or else defer judgement to a later enquiry whilst further research is done. There has been much criticism of the COBA procedure (see, for example, Nash, 1990). Some of this has related to the value of small time savings, since large numbers of drivers saving a few minutes each can count for the same as a smaller number saving very large amounts of time. Yet, people may not even perceive small time savings of a minute per journey. This is important since, for most road schemes, time savings constitute the largest share of project benefits. Hopkinson (1989) has argued that standard values for time savings are taken out of context. If individuals were asked the value they placed on saving 5 minutes in the knowledge that this saving would be produced by the destruction of a wood, then a different value might be tendered than when, for instance, the time saving is made by rationalizing traffic light sequences in a city. Alternatively, if the COBA procedure were changed to capture the environmental effects of a road scheme, then standard values should be used if individuals are thought to net-out environmental effects before stating benefits.

12.3.4 CBA of the Harrogate-Knaresborough Bypass

This section reports the results of applying the COBA procedure to alternative routes for the Harrogate-Knaresborough (H-K) bypass, and the estimates of the preservation benefits for Birkham Wood. The initial preferred route for the H-K bypass, which ran through the middle of the wood, was the subject of a public inquiry. At this inquiry, a number of alternative routes were suggested by North Yorkshire County Council and protesters, the latter being very unhappy about the destruction of the wood. Therefore the inquiry recommended that an amendment to the preferred route be sent to the secretary of state for approval (this is the "proposed route", P). However, protests continued, with arguments being made for alternative routes which either avoided the wood entirely (routes C and D) or else damaged it to a lesser extent than route P (route E). Of key importance to each option were time savings, construction costs, agricultural land severance (that is, cutting off access to farmers), agricultural land take, woodland severance and woodland land take.

As shown in Table 12.4, route P has the highest NPV, but also the largest quantitative impact on the wood. Routes C and D both avoid all impacts on the wood, but D is in every way inferior to C, since it has a lower NPV, higher agricultural land take and a higher degree of farm land severed. Route D is therefore excluded from further consideration. Route E has a greater impact on the wood than route C, but much less than route P since, although 1.8 acres are lost with route E, the wood is cut into one very big remnant and one very small remnant, whilst route P cuts the wood in half. The impact on agriculture is much less with route E than route C. Route E might thus be seen as a compromise between agricultural, conservation and Treasury interests; arguing for route E to replace route P, rather than route C to replace route P, would therefore be easier.[9]

If route E is chosen, then the opportunity cost of reducing damage to the wood is the difference between the NPVs of route E and route P. This comes to £3.45 million, or 5.8% of NPV of the proposed route. This sum is a present value amount; the equivalent amount in current annual terms depends on the discount rate. At the COBA rate of 8%, this is £276,000 per annum into perpetuity. In order to find out if preservation values are at least as great as this amount, a CVM exercise was undertaken.

Table 12.4 Route Options for the Harrogate-Knaresborough Bypass

	Length (km)	Cost (£m)	NPV (£m)	WLT (acres)	WLS (%)	ALT (acres)	AS (acres)
Option							
P	2.89	1.38	59.17	2.2	50	18.0	41
C	3.10	1.93	54.06	0.0	0	22.6	157
D	3.36	2.16	51.26	0.0	0	25.6	181
E	2.98	1.52	55.72	1.8	5	19.2	102

Notes: WLT = woodland take (area of woodland lost); WLS = percentage of woodland severed; ALT = agricultural land take; AS = agricultural land severed. All NPV figures are positive.

An initial problem in designing the CVM survey was to decide on the relevant population. The local population of Harrogate District is the most obvious candidate: 140,000 persons. However, those living further away from the site might also benefit from preserving the wood. North Yorkshire has a population of 667,000, whilst in the whole of Yorkshire there are 4.8 million people. Perhaps only those interested in conservation would benefit. In the Yorkshire area, around 80,600 are registered with conservation groups.[10] Table 12.5 shows what mean bids would be required per annum to give an aggregate WTP of £276,000 for different definitions of population. Some of these required bids are clearly very small, especially that for the general public in Yorkshire. In the CVM survey reported here, the population of Harrogate District was sampled.

One thousand CVM questionnaires were sent out. As may be seen, both WTP and WTA scenarios were used, but each respondent was asked for only one type of bid. A test for the impact of small changes in questionnaire wording was included: one half of all those sampled were told that the woodland was "an ancient woodland of national importance" in the initial question; the other half were not. All respondents were given a map of the wood showing routes P, C and E.[11] Respondents were asked to rank these routes, and to assist their decision they were provided with information on cost, woodland losses, woodland severed, and farmland lost and severed. Questions were also included on past rates of use of the wood, reasons for use, reasons for maintaining the wood, expected rate of use of new bypass, attitude to a new bypass irrespective of route, and socio-economic variables. The bid vehicle used was a once-and-for-all payment to a trust fund and reasons for zero bids were sought.

Table 12.5 Bids Required for the Preservation of Birkham Wood

Population Group Affected	Required WTP Mean Annual (£)
General Public	
Harrogate District	1.97
North Yorkshire	0.41
Yorkshire	0.06
Registered Conservationists	
Yorkshire	3.42
National	0.17
Total	
Harrogate Locals plus Registered Conservationists in Yorkshire	1.27

Source: Hanley et al., 1991.

Two mailings resulted in a response rate of 38.5%. A follow-up survey of non-respondents indicated that most would be classified as protest bidders. Of 500 WTP surveys, 161 non-protest bids were returned; for the WTA scenario, 119 non-protest bids were returned. Protest bidding was much more prevalent under the WTA scenario (as the discussion in Chapter 3 predicts). The two most common motives for protesting under WTA were: (i) no amount of money could compensate for the loss of woodland; and (ii) money should not come into such issues.

Some descriptive data from the sample now follows. Respondents had a mean household income of £17,330. The mean number of visits paid to Birkham Wood was 2.74 per annum, with the most common motive for visiting being to take a walk. When asked to indicate why the wood should be preserved, the highest score was given to the motive "Nature conservation". A big majority of the sample (80%) was in favour of the bypass in principle. However, 55% were opposed to route P, whilst a further 20% were unsure, despite route P being shown as the cheapest route. The route option avoiding the wood entirely received the most votes as which that respondents would prefer.

WTP bids were recorded as shown in Table 12.6, with protests having been excluded. The 95% confidence interval is £6.40 to £31.48. If the highest bid of £1,000 is excluded (it is more than 10 standard deviations from the mean), then mean WTP falls to £12.89 and the standard deviation to £20.97. A bid curve was estimated to explain WTP bids. Table 12.7 shows that WTP is well explained by the independent variables used. WTP rises significantly with income, membership of conservation groups and annual visits to Birkham Wood, which all seem intuitively correct. Expected use rate of bypass and approval of bypass in general are both insignificant. The change in wording ("info") also has no significant effect. However, WTP rises with increasing values of pref1, and with increasing familiarity with the current controversy surrounding Birkham Wood and the H-K bypass.

Table 12.6 WTP Birkham Wood Study

	Mean (£)	95% Trimmed Mean (£)	Range (£)	Std. Dev. (£)	N
WTP	18.94	9.93	0-1000	80.55	161

As explained above a mean annual bid of at least £1.97 was necessary from the population of Harrogate district to make route P no longer the preferred choice. The mean bids from the CVM survey above are once-and-for-all values, so should represent the discounted sum into perpetuity of preservation benefits. If the discount rate is 8% and if the mean value of £12.89 is used, then this converts to an annual WTP of £1.03, which is clearly less than the "required" amount (the 95% confidence interval becomes £0.76 - 1.29). The figure of £12.89 excludes the one bid of £1,000 recorded in the sample. If this bid is not excluded, mean once-and-for-all WTP is £18.94, which gives an annual sum of £1.52/person, with a confidence interval of £0.48 - £2.51. This illustrates how at times there can be considerable difficulty in using CVM results in CBA. The required amount lies within the 95% confidence interval if the one bid of £1,000 is included. This reinforces the question posed by Kahneman and Knetsch, reported in Chapter 3: what if people's once-and-for-all bids actually represent annual amounts (because people forget they are supposed to be implicitly discounting a infinite stream of benefits)? If this is so, then including or excluding the £1,000 bid makes no difference: the route through the wood is massively out-voted in CBA terms.[12]

Table 12.7 Bid Curve for Birkham Wood Study

Variable	Coefficient	t-Statistic
constant	-11.0240	- 2.08**
info	- 1.2910	- 1.47
familiar	1.2950	1.69*
appByP	- 1.9200	- 1.41
appRtP	3.9330	2.48**
userate	0.9800	1.41
visits	0.6840	5.21
pref1	3.2650	2.53**
conserve	2.6480	1.66*
income	0.0002	2.12

Notes:

*Significant at 90% level.
**Significant at 95% level.
R^2 (adj.) = 35.7% F = 9.08
info: dummy variable for questionnaire wording.
familiar: knowledge of controversy, 1 familiar to 5 unfamiliar.
appByP: approve of bypass in general? 0 yes, 1 no.
appRtP: approve of route P? 0 yes, 1 no.
userate: expected bypass use: 0 more than twice daily to 7 never.
visits: annual number of visits to Birkham Wood.
pref1: first choice for bypass route 0=P, 1=A, 2=B
conserve: membership of conservation groups.

An analysis of WTA bids from the survey illustrates the problems of using this format in CVM work. Bids ranged from £700,000 million (!) to zero. If the 5% highest bids are excluded, the mean falls to a mere £196,552, which is obviously well in excess of the required preservation value. Common motives for protests have already been mentioned.[13] Many more protests were tendered under the WTA than under the WTP scenario: 45 and 6 respectively. There are three possible responses to this WTA data:

1.   The economic value of preserving Birkham Wood is very high on WTA grounds, and much higher than on WTP grounds. This

difference is in part attributable to the phenomenon of loss aversion (see Chapter 3).

2.   By bidding such large compensation sums, individuals are signalling that a CBA comparison is inappropriate as a means of deciding the fate of Birkham Wood.

3.   As the WTA mean is so great and the confidence interval so wide (-£5.8 E+09 to +£1.75 E+10), WTA should be rejected.

12.3.5 Conclusions

The size of the population over which to sample and over which to aggregate preservation benefits is again shown to be important in this case study. Whilst the environmental effects of new roads are currently excluded from government CBA in the UK, some clearly could be estimated. Again though, we note that inclusion of environmental effects would not necessarily result in these effects being minimized, given a CBA framework. Finally, the large empirical divergence between WTP and WTA raises the question as to which measure should be used, which in turn begs the question of the current allocation of property rights. If the residents of Harrogate district have the right to a preserved wood, then WTA is the correct measure; on CBA grounds the current "preferred route" would thus be rejected.

12.4 THE PRESERVATION OF WETLANDS

In this section, three studies of preservation benefits for wetlands are presented. They cover the Flow Country of Caithness and Sutherland in Scotland and two studies of coastal wetlands in Louisiana.

12.4.1 The Scottish "Flow Country"[14]

The Flow Country of Caithness and Sutherland is a large area of blanket peat bog, covering some 401,375 ha in the far North of Scotland. The area is characterized by many small lakes (lochans), which are hydrologically linked to each other. Many parts of the Flows have been designated as SSSIs due to their great conservation value: many specialized wetland plants are found here, including sphagnum mosses and sundews. The area is also of great value for its birds, especially waders and waterfowl. The major wading species are the greenshank (70% of UK population), dunlin (25% of UK population) and golden plover. Arctic skuas, merlins and golden eagles are amongst the rarer birds found in the Flows. The landscape of the Flow

Country is unique in Scotland.   Large, open vistas of watery land, interspersed with solitary mountains (such as Ben Klibreck) rising abruptly above the bog.   Views are extensive in all directions, and the area is very sparsely populated, even by Scottish standards.

Recently, however, this unique ecosystem has been subject to increasing change, predominantly caused by forestry planting.   Most of this planting is being done by the private sector using only one or two species (principally lodge pole pine and sitka spruce), typically in square or rectangular blocks. The effect on the landscape is striking and has produced many protests from conservationists who have also argued that afforestation creates environmental damages.   These include:

(i)   The displacement and loss of the resident flora and fauna.   Displaced peatland birds are not easily absorbed into neighbouring areas.   By 1987, the Nature Conservancy Council estimated that 912 (19%) pairs of golden plovers, 791 (17%) pairs of dunlins and 130 (17%) pairs of greenshank had been lost due to afforestation since 1979.

(ii)   Soil and water conditions are irreversibly altered, with shrinking and drying of peat, acidification of water, and a tendency to wet weather spates with rapid subsidence to low water levels thereafter.

(iii)   A large increase in sedimentation and erosion rates.

(iv)   A net increase in carbon dioxide emissions.   Peatbogs lock up an amount of carbon comparable to forests at the world level.   This carbon is released as CO when the bog is drained.   Whilst growing trees absorb carbon dioxide, and store carbon, the net effect on carbon release is thought to be positive (Silvola, 1986).

These environmental effects are to all intents and purposes irreversible. Peatbogs, their resident species and associated landscape qualities cannot be recreated except perhaps over a very long time period; whilst the act of draining parts of the Flows has destroyed some of the hydrological inter-connections linking together the lochans: actions in one part of the Flows have impacts on the whole area.   Hanley and Craig (1991a, 1991b) applied the Krutilla-Fisher model of irreversible development to forestry in the Flows.   From Chapter 9, it will be recalled that the Krutilla-Fisher model in infinite time can be written as:

$$NPV_d = D/(i-g) - C - P/(i-r) \qquad (12.3)$$

where $g<0$, $r>0$, D and P are year one development and preservation benefits respectively, and g and r are the associated growth/decay rates.   The discount rate is given as i, and C is the year zero capital cost. The value for D here is the net present value of forestry, excluding external costs and benefits. This was calculated for a "representative hectare" of the Flows, on a perpetual rotation basis.

The principal problems facing foresters in this area are those of shallow soils and high winds. Combined these increase the probability of trees being blown down before they are ready to be harvested (typically around 45 years after planting under these conditions). This probability is reflected in a Windthrow Classification scheme, which runs from 1 (very low probability) to 6 (very high probability). Some 86% of the core peatland area in the Flows is rated as class 5. This effectively rules out thinning the crop (as the trees derive most support by leaning on each other), which in turn eliminates an important source of revenue. Annual expenses from operating the forest were also included, along with the expected return from clear felling at the end of the rotation. Year 0 costs (C, above) include land purchase and road construction.

An important consideration for forestry in the Flows is the existence of government grants for planting. Up until 1988, private planters could receive two forms of state support; namely a tax concession and a capital grant per ha of land planted. The tax concession was taken away in 1988, but rates of grant were increased. These capital grants are excluded from the calculations of net social benefit, since they represent transfer payments from the government to foresters, and not real resource costs or benefits (see Chapter 1). However, their existence has been very important in terms of the level of actual planting in the Flows. Values for P were estimated using contingent valuation. A CVM survey was carried out by post in 1990. A stratified random sample of 400 households in Scotland was taken. Respondents were told about the Flow Country and about the conflicts between forestry (and therefore local employment) and conservation. They were also shown a map of the area. The bid vehicle used was a trust fund, with respondents stating their maximum WTP as a once-and-for-all sum. Again, protest bidders were identified.

Results

In the results reported here, no real growth in timber prices or in preservation benefits is initially assumed, so that both g and r are set equal to zero. The net benefits of afforestation (D) were calculated using a clear-fell value of £5,921/ha (in 1990 prices) and a real discount rate of 6%.[15] Excluding transfer payments showed that further afforestation is economically inefficient in the area since the NPV of the infinite rotation is negative, at -£895/ha, even excluding preservation benefits. This result is very stable with respect to land prices: even at a zero price (implying no opportunity costs for land use), the outcome is still negative. It echoes many of the empirical findings of Krutilla and Fisher (1985), who discovered that many wilderness development projects failed the Kaldor-Hicks test even if environmental costs were ignored.

In the CVM survey, 159 replies were returned, 129 of which were complete and thus usable. Of these, 78 individuals stated a positive WTP for preservation of the Flow Country. A further 22 genuine zero bids were tendered, and 29 protest bids. WTP results are shown in Table 12.8. The maximum bid of £1,000 was excluded from all the measures (except for "range"); the next highest bid was £100. A bid curve was estimated to try to explain bids. Information collected from respondents included their household pre-tax income, their age, whether they had ever visited the Flow Country ("User" below, 1=yes, 0=no), and whether they were a member of a conservation group or not ("Conserve" below, 1=yes, 0=no).

Table 12.8 WTP Flow Country Study

	Mean (£)	95% Confidence Interval (£)	Range (£)	Std. Dev. (£)	N
WTP	16.79	12.82-20.76	0-1000	19.69	129

Table 12.9 shows that 25% of the variation in WTP is explained. Income and "conserve" are both significant and increase WTP, which is plausible, whilst having visited the site ("user") also increases WTP, but is insignificant at the 95% level. Age is clearly unimportant. The sample was split according to whether respondents had visited the site or not, so as to see whether non-users placed significant value on preservation. Unfortunately, non-users were not asked whether they ever intended to visit the site, so these individuals' bids are not existence values in the standard meaning of the phrase. However, those who had visited the site cited a higher mean bid (£24.59) than those who had not (£12.15); while the mean bid of non-users was significantly different from zero. Given the relatively low numbers of actual visitors to the Flows, this is an important finding.

When preservation benefits are taken away from development benefits, the net present value of development becomes even more negative, at minus £1,222/ha. This figure was obtained by first converting CVM bids into annual equivalents, using a 6% discount rate,[16] aggregating them over the adult Scottish population, and finally dividing the result by the number of hectares of the area being preserved to get a population bid per hectare. However, this whole procedure was rather reduced in relevance, since the

Table 12.9 Bid Curve for Flow Country Preservation.

Variable	Coefficient	t-Statistic
constant	2.9600	0.37
user	5.7200	1.52
conserve	10.9000	2.41*
income	0.0005	2.25*
age	0.0070	0.05

Note: *Significant at 95% level R^2(adj.) = 25%, F = 7.61

NPV of afforestation was negative even before preservation benefits foregone were included.

This result was found to be stable with regard to all of the variables used in the calculation. Only if the discount rate were reduced to 2% would the net present value of D become positive: the NPV of (D-P), though, is still negative. If timber prices are allowed to grow at 2% per annum, then the NPV of D remains negative also. This all assumes a zero growth rate for preservation benefits, which is unrealistic. In fact, assuming a rate of growth of 2% per annum in real incomes, the value of r in this case was calculated to be +0.73%.

According to this study new afforestation, especially when funded partly by the taxpayer, is inferior to leaving the Flow Country as it is: a haven for birds and a very special landscape. This was found to be the case even when environmental effects were ignored. The estimation of preservation benefits was done using a CVM approach with a trust fund bid vehicle. Due to the problems of deciding how individuals treat once-off payments to hypothetical funds, a comparison of this mechanism with annual payments would be of interest (Kahneman and Knetsch, 1992).

12.4.2 Louisiana Wetlands

About 40% of the coastal wetlands in the USA are found along the Gulf of Mexico coast of Louisiana. These wetlands provide many important functions, which include storm protection, waste assimilation, commercial fishing and flood control. They also provide many recreational opportunities. Such wetlands are under threat from a number of development activities, including draining, commercial development and salt-water intrusion. According to Scaife et al. (1983), over 100 square kilometres of Louisiana wetland are lost each year. In this section, two studies are reviewed. The first, by Costanza et al. (1989), estimates commercial and recreational values, and compares these with "contributory values". These are the contributions of the component parts of the ecosystem to the functioning of that system, and the contribution of the ecosystem as a whole to connected systems. The notion, which derives from Norton (1986), avoids the problem of a lack of information on the part of potential beneficiaries of preservation (only if you know about the importance of wetlands do you state a positive WTP to preserve them) and is measured here in terms of primary energy output. The second study, by Bergstrom et al. (1990), concentrates on recreational use values for wetlands.

Costanza et al. Study
Costanza et al. use a system of energy accounting to estimate the total amount of energy captured by the ecosystem as an upper bound on its capability of providing useful work to the economic system. The gross primary production of the system, its capture of solar energy, is converted to fossil fuel equivalents, which are then converted to dollar values by multiplying by the ratio of gross national product for the USA to determine total fossil fuel equivalent energy use. This process was used to measure the contributory value of a range of wetland types, giving for example 48,000 kcal/m^2/year as gross primary production for salt marsh, which converts to $624/ha. Coastal erosion reduces gross primary production, giving a loss of $538/acre/yr for salt marsh. The present value of this loss depends on the discount rate: at 8%, the value per acre is $6,700; at 3%, it is $18,000. Costanza et al. (p.340) state that:

> Standard economics has too often operated on the assumption that the only appropriate measures of value are the current public's ... preferences. This yields appropriate values only if the current public is fully informed. The public is most likely far from being fully informed about the ecosystem's contribution to their true well-being, and they may therefore be unable to directly value the ecosystem's services.

More conventional preference-based measures of economic value were also calculated. These related to reductions in value for a number of activities. Their values at two discount rates are shown in Table 12.10. Three points can be noted. First, storm protection benefits dominate WTP-based measures at either discount rate. Second, preservation benefits are much higher with the lower discount rate (which of course they must be, since preservation benefits stretch far into the future). Finally, contributory value estimates are roughly three times the size of WTP measures. Costanza et al. admit to misgivings over the fossil-fuel equivalent to dollar-value conversion, noting that only part of primary energy production is used. The contributory value figures are upper bounds then, even if one does accept the dollar conversion.

Table 12.10 Wetland Preservation Values in Louisiana

	Present Value (1983 dollars, per acre)	
WTP Based Measures	8%	3%
Commercial fishing	317	846
Trapping	151	401
Recreation	46	181
Storm protection	1,915	7,549
TOTAL	2,429	8,977
Contributory Value[1]	6,400-10,600	17,000-28,200

Note: [1]Depends on type of wetland ecosystem.
Source: Costanza et al, 1989, p.354.

Bergstrom et al. Study
In another study of Louisiana wetlands, Bergstrom et al. estimated recreational use values, both in terms of current and future utilization of the wetland. Over an area of 1.2 million ha of freshwater marsh, saltwater marsh, open water and dry land, recreational uses include waterfowl hunting, freshwater and saltwater fishing, and shrimp and crab fishing. Sampling at 88 boat-launch sites enabled a sampling frame of possible respondents to be drawn up. Some 3,842 questionnaires were then mailed to this sample, of which 55.2% responded with usable replies. Respondents were asked about their current expenditures on recreational activities in the study area (such as accommodation and petrol purchases). Dichotomous choice CVM questions were posed, where respondents were asked whether they would be willing to pay a given amount under three scenarios: (i) that a wetlands management strategy be introduced which would maintain catches at current levels; (ii) that a strategy be introduced which resulted in catches per day at 50% of current levels; and (iii) that a strategy be introduced which preserved catches at 25% of current levels.

This series of questions, as the authors point out, implies that recreationalists have no property rights over wetlands preservation: they must either pay to have wetlands protected or else watch them be degraded.

However, the alternative working assumption, that individuals have a right to preserved wetland, would require WTA measures of the value of protection. As the discussion in Chapter 3 hopefully made clear, there are many problems over WTA measures in CVM work.

Recreational expenditures were on average about $42 per person per day.[17] Data on recreational expenditures would be of interest (i) if travel cost analysis was desired (ii) if the estimate of consumers' surplus from the CVM study was to be increased by actual expenditures, to give an estimate of total value; and (iii) if policy analysts were interested in regional income and employment effects of wetland preservation. In the analysis of the CVM data, a single logit bid equation was estimated by pooling responses from each of the three scenarios listed above. Explanatory variables in the bid curve included the amount to which respondents were giving a "yes" or "no" response to (the "posted price") variables relating to past catch levels, income, and a dummy variable for whether a respondent was a member of an outdoor club. A log-log functional form was used. Posted price was negatively and significantly associated with the probability of a yes response (as is to be expected). Other important variables were annual fish catch, income and outdoor club membership.

The area under the bid curve was then approximated to give an estimate of consumers' surplus, by integrating the bid curve over the range of $p=0$ to $p=p^{max}$ where p is the posted price and p^{max} is the maximum posted price. This implicitly assumes that the probability of a yes response at some $\bar{p}>p^{max}$ is zero. This procedure gave an estimate of $360 per recreationalist per annum for wetlands preservation.

Bergstrom et al. calculate that annual recreational use of the study area corresponds to 1,810,488 user-days per annum. Given that their sample contains a mean trips per annum of 23.7, this implies a population of about 76,000 users. Using the CVM estimates, this implies a consumers' surplus of $27,360,000 per year for recreational use. Added to actual expenditure, this implies a total economic value of recreational use of $145 million per annum. These figures may be converted to a per hectare or per acre basis: for total economic value is thus calculated at $110/acre/year. This gives a misleading impression of the value lost if a single acre is destroyed, since each acre is connected with the whole, whilst some areas are clearly more valuable than others. The authors sound a strong caution (p.144) about the use of per acre figures for management purposes, preferring to stress values per user. Note that all the figures reported here exclude existence benefits. The consumers' surplus figures, Bergstrom et al. point out, are comparable to figures produced for a similar area by Farber and Costanza (1987).

Conclusions

These two studies of the benefits of wetlands preservation raise some important points. First conventional economic value figures are based on the preferences, income and alternative consumption possibilities of each individual; if individuals are uninformed about preservation benefits, then they may place a low value on preservation. Costanza et al. offer the alternative of contributory value, but there are difficulties in applying this, as they admit. Bergstrom et al. make the very good point that per hectare figures for preservation benefits can be misleading. This will be so where they are used to measure the marginal effects of habitat loss, since they represent average values. A one hectare reduction in the area of a large expanse of habitat will probably be less costly than the average. A further problem is the "homogeneity assumption": that average WTP is a poor representation of the value of a given hectare, if the physical characteristics of this particular hectare are very different from their average values across the wetland.

REFERENCES

Bergstrom J, Stoll J, Titre J, and Wright V (1990) "Economic value of wetlands-based recreation" *Ecological Economics* 2 (2): 129-147.

Costanza R, Farber S and Maxwell J (1989) "Valuation and management of wetland ecosystems" *Ecological Economics* 1 (4): 335-362.

Department of Transport (1989) *Roads for Prosperity* London: HMSO.

Farber S and Costanza R (1987) "The economic value of wetlands systems" *Journal of Environmental Management* 24: 41-51.

Hanley N and Craig S (1991a) "The economic value of wilderness areas: an application of the Krutilla-Fisher model to Scotland's Flow Country" in F Dietz, F van der Ploeg and J van der Straaten (Editors) *Environmental Policy and the Economy* Amsterdam: Elsevier.

Hanley N and Craig S (1991b) "Wilderness development decisions and the Krutilla-Fisher model: the case of Scotland's Flow Country" *Ecological Economics* 4 (2): 145-164.

Hanley N and Munro A (1992) "The effects of information in contingent markets for environmental goods" Institute for Economic Research, Queens University, Kingston, Canada.

Hanley N, Munro A and Jamieson D (1991) Environmental Economics, Sustainable Development and Nature Conservation. Report to Nature Conservancy Council, Peterborough, England.

Harris S (1989) "Taking stock of brock" *BBC Wildlife* 7 (7).

Hopkinson P (1989) "Prospects for valuing the environmental effects of road schemes in monetary terms" Institute for Transport Studies, University of Leeds.

Kahneman D and Knetsch J (1992) "Valuing public goods: the purchase of moral satisfaction" *Journal of Environmental Economics and Management* 22: 71-89.

Kent M (1989) "Habitat conservation: what can we learn from the island biogeography theory?" *Geography Review* 2 (4): 2-6.

Krutilla J and Fisher A (1985) *The Economics of Natural Environments* Washington, DC: Resources for the Future.

Nash C (Editor) (1990) Appraising the environmental effects of new roads: a response to the SACTRA committee. University of Leeds: Institute for Transportation Studies, Working Paper 293.

Nature Conservancy Council, NCC (1990) "The treatment of nature conservation in the appraisal of trunk roads" Submission to SACTRA. NCC, Peterborough.

Norton B (1986) "On the inherent danger of undervaluing species" in B Norton (Editor) *The Preservation of Species* Princeton, NJ: Princeton University Press.

Reh W and Seitz A (1990) "The influence of land use on the genetic structure of populations of the common frog" *Biological Conservation* 54: 239-249.

Scaife W, Turner R and Costanza R (1983) "Coastal Louisiana recent land loss and canal impacts" *Environmental Management* 7: 433-442.

Silvola J (1986) "Carbon dioxide dynamics in mires reclaimed from forestry in eastern Finland" *Annals of the Botanical Society of Finland* 23: 59-67.

Smith V K and Kaoru Y (1990) "Signals or noise? Explaining the variation in recreation benefit estimates" *American Journal of Agricultural Economics* May: 419-433.

Spash C L and Simpson I A "Protecting sites of special scientific interest: intrinsic and utilitarian values" Economics Discussion Paper 92/13, University of Stirling.

Whitby M (1991) "The changing nature of rural land use" in N Hanley (Editor) *Farming and the Countryside: an Economic Analysis of External Costs and Benefits* Oxford: CAB International.

Zande A, Keurs W and van der Weijen W (1980) "The impact of roads on densities of four bird species in an open field habitat" *Biological Conservation* 18: 299-321.

ENDNOTES

1.   This chapter was co-authored with Alistair Munro, Department of Economics, University of East Anglia.

2.   This and the following section (on ancient woodlands) are based on material contained in Hanley, Munro and Jamieson (1991). Thanks are due to the Nature Conservancy Council (now English Nature) for funding the original study. We also thank Peter Hopkinson for his comments on an earlier draft of this chapter.

3.   An example being the fund set up by the RSPB to purchase Abernethy Forest in the Cairngorms.

4.   In the major heathland counties abutting and including Dorset, there are 5.9 million residents. At a 6% discount rate, the WTP_c bid has an annual equivalent of £1.53, implying a preservation value of £9.03 million if the sample were representative of this population. However, as Kahneman and Knetsch argue, the one-off bid might be very close to the annual value; this raises aggregate WTP to £150 million.

5.   This figure will be biased upwards due to the omission of substitute sites and also due to the use of an OLS estimator when the dependent variable is truncated at 1 visit, as it is here.

6.   These impacts include (a) a direct loss under tarmac of ecologically valuable land; (b) site severance and habitat fragmentation; (c) alteration of local topography; (d) changes in micro-climate; (e) increased development pressure; (f) off-site increase in sand and gravel extraction; (g) increased animal fatalities; and (h) increased local air, noise and water pollution.

7.   Predicted time savings are valued according to the guidelines in Highways Economics Note 2. This sets out standard values for work and non-working time.

8.   Road impact assessments will take account of:
- property demolition
- land take
- traffic noise
- visual impact
- air pollution
- barrier effects
- effects on agriculture
- impact on heritage
- ecological impact
- disruption during construction
- view from road, and
- driver stress.

9.   This argument assumes that developers have the property rights (or at least the advantage) and therefore need to be placated. If conservationists had absolute property rights they could refuse any development of the woods.

10.   1990 data for Friends of the Earth, World Wide Fund for Nature, Royal Society for the Protection of Birds, Woodland Trust, Yorkshire Wildlife Trust, and Harrogate Society.

11.   For clarity, these were termed P, B and A respectively in the survey. This was to prevent people from wondering what had happened to routes B and D!

12.   Also, this survey ignores existence and user benefits to those living outside the Harrogate district.

13.   No amount of money could compensate for the loss of the wood (45% of protests); and impossible to formulate a monetary equivalent (30% of protests).

14.   A full account of this case study may be found in Hanley and Craig (1991a) and (1991b).

15.   The 6% rate of discount is the standard UK government approved test rate for projects.

16.   Individuals may have used another discount rate, even if they employed an implicit discounting procedure in calculating the value to them of the stream of preservation benefits.

17.   All values in the Bergstrom study are in 1986-87 dollars.

13 COST-BENEFIT ANALYSIS AND THE GREENHOUSE EFFECT

13.1 SCIENTIFIC BACKGROUND

The greenhouse effect refers to the phenomenon whereby carbon dioxide and other gases trap long-wave infra-red radiation (heat) in the atmosphere, thereby warming the earth. The infra-red radiation emitted by the earth can be trapped by atmospheric carbon dioxide (CO_2), nitrous oxide (N_2O), chlorofluorocarbons (CFCs), methane (CH_4), ozone (O_3), and other gases. The concentration of these greenhouse gases (GHGs) in the atmosphere reduces the re-radiation of heat into space. The operation of this natural, radiative balance mechanism has become a problem because of the rate at which anthropogenic emissions of infra-red trapping gases have increased, creating a stock in the atmosphere.

The greenhouse effect is one of the better understood features of the atmosphere. Since the work of John Tyndall, circa 1861, water vapour and carbon dioxide have been recognized as radiative absorbers affecting climate (Idso, 1982). Anthropogenic emissions of CO_2 from fossil fuel combustion were hypothesized as climate altering in 1896 (Jamieson, 1988). At that time a doubling of CO_2 was expected to cause a 4°C to 6°C increase in temperature (remarkably close to current predictions, see below). Surface warming due to the GHGs does maintain a livable climate; their entire removal from the atmosphere (if possible) would reduce the earth's surface temperature by 33°C (Frior, 1989).

Carbon dioxide has formed the central concern in the discussion of atmospheric pollution and climatic change since at least 1957 (Revelle and Suess, 1957). While CO_2 remains the most important single gas expected to cause increases in global temperature, more recently several other gases have been recognized as substantial sources of climate forcing (Marland and Rotty, 1985). Cumulative climatic effects of other GHGs are likely to be of comparable magnitude to that of CO_2 (Dowd, 1985). Figure 13.1 shows how, during the 1970s, CFCs, CH_4 and N_2O had a warming effect that was

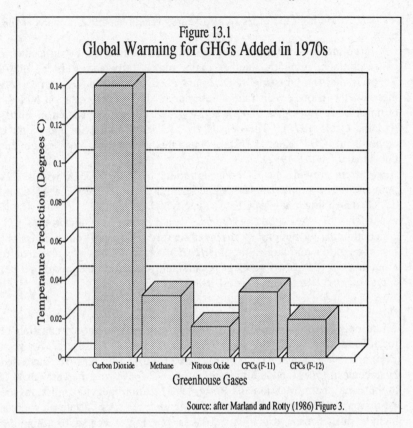

Figure 13.1
Global Warming for GHGs Added in 1970s

Source: after Marland and Rotty (1986) Figure 3.

equivalent to 70% of that of CO_2 alone. Thus, in order to understand the potential for anthropogenic impacts on global climate, background information is required on a host of gas species.

Carbon Dioxide
CO_2 is a product of complete combustion which industry regards as "good" in comparison to toxic carbon monoxide from incomplete combustion (Henderson-Sellers, 1984). Fossil fuel sources of CO_2 in order of importance are coal, oil and natural gas. Natural sources are vegetative decay and atmospheric oxidation of methane; natural sinks are biomass via photosynthesis and solution in water bodies (e.g., the oceans). Atmospheric CO_2 has increased steadily with industrialization from 280-300 parts per million (ppm) by circa 1880 to current levels of 355ppm (IPCC, 1992). The principal cause of the increase in atmospheric CO_2 in recent years has been the combustion of fossil fuels (Detwiler and Hall, 1988). Atmospheric

residence time is in the order of 500 years (Wuebbles and Edmonds, 1988, p.9).

A large amount of CO_2 emissions are unaccounted for by atmospheric concentrations, implying another major sink (Rotty and Reister, 1986). Theories that the "missing" CO_2 is absorbed by biota have been largely discounted. Biota are in fact a net source, due to deforestation and the burning of fuel-wood, a major energy source in less developed countries (Adams et al., 1977). The oceans are too small a sink for the required amounts of CO_2 (Kerr, 1977). Thus, the global CO_2 budget remains unbalanced (IPCC, 1992).

At current growth rates CO_2 concentrations by the year 2000 will be 373 ppm and the accompanying surface temperature will rise between 0.5°C and 0.8°C, depending on ocean heat capacity (Hansen et al., 1986). Rapid expansion of the world economy could triple or quadruple CO_2 concentrations by the end of the next century. To keep future emissions low enough to avoid large atmospheric CO_2 concentrations may also require reductions in the growth rates of population, production of goods, and per capita income (Rotty and Reister, 1986).

Nitrous Oxide

Anthropogenic production of N_2O occurs primarily in the combustion of fossil fuels, especially coal, and in the use of nitrogen fertilizers. Between 1950 and 1980, global annual production of nitrogen in fertilizer increased by seventeen times, and is implicated in the 0.2-0.4%/year increases of N_2O in the atmosphere (Marland and Rotty, 1985). Anthropogenic emissions are estimated to be approaching 50% of natural releases. Natural sources include soils, oceans, estuaries and lakes, burning of vegetation, lightning and volcanoes. The main sink for N_2O is photodissociation in the stratosphere by oxygen giving nitrogen oxide and nitrogen dioxide. The atmospheric life-time of N_2O is estimated at about 150 years.

Chlorofluorocarbons (CFCs)

CFCs are used as aerosol propellants, refrigerants, solvents, foam-blowing agents, plastics and resins. Important sinks are the oceans, desert sands and chemical scavenging in the stratosphere. The lifetimes of Group I CFCs, F-11 and F-12, in the atmosphere are 75 years and 110 years respectively (Wuebbles and Edmonds, 1988; National Research Council, 1984). On a molecular basis, CFCs are about 100,000 times more effective than CO_2 as contributors to the greenhouse effect, and may be equally important as a cause of climate forcing by the year 2000 (Cumberland, 1982). If the rates of increase were 10%/year, i.e., pre-1973 growth rates (twice current Group I growth rates), the temperature increase attributed to CFCs would be 0.3°C for 1990, and 0.7°C by 2000 (Forziati, 1982).

Under the Montreal Protocol (signed 1987, effective 1989, London amendment 1990, Copenhagen amendment 1992), certain signatories undertook to reduce emissions of CFCs, but the agreement is complex and allows developing countries and the former Soviet Union to increase emissions. Without the Protocol, Group I CFCs would have doubled over their 1986 levels by 2009; given adherence to the original Protocol (that is, a 50% reduction in CFCs in developed countries) and no increase in developing countries' exports of CFC-related products, emissions could range from a 20% increase to a 45% decrease from 1986 levels (Office of Technology Assessment, 1989). The inadequacies of the original agreement were recognized at the London conference in July 1990 where a complete phase-out by the end of this century of CFCs and halons was agreed. This agreement also established a fund to aid developing countries in reaching the targets set. At Copenhagen the phaseout of CFCs was advanced to January 1996 and halon phaseout to January 1994 and carbon tetrachloride to January 1996 (DOE, 1992).

Methane
The atmospheric concentration of CH_4 has doubled over the last century. The lifetime of atmospheric methane has been increasing (due to the depletion of OH radicals that remove CH_4 from the atmosphere) and is currently estimated at 9-13 years (IPCC, 1992). Anthropogenic sources include production and transportation of coal, oil and gas, enteric fermentation, rice paddy fields, biomass burning, landfills and sewage treatment. Concentrations of CH_4 started increasing rapidly 100 to 200 years ago after being constant for perhaps 20,000 years or more. The trend in CH_4 appears to coincide with the changing trends of population and may be caused largely by industrial and agricultural activities associated with the production of food and energy. The growth of atmospheric CH_4 is estimated at 1.0-1.9%/year (Khalil and Rasmussen, 1987).

Table 13.1 summarizes the preceding discussion. Ozone is excluded as currently its greenhouse role is relatively small, but its importance in atmospheric chemistry and as a potential source of future warming should be remembered. The relative sizes of sources and sinks, trace gas abundance in the atmosphere and emission trends are all changing over time, as is the mixture of gases contributing to climate forcing. Additional uncertainty surrounds the role of sources and sinks. For example, while forests are referred to as a sink for CO_2, deforestation throughout the globe currently makes forests a net source of CO_2.

13.2 PHYSICAL IMPACTS

Mean global temperature has in the past been much warmer than at present: 1°C during the Holocene climatic optimum (5000 to 6000 years ago), 2°C higher during the last interglacial warming (125,000 years ago), and 3°C to 4°C higher during the Pliocene (3 to 4 million years ago) (MacDonald, 1988). However, over the last 10,000 years, from the Holocene to the Little Ice Age, the mean temperature of the northern hemisphere has varied by no more than about 2°C (Gates, 1983). The earth's mean surface temperature has increased between 0.5°C and 0.7°C since 1860 (Abrahamson, 1989, p.10), coinciding with the increased combustion of fossil fuels due to industrialization. Hansen et al. (1986) predict the warming of most mid-latitude northern hemisphere land areas at between 0.5°C to 1.0°C by 1990-2000, and 1°C to 2°C by 2010-2020. The evidence from more than 100 independent studies gives estimates of average global warming within the 1.5°C to 4.5°C range for a double CO_2-equivalent scenario (Jamieson, 1988).[1] Such a doubling is expected sometime in the next century. Thus, global warming due to the release of GHGs represents a potentially drastic temperature increase over a relatively short period of time.

Yet, there appears to be a period during which aggregate benefits from greenhouse gas emissions dominate costs. Most obviously, society benefits from the relatively cheap use of fossil fuels, but there are other benefits as well. An average global warming of 0.5°C is expected to produce net benefits in terms of heating, agriculture and water use (d'Arge, 1975). Research suggests that Great Lakes fish may benefit, with Walleye yields in Lake Michigan increasing 29-33%, although trout may simultaneously decrease by 2-6% (Mlot, 1989). Idso (1983) maintains that increased levels of atmospheric CO_2 will increase future well-being via crop fertilization. This is achieved if escalated CO_2 concentrations enhance crop productivity (by increasing rates of photosynthesis), and reduce water use (by decreasing rates of transpiration). The projected yield increases range from 16% for corn to 60% for cotton under a CO_2 doubling (Seneft, 1990). In the past an argument has been put forward in favour of deliberately increasing mean global temperature to reap the benefits of delayed glaciation and increased agricultural range (Calendar, 1938, p.236). More recently, a similar line of reasoning can be found in Crosson (1989) where the costs of stopping warming are to be weighed against the potential loss from doing so too soon.

Such benefits are often ignored and would of themselves imply serious economic impacts, for example, on world trade. However, as temperature increases, benefits are likely to diminish. The positive CO_2-fertilization effect will only prove beneficial while CO_2 remains a dominant gas in climate forcing. As other gases become relatively more important, this benefit will diminish, at the same time as negative impacts of global warming on crop yields increase. Crop yields will also be affected by water shortages caused by global warming. Agriculture and, particularly, forestry will be more susceptible to serious decline if climate change occurs rapidly. For example, in North America each 1°C rise in temperature translates into

Table 13.1 Summary of the Principal Greenhouse Gases

	Principal Greenhouse Gases			
	CO_2	CH_4	CFCs (F11 & F12)	N_2O
Main Anthropogenic Sources	Fossil fuel	Rice paddies, cattle, fossil fuel	Propellants, foams, fridges	Fossil fuel, fertilizer
Main Sinks	Oceans and Forest	Chemical scavenging	Stratospheric photodissociation	
Atmospheric Lifetimes (years)	500	9 to 13	75 and 110	150
Climate Forcing (% of total change in temperature)	50	11	19	6
Atmospheric Increase (% per year)	0.4	1.0-1.9	4.0	0.3

Source: adapted from Spash (1990), Table 2.5.

a range shift of about 100 to 150 kilometres (Roberts, 1989). The rate of northward dispersal of trees due to historical warming (shown by fossil records) is 10 to 45 kilometres a century, with Spruce the fastest at 200 kilometres. Abrahamson (1989) estimates, given current gas emissions, that global warming is proceeding at between 0.15°C and 0.5°C per decade. Thus, almost all forest species in North America will expand into colder northern climates at slower rates than their current range becomes uninhabitable. A similar problem may exist for agriculture, but no thorough analysis of adaptive capacity has yet been conducted for the agricultural sector (Parry, 1990). Wildlife will also be forced to migrate as ecosystem characteristics change.

Costs will also escalate as the ability to adapt is restricted by the absolute size and increasing *rate* of sea-level rise. Studies suggest the rate of change of sea level will be relatively small in the first quarter of the next century compared to the last quarter, a situation which is true for a variety of underlying emissions scenarios (Titus, 1989). The absolute rise is estimated at between two-thirds of a metre to over three and a half metres by 2100 (Thomas, 1986; Titus 1989). Cost estimates for protecting against a one meter rise include $4.4 billion for the Netherlands (Goemans, 1986), and up to $100 billion for the east coast of the United States (Jaeger, 1989). Broadus, (1986) provide an indication of the damages to unprotected nations from a one meter rise. These include the loss of around one-tenth of the land area in both Bangladesh and Egypt, resulting in the dislocation of over 16 million people. Meanwhile, other expectations are that low-lying islands, such as the Maldives, would disappear completely.

The intertemporal asymmetry of impacts is apparent as initial benefits to most regions, from slight global warming, turn into very large economic costs as warming continues. Population migration will undoubtedly occur as land is lost to rising seas and storm surges, and agricultural productivity is reduced in semi-arid regions. The more extreme and rapid the temperature increases, the greater are the costs and the fewer the benefits. Thus, not only will the damages of preceding generations' greenhouse gas releases be placed upon those in the distant future, but the cost of continuing to release those gases will escalate (d'Arge and Spash, 1991).

The majority of evidence concerning global warming limits itself to a double CO_2-equivalent scenario and ignores what happens beyond that point. There is, as Crosson (1989) has noted, no reason to believe that global warming will stop there. The lifetimes of key GHGs in the atmosphere run into centuries, as shown earlier. Emissions of GHGs prior to 1985 have already committed the earth to a warming of 0.9°C to 2.4°C, of which about 0.5°C has been experienced. The warming yet to be experienced is unrealized warming of 0.3°C to 1.9°C, and is unavoidable (Ciborowski, 1989). Emissions of the principal GHGs are increasing at rates between 0.3 and 5 % per year. Within 50 years we are likely to create an irreversible increase of 1.5°C to 5°C and, in the 40 years following that, a further 1.5°C to 5°C increase (Ciborowski, 1989). As Cline (1991) reports, a sixfold increase in CO_2 has been estimated by 2250 and an eightfold increase by 2275 associated with central estimates of 7.5°C and 10°C respectively. Beyond this point the role of ocean uptake is hoped to be our saviour, with CO_2 levelling out at 3.5 times pre-industrial levels in 750 years time (given that the system is not chaotic). The implication is of continually rising temperatures and associated damages for at least the next 250 years followed by 500 years of stabilization.

13.3 CBA OF GREENHOUSE GAS CONTROL[2]

Faced with the threat of global warming, society has three options: do nothing, prepare to adapt, or reduce emissions of GHGs. The first implies that the greenhouse effect is either unimportant or beneficial. The second and third options take the problem seriously enough to warrant action, and could be carried out simultaneously. Adaptation would include measures such as strengthening sea defences, changing cropping patterns, organizing population migration and increasing irrigation. A policy solely relying on adaptation implies that it will be within the bounds of human ability to adapt to all future consequences and to offset undesirable physical effects. Irreversible damages, uncertainty and ignorance of future consequences argue in favour of controlling GHGs. However, to the extent that global warming is already irreversibly underway, society has no choice but to adapt. The third option is the one most commonly studied by economists and is the subject of this section.

GHG emissions could be reduced by cutting CO_2, CH_4, CFC and N_2O emissions and/or by increasing sinks for GHGs (e.g., increasing CO_2 absorption by reforestation). A stream of costs and a stream of benefits are associated with such actions. Optimal levels of GHG reductions could, in principle, be deduced from an examination of how costs and benefits of control vary with the level of reduction. Control costs will be higher the greater are the reductions in emissions and the quicker a given reduction is attempted. The marginal benefits of reducing GHGs will fall with the level of control, since fewer damages are avoided per unit of GHG reduced. The optimal level of control will occur when the marginal benefits of GHG reductions, in present value terms, are just equal to marginal control costs.[3] This is shown in Figure 13.2, where marginal control costs are shown as rising with the level of emission reduction, and marginal benefits are shown as falling. The emission reduction E^* is the optimal target. If the assumptions concerning control costs and benefits are correct, this analysis implies that the optimal reduction in GHGs will be less than 100%, since the output associated with GHG production is valued more highly the scarcer it

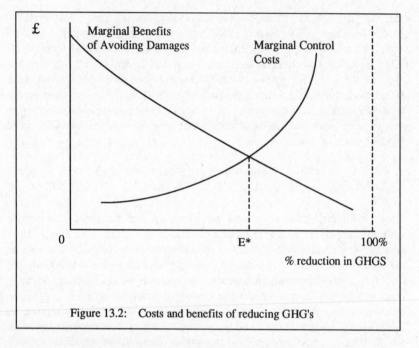

Figure 13.2:   Costs and benefits of reducing GHG's

becomes. However, E* in Figure 13.2 is an impractical policy goal because no authority can accurately estimate marginal benefits or marginal costs. CBAs of controlling GHGs can therefore only be one input to indicate the degree of control required.

The earliest example of a CBA of GHG control is d'Arge (1975), but the area remained very quiet throughout the 1980s (a notable exception is Cumberland et al., 1982). Since the early 1990s numerous studies have appeared and the literature on this subject is growing rapidly. Approaches range from the country specific (Ingham and Ulph, 1991) to world models (Manne and Richels, 1991), and from partial equilibrium (IEA, 1989) to general equilibrium studies (Bergman, 1991). The almost exclusive focus of these studies is the control cost of CO_2 reductions. Surveys of this work may be found in Hoeller et al. (1991) and Ayres and Walter (1991). The studies chosen here serve to illustrate the issues which such work must address.

Studies by Nordhaus
Perhaps the best-known CBA work on reducing GHGs is that of Nordhaus (1982, 1991a, 1991b). In his most recent studies, Nordhaus divides the USA into three sectors by susceptibility to climate change: (i) very susceptible, such as agriculture; (ii) medium susceptibility, such as construction; and (iii) unsusceptible, such as finance. These sectors accounted for 3%, 10% and

87% respectively of US Gross National Income (GNI) in 1981. The economic benefits of emissions reductions in the high and medium sensitivity sectors is slight (only 0.25% of GNI, or $6.23 billion for double CO_2-equivalent) because these account for a low proportion of total GNI. Marginal damage costs under three scenarios are $1.83/ton CO_2 for low damages (i.e., 0.25% of GNI), $7.33/ton CO_2 for medium damages (i.e., 1% of GNI) and $66/ton CO_2 for high damages (i.e., 2% of GNI). Nordhaus excludes undesirable effects of global warming on non-marketed resources (such as wildlife), viewing such impacts as too difficult to value. However, he states, "my hunch is that the overall impact upon human activity is unlikely to be bigger than 2% of total world output" (Nordhaus 1991b, p.933). In calculating control costs, he assumes GHG reductions will be achieved by methods offering the lowest control cost. He argues that control costs will depend on how fast reductions in GHGs are required, and that marginal control costs will increase steeply beyond a 10% reduction. Thus, Nordhaus calculates the optimal control policy for the greenhouse effect as being to cut CFCs by 9% and CO_2 by 2% under the medium damages scenario (assuming a 1% discount rate).

Such minimalist recommendations have been criticized as misleading, for example, by Daily et al. (1991) and Ayres and Walter (1991). The latter make three main points. First, up to a certain point, the costs of reducing GHGs are negative. In other words, society would be better off reducing its use of substances generating GHGs. This principally means cutting energy demand, since energy production and consumption comprise the single largest source. There are two reasons for this conclusion: (i) due to market distortions energy is currently overused, and (ii) profitable opportunities for energy conservation exist but are currently ignored. Ayres and Walter provide case-study evidence for Italy and the US; whilst Fitzroy (1992) cites similar evidence produced by Flavin and Lenssen (1990). Thus, some GHG emissions can be cut at no net cost. As shown in Figure 13.3, this implies, ceteris paribus, a higher optimal level of emission reduction than the case where control costs are always positive.

The second criticism that Ayres and Walter make is that cutting GHG emissions has environmentally beneficial side-effects, which add to the benefits of cutting GHGs. If a carbon tax were imposed, European coal consumption would be cut, since coal would face a higher tax rate than either oil or natural gas due to its relatively high carbon content by weight. Reduced coal use would reduce SO_2 emissions and so mean lower acid deposition. If the strategy to reduce GHG concentrations involved afforestation, this would generate a stream of non-market amenity benefits, depending on the type of forestry planted. In fact, the UK Forestry Commission has started to include carbon absorption benefits in its investment appraisals of new tree planting (Whiteman, 1991). Similarly, CFC reductions will help reduce stratospheric ozone depletion.

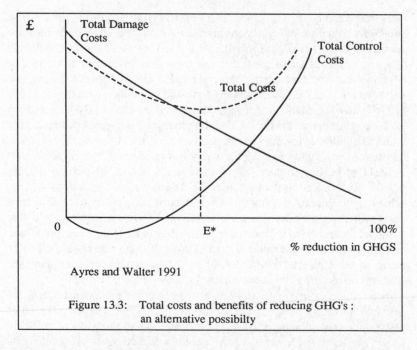

Ayres and Walter 1991

Figure 13.3:   Total costs and benefits of reducing GHG's :
an alternative possibilty

Finally, Ayres and Walter criticize Nordhaus' estimates of the benefits of
cutting GHGs as excessively conservative. They revise his estimates of the
area of land lost upwards by a factor of ten, and increase the value of land
lost in LDCs, such as Bangladesh. They also add an amount to cover the
cost of resettling refugees forced to move as a result of sea-level rise.
Nordhaus extended his estimates for the US economy to the world level, and
Ayres and Walter target their criticism at these world figures. As d'Arge
and Spash (1991) have pointed out, developing countries are more
susceptible to global warming with extensive dependence upon climate
sensitive production, a limited ability to adapt, and a sizeable population of
subsistence farmers. Fitzroy (1992) has also argued that the benefits of
reducing global warming are underestimated in Nordhaus, since climate
change combined with soil erosion in food-producing regions would reduce
world food supplies at a time when the world population will have doubled.
Declining levels in major world aquifers would aggravate this situation.
Even without attempting to include non-market effects, the Ayres and
Walter's revisions result in costs of global warming ten times greater than
the medium damage scenario estimates given by Nordhaus (that is, 2.5% of
gross world income).[4]

Carbon Tax Studies
Most studies of reducing global warming have centred around the cost

efficiency of achieving a given reduction in CO_2 emissions, thus avoiding benefit estimation altogether. For example, a common target has been the Toronto agreement's level of a 20% cut in CO_2 emissions by 2005. Two key parameters in all such studies are (i) the assumptions about underlying economic growth rates, and (ii) the method by which emissions reductions are to be achieved. If controls act to reduce the growth of GDP, a base-case no-intervention growth rate is needed as a comparator. This indicates that countries with high growth rates (e.g., fast developing countries like Malaysia and China) may have the most to lose in terms of common measures of GDP. Background assumptions will be included concerning energy supply and demand, and the development and cost of low-carbon backstop technologies. The method for achieving the target is crucial to the cost, with the general expectation in the pollution control literature that a market mechanism (e.g., tax or tradeable permit) will be the lowest cost option.

One of the best known world studies is Manne and Richels' (1991) dynamic optimization model, which divides the world into five regions with nine energy sectors. This model, which predicts CO_2 emissions from fossil fuel sources through to the year 2100, has been used to examine the cost of various policy options. The target assumed is a 20% reduction of CO_2 emissions by 2020, with that level maintained until 2100. This is compared to a "do nothing" scenario where GDP grows at around 2% per annum (pa), and energy efficiency grows at between 0.5% and 2% pa depending on region (thus total energy demand per unit of GDP is falling). CO_2 emissions in the absence of action rise at 0.7-2.1% pa. The principal policy simulation is of a tax levied on the carbon (C) content of fuels. This hits a peak of $400/tonne C, then falls to $250/tonne by 2100. The cost in terms of reduced GDP is between 2% and 10.5% by region. Whalley and Wiggle (1991) consider a wide range of possible taxes, all aimed at a 50% reduction in global CO_2 emissions. A production tax high enough to hit this target produces much larger losses in developing countries than in the EC or North America: the loss in the present value of GDP over the period 1990-2030 is 7.1% in the LDCs, 4% in Europe and 4.3% in North America.

While many modelling exercises carried out so far show how increasing rates of tax are required for greater emissions reductions, even quite small reductions in CO_2 emissions imply large rises in fossil fuel prices. Manne and Richel's $250/tonne C tax would increase coal prices by a factor of five. In the case of the UK, Ingham and Ulph (1991) also find that high tax rates on the carbon content of fossil fuels are necessary for a 20% reduction in CO_2. For example, oil prices would need to rise by 57-128% in real terms, depending on underlying assumptions.[5] In Sweden, Bergman (1991) uses a computable general equilibrium model to calculate the costs of reducing CO_2 emissions by a carbon tax. For a reduction in annual emissions from 88 million tonnes to 63 million tonnes by the year 2000, the costs are about

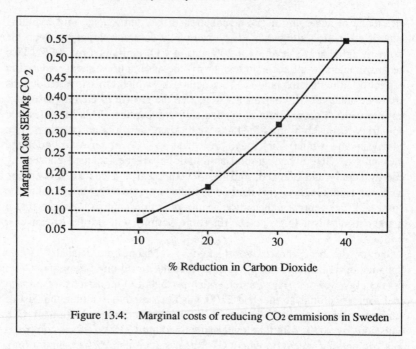

Figure 13.4:   Marginal costs of reducing CO2 emmisions in Sweden

4.5% of GDP. Bergman also finds that higher tax rates are necessary to cut CO_2 by increasing amounts, since the marginal control cost schedule is rising, as Figure 13.4 shows.

Conrad and Schroder (1991) use a general equilibrium approach to estimate the costs of hitting the Toronto target for Germany. This implies an annual reduction of 1.17% in CO_2 emissions if the target is to be met by 2005. Conrad and Schroder find that the cost, in terms of loss of GDP, depends on what sort of tax is used. If only the "energy intensive industries" are taxed (such as iron and steel, and refining), then the cost is higher, at 32 billion DM by 1996, than if all sectors are taxed (which costs 22.8 billion). This is because restricting the tax base reduces substitutions in energy use relative to the "tax everyone" case. Tradeable permits for CO_2 emissions have received much less attention; Manne and Richels (1991) present some results for such a system, but Schelling (1992) casts doubts over whether trades would actually occur.

The above discussion on policy has been in terms of a tax on CO_2 generation.[6] Some commonly cited alternatives are reforestation, preventing deforestation and cutting CFCs. Deforestation, particularly in the Amazon, is a major source of CO_2 emissions, at around 3 billion tonnes a year. This occurs due to the burning of felled timber releasing CO_2, the oxidation of carbon in the soil and a reduction in carbon absorption in following years. Reforestation would lock up CO_2 released from industrial sources. There appears to be wide disagreement over the costs of reducing CO_2 emissions by increasing tree cover. Nordhaus estimates the cost of preventing further deforestation as much lower than costs of reforestation (although his cost figures are very partial, excluding additional benefits and costs of deforestation/reforestation). For reforestation, Nordhaus' cost figures are $40 per tonne C in tropical areas and $115 in marginal areas of the US. Bloc et al. (1989) produce a much lower average figure of $0.7 per tonne C, whilst Dixon et al. (1989) give a figure of $4 to $8 per tonne C.

Finally, cutting CFC emissions is a most cost-effective way of achieving reductions in GHG emissions, in that (i) marginal control costs appear low and (ii) cutting CFCs is essential to prevent further depletions of the stratospheric ozone layer. Nordhaus finds that the marginal costs of cutting CO_2-equivalent emissions by reducing CFCs are about $5 per ton of CO_2 up to a 60% reduction in CFC use. Thereafter, marginal control costs rise steeply. However, UNEP (1991) reports that by 1997 CFCs could be completely phased out, along with other halocarbons, at little or no cost.

Economists have been able to produce estimates of the costs of reducing GHG emissions, but for the most part have avoided estimating the benefits of that control. Thus most work has been in terms of cost-effectiveness analysis, rather than cost-benefit analysis. This is because estimating the benefits of reducing GHGs is fraught with problems. There are many areas of uncertainty, for example, concerning regional impacts of climate change, how people and natural systems will adapt, and the nature of the world's economies in the distant future. There are also the standard problems of valuing non-market effects such as the displacement of wildlife and the human misery of environmental refugees. Both these areas are receiving attention and pose philosophical and political questions. Another such frontier research area which has received little attention is how to treat long-term damages incurred by future generations.

13.4 RESPONSIBILITIES TO FUTURE GENERATIONS

Earlier in this chapter we argued that the greenhouse effect could have serious impacts upon future generations while actually benefiting their predecessors. The standard application of cost-benefit analysis to the greenhouse effect, even if all costs and benefits could be calculated, would give the impression that the future is almost valueless. As Nordhaus (1991a, p.936) has stated,

> The efficient degree of control of GHGs would be essentially zero in the case of high costs, low damages, and high discounting; by

contrast, in the case of no discounting and high damages, the efficient degree of control is close to one-third of GHG emissions.

The distribution of net costs in the future, and net benefits now, makes the emission of GHGs appear falsely attractive. Following Spash (1993), four reasons for giving less weight to the expected future damages of global warming, than if they were to occur now, can be advanced and criticized. These concern who constitutes the electorate, uncertainty over future preferences, the extinction of the human race, and uncertainty over future events.

First, taking into account the benefits to unborn generations of greenhouse gas abatement may be considered to widen the concept of democratic voting in an unacceptable way. Yet, if future voters are ignored, resources will be wasted because investments will be needed to reverse the effects of actions which shifted damages to the future. Unfortunately, once GHGs are emitted they are almost entirely beyond our control; that is, the action is irreversible (Spash and d'Arge, 1989).

Second, if the vote of future generations over greenhouse gas control is to be included in some manner, the argument has been put forward that this is impossible since future preferences are unknown. However, current individuals can recognize that certain actions will harm future persons despite indeterminacy concerning their identities and our ignorance of their special needs. For example, the destruction of the Maldavian's homeland and the dislocation of millions of people in Egypt and Bangladesh might qualify as such wrongs.

Third, the argument has been made that due to the inevitable extinction of the human race, the future must be regarded as less important; for example see Heal (1986). As the human race will no longer exist, the degradation due to global warming can therefore be dismissed or at least discounted. Resources used for greenhouse gas control are then better used for increased consumption for the immediate generation. This approach in the case of global warming is in line with a self-fulfilling expectation.

Fourth is the case where uncertainty over the impacts of global warming are such that there is a positive probability that no damage will occur, a probability which might be increasing over time. From an economic perspective, the suggestion has been made that when deciding to undertake an emissions abatement project, the future should be discounted at some positive rate to account for risk. However, except under special circumstances, there is no well-defined way to adjust the discount rate such that it will make the appropriate adjustment for risk in the present value of uncertain future benefits and costs in each period, as was argued in Chapter 8. On moral grounds, the fourth argument is equivalent to justifying actions which can harm others because there is a chance they will remain unharmed (Routley and Routley, 1980).

Cost-benefit analysis as commonly applied would use an arbitrary but positive social discount rate. Thus, implicitly, some concern for the future effects of global warming would be shown, but the extent of this concern would depend upon the discount rate chosen. The problem which faces economists, in falling back on the use of a positive rate, is that their policy conclusions still have serious long-term implications which raise the need for a moral justification for the procedure.

However, there is a persistent view that the current generation should be unconcerned over the loss or injury caused to future generations because they will benefit from advances in technology, investments in both man-made and natural capital, and direct bequests. Adams (1989, p.1274) has raised this exact issue in terms of alleviating our responsibilities for global warming. While fossil fuel combustion implies foregone opportunities for future generations, they "typically benefit (in the form of higher material standards of living) from current investments in technology, capital stocks, and other infrastructure". However, this line of reasoning confuses actions taken for two separate reasons. That future generations may be better-off has nothing to do with societies consciously deciding to compensate the future.

If society has in fact been undertaking investments with the express purpose of compensating future generations for global warming, the lack of publicity has been conspicuous. More importantly this would imply that the extent to which the future will be better off has in some sense been balanced against *all* the long-term environmental problems. That is, society cannot take global warming and see the future as better off, and then ignore global warming and take ozone depletion as compensated, and then ignore ozone and balance nuclear waste against supposed future well-being. Each case of long-term damage implies compensation which is distinct from catering for the general needs of future individuals.

This distinct nature of such compensatory transfers has been neglected (Spash, 1993). The greenhouse effect as characterized earlier creates an asymmetric distribution of losses and gains over time. Intergenerational compensation would counterbalance the negative outcomes of global warming by positive transfers, while not interfering with basic transfers. For example, assuming egalitarianism, the maintenance of the same welfare level fails to compensate for global warming. Yet the suggestion has been made that spreading the costs of global warming equitably across generations is an acceptable solution (Crosson, 1989).

Assume individuals of a nation are accepted to have a right to live in their own homeland. A sea-level rise due to global warming floods the Maldives and violates this right. Of course the Maldavians can be relocated and compensated, but this approach is unacceptable given the previously stated right. The objection free-market economists might raise to the imposition of such rights is that freely contracting parties are prevented from entering into agreements of their own free will. That is, the individual is his/her own best judge of welfare changes. If the Maldavians believe they are better off in their new homeland, then who is to deny the acceptability of this exchange. The difficulty in the intergenerational context is that the individuals who will be impacted are unavailable for comment. In order to protect these individuals from unjustified harm, rights could be used, so that what appeared to be a problem for the use of rights can be viewed as an argument in their favour.

The appeal to the "safe minimum standard" can be viewed as an example of constraining economic trade-offs by introducing rights. This standard advocates the protection of species, habitats and ecosystems unless the costs of doing so are "unacceptably large". In the case of global warming Batie and Shugart (1989) argue that the safe minimum standard would support emission reductions despite apparently high costs. However, the withdrawal of the right of, say, a species to exist at some cost implies a basis of the right within utilitarian morality. This view contrasts with rights in the context of a deontological philosophy.[7]

If rights which protect future individuals from the results of our greenhouse gas emissions are accepted to exist, the scope for trade-offs commonly assumed in economics will be drastically reduced. Compensation payments are no longer licences for society to pollute, provided the damages created are less than the amount of compensation. In which case compensation cannot be used to excuse the continuation of GHG emissions. Irreversible damages which will occur regardless of GHG emissions reductions would require compensation. In order to protect the future from potential infringements upon this right, actions with uncertain intertemporal consequences would have to be avoided, and environmentally benign production and consumption processes encouraged.

Stopping the build-up of GHG emissions in the stratosphere is complicated by the delay in transportation. That is, concentrations would continue to increase for over one hundred years. For example, in the case of chlorofluorocarbons, total emissions in the world would have to be reduced by approximately 85% immediately in order to stabilize the concentration of CFC-12 (Hoffman, 1986). Due to the cost of enforcing the rights of future generations to remain unharmed, the current generation has a vested interest in denying those rights. Continuing to emit GHGs at current rates denies the future the right to remain undamaged and asserts the dominance of the current generation. The current generation is in effect being asked to change the present rights structure, as found within society, in a manner detrimental to its own interest. The dictatorship of the current generation allows the imposition of damages regardless of the gain now and the extent of future damages. Yet, the abolition of slavery is an example of just such a change within society.

By appealing to CBA, economists are attempting to take losses and gains of controlling harmful activities directly into account. In doing so the rights of future generations are violated when the costs of controlling the greenhouse effect are deemed to exceed the benefits of that control. The use of cost-benefit analysis therefore denies the existence of inalienable rights. Reliance upon the potential compensation principle prevents actual compensation and allows the welfare of a subgroup of individuals to be reduced. Even the Pareto criterion allows harm to be inflicted, but at least this harm must then be compensated for by resource reallocation. That is, harm and good are seen as equivalent. However, harm is recognizably different from good and the deliberate infliction of harm is morally objectionable. If rights preventing harm to future individuals are accepted, actual compensation is required if these rights are violated. If at all possible, these rights should not be violated and people should be freed from actions which deliberately externalize the risk of damages by imposing it upon others. This can be viewed as a stricter definition of the Pareto criterion because it prevents harm, rather than allowing harm which is then actually compensated. These issues begin to reflect upon the role of CBA and some of the problems apparent with WTA measures (see Chapter 12) where a structure of rights enforces a compensation principle.

13.5 CONCLUSIONS

Global warming is one of the most serious environmental threats humanity currently faces. CBA runs into problems due to uncertainty in the estimation of benefits, attitudes towards future generations and, more fundamentally, the very size of the problem (there is a point at which marginal welfare analysis loses its theoretical basis). These problems prevent a clear answer as to what should be done and economics cannot, of course, provide a complete answer. The costs of reducing CO_2 emissions may be quite high, but because the benefits of reducing emissions are beyond economists' ability to estimate, the extent to which control options should be adopted, on efficiency grounds alone, is unknown. Thus, a practical way forward is to adopt "no regret" or "double dividend" policies. These are actions which can be justified on their own account, but which also reduce global warming. Such policies include solving third world food insecurity, increasing energy efficiency, cutting CFC emissions, preventing deforestation, and encouraging reforestation. If planting a broadleaved forest on farmland in the English Midlands is justified on CBA grounds, regardless of its impact on global warming, then GHG reductions are an added bonus. Similarly, if it is known that energy prices are below their marginal social cost (excluding global warming impacts), then raising energy prices will make utilization more efficient and reduce GHG emissions.

In addition to no regret policies, reducing GHG emissions is desirable even if the costs of doing so are known to be large. This will be so if society is risk averse. The cost of reducing GHG emissions by 75% might be known to be $1 trillion. The costs of not reducing GHG emissions might range from $0.25 trillion to $10 trillion, with an expected value of $0.8 trillion. If society is risk averse, it will prefer to incur the certain loss of $1 trillion (the "certainty equivalent") to the expected loss of $0.8 trillion. In a fragmented world, risk aversion leads to risk externality; that is, the risk is placed upon "other" societies.

Externalizing the harm created by our actions can be viewed as having led us to the dramatic risks of damages faced by the world under global warming. Whether this issue materializes in the devastating form some predict or not, the moral implications go to the heart of modern industrial society. Economic analysts are in the uncomfortable position of justifying immoral actions if society or individuals can potentially (but not actually) transfer resources to those harmed. Unfortunately, current models tend to perpetuate the myth that the consequences of such actions will be felt by those on the other side of the world and living in the distant future so that even the potential need for such considerations can be discounted. The rising popularity of global warming as a matter for economists to consider will either force these matters into open debate or show how blinkered our minds can remain to the potential consequences of our actions.

REFERENCES

Abrahamson P H (editor) (1989) *The Challenge of Global Warming* Washington, D.C.: Island Press.

Adams J A S, Mantovani M S M and Lundell L L (1977) "Wood versus fossil fuel as a source of excess carbon dioxide in the atmosphere: a preliminary report" *Science* 196 (4291): 54-56.

Adams R M (1989) "Global climate change and agriculture: An economic perspective" *American Journal of Agricultural Economics* 71 (5): 1272-1279.

Ayres R U and Walter J (1991) "The greenhouse effect: Damages, costs and abatement" *Environmental and Resource Economics* 1 (3): 237-270.

Barry B (1983) "Intergenerational justice in energy policy" in D Maclean and P G Brown (editors) *Energy and the Future* Totowa, NJ: Rowan and Allanheld.

Batie S S and Shugart H H (1989) "The biological consequences of climate changes: An ecological and economic assessment" in N J Rosenberg, W E Easterling, P R Crosson and J Darmstadter (editors) *Greenhouse Warming: Abatement and Adaptation* Washington, DC: Resources for the Future.

Bergman L (1991) "General equilibrium effects of environmental policy: a CGE-modelling approach" *Environmental and Resource Economics* 1 (1): 43-62.

Bloc K, Hendriks C and Turkenberg W (1989) "The role of carbon dioxide removal in the reduction of the greenhouse effect" in IEA *Energy Technologies for Reducing Emissions of Greenhouse Gases* Paris, International Energy Authority.

Broadus J M, Milliman J D, Edwards S F, Aubrey D G and Gable F (1986) "Rising sea level and damming of rivers: Possible effects in Egypt and Bangladesh" in J G Titus (editor) Effects of Changes in Stratospheric Ozone and Global Climate, IV. US Environmental Protection Agency.

Bromley D W (1991) "Entitlements, missing markets, and environmental uncertainty: Reply" *Journal of Environmental Economics and Management* 20 (3): 297-302.

Calendar G S (1938) "The artificial production of carbon dioxide" *Quarterly Journal of the Royal Meterological Society* 64: 223-240.

Ciborowski P (1989) "Sources, sinks, trends and opportunities" in D E Abrahamson (editor) *The Challenge of Global Warming* Washington, DC: Island Press.

Cline W R (1991) "Scientific basis for the greenhouse effect" *Economic Journal* 101 July: 904-919.

Cline W R (1992) *The Economics of Global Warming*. Harlow, Essex: Longman.

Conrad K and Schroder M (1991) "The control of CO_2 emissions and its economic impact: An AGE model for a German state" *Environmental and Resource Economics* 1 (3): 289-312.

Crosson P R (1989) "Climate change: Problems of limits and policy responses" in N J Rosenberg, W E Easterling, P R Crosson and J Darmstadter (editors) *Greenhouse Warming: Abatement and Adaptation* Washington, DC: Resources for the Future.

Cumberland J H (1982) "Overview" in J H Cumberland, J R Hibbs and I Hoch (editors) *The Economics of Managing Chlorofluorocarbons: Stratospheric Ozone and Climate Issues* Baltimore, MD: Johns Hopkins Press.

Daily G C, Ehrlich P R, Mooney H A and Ehrlich A H (1991) "Greenhouse economics: Learn before you leap" *Ecological Economics* 4: 1-10.

d'Arge R C (editor) (1975) Economic and Social Measures of Biological and Climatic Change, Vol. 6, Climate Impact Assessment Program, US Department of Transport.

d'Arge R C and Spash C L (1991) "Economic strategies for mitigating the impacts of climate change on future generations" in R Costanza (editor) *Ecological Economics: The Science and Management of Sustainability* New York: Columbia University Press.

Detwiler R P and Hall C A S (1988) "Tropical forests and the global carbon cycle" *Science* 239 (January): 42-47.

Dixon P, Johnson D, Marks R, McLennan P, Schodde R and Swan P (1989) "The feasibility and implications for Australia of the adoption of the Toronto proposal" Report to CRA, Sydney, Australia.

DOE (Department of the Environment) (1992) Press release 25th November, 1992 London.

Dornbusch R and Poterba J (1991) *Economic Policy Responses to Global Warming* Cambridge, Ma: MIT Press.

Dowd, R M (1985) "The greenhouse effect" *Environmental Science and Technology* 20 (8): 767.

Fisher A C (1981) *Resource and Environmental Economics* Cambridge: CUP.

Fitzroy F (1992) "Economic aspects of global warming: a comment" *Green Values: Scottish Environmental Economics Discussion Group Newsletter* 5.

Flavin C and Lenssen N (1990) *Beyond the Petroleum Age: Designing a Solar Economy* Washington DC: Worldwatch Institute.

Forziati A (1982) "The chlorofluorocarbon problem" in J H Cumberland, J R Hibbs and I Hoch (editors) *The Economics of Managing Chlorofluorocarbons: Stratospheric Ozone and Climate Issues* Baltimore, MD: Johns Hopkins Press.

Frior J W (1989) "The straight story about the greenhouse effect" Presented at the Western Economic Association International Meeting, June 18-22, Lake Tahoe, California.

Gates D M (1983) "An overview" in E R Lemon (editor) *CO_2 and Plants: The Response of Plants to Rising Levels of Atmospheric Carbon Dioxide* Boulder, CO: Westview Press.

Goemans T (1986) "The sea also rises: The ongoing dialogue of the Dutch with the sea" in J G Titus (editor) Effects of Changes in Stratospheric Ozone and Global Climate, IV. US

Environmental Protection Agency.

Hansen J, Lacis A, Rind D, Russell G, Furg I, Ashcroft P, Lebedeff S, Ruedy R and Stone P (1986) "The greenhouse effect: Projections of global climate change" in J G Titus (editor) Effects of Changes in Stratospheric Ozone and Global Climate, IV. US Environmental Protection Agency.

Heal G (1986) "The intertemporal problem" in D W Bromley (editor) *Natural Resources, Economics Policy Problems and Contemporary Analysis* Boston: Kluwer Nijhoff Publishing.

Henderson-Sellers B (1984) *Pollution of Our Atmosphere* Adam Hilger, Bristol.

Hoeller P, Dean A and Nicolaisen J (1991) "Macroeconomic implications of reducing greenhouse gas emissions: a survey of empirical studies" *OECD Economic Studies* 16: 45-78.

Hoffman J S (1986) "The importance of knowing sooner" in J G Titus (editor) Effects of Changes in Stratospheric Ozone and Global Climate, I, US Environmental Protection Agency.

Idso S B (1982) *Carbon Dioxide: Friend or Foe?* Tempe, Arizona: IBR Press.

Idso S B (1983) "Carbon dioxide and global temperature: What the data show" *Journal of Environmental Quality* 12 (2): 159-163.

Ingham A and Ulph A (1991) "Carbon taxes and the UK manufacturing sector" in F Dietz, F van der Ploeg and J van der Straaten (editors) *Environmental Policy and the Economy* Amsterdam: Elsevier.

International Energy Authority (1989) *Energy and the Environment* Paris: IEA.

Intergovernmantal Panel on Climate Change (IPCC) (1992) *Climate Change 1992: The supplementary report to the IPCC scientific assessment* Cambridge: Cambridge University Press.

Jaeger J (1989) "Developing policies for responding to climate change" in D E Abrahamson (editor) *The Challenge of Global Warming* Washington, DC: Island Press.

Jamieson D (1988) Managing the Future: Public Policy, Scientific Uncertainty, and Global Warming. Working Paper, Center for Values and Social Policy, Department of Philosophy, University of Boulder, CO.

Kerr R A (1977) "Carbon dioxide and climate: carbon budget still unbalanced" *Science* 197 (4311): September.

Khalil M A K and Rasmussen R A (1987) "Atmospheric methane trends over the last 10,000 years" *Atmospheric Environment* 21 (11): 2445-2452.

MacDonald G J (1988) "Scientific basis for the greenhouse effect" *Journal of Policy Analysis and Management* 7 (3): 425-444.

Manne A and Richels R (1991) "Global CO_2 emission reductions: The impacts of rising energy costs" *The Energy Journal* 12 (1): 87-102.

Marland G and Rotty R M (1985) "Greenhouse gases in the atmosphere: What do we know?" *Journal of Air Pollution Control Association* 35 (10): 1033-1038.

Mlot C (1989) "Great lakes fish and the greenhouse effect" *BioScience* 39 (3): 145.

National Research Council (1984) *Causes and Effects of Changes in Stratospheric Ozone: Update 1983* Washington, DC: National Academy Press.

Nordhaus W (1982) "How fast should we graze the global commons?" *American Economic Review Association Papers and Proceedings* 72 (2): 242-246.

Nordhaus W (1991a) "To slow or not to slow: The economics of the greenhouse effect" *Economic Journal* 101: 920-938.

Nordhaus W (1991b) "A sketch of the economics of the greenhouse effect" *American Economic Review* 81 (2): 146-150.

Office of Technology Assessment (1989) "An analysis of the Montreal protocol on substances that deplete the Ozone Layer" in D E Abrahamson (editor) *The Challenge of*

Global Warming Washington, DC: Island Press.

Parry M (1990) *Climate Change and World Agriculture* London: Earthscan.

Pojman L P (1989) *Ethical Theory: Classical and Contemporary Readings* Belmont, Ca: Wadsworth.

Revelle R and Suess H E (1957) "Carbon dioxide exchange between atmosphere and ocean, and the question of an increase in atmospheric CO_2 during the past decades" *Tellus* 9 (18): 18-27.

Roberts L (1989) "How fast can trees migrate?" *Science* 243: 735-737.

Rotty R M and Reister D B (1986) "Use of energy scenarios in addressing the CO_2 question" *Journal of Air Pollution Control Association* 36 (10): 1111-1115.

Routley R and Routley V (1980) "Nuclear energy and obligations to the future" in E Partridge (editor) *Responsibilities to Future Generations* New York: Prometheus Books.

Schelling T (1992) "Some economics of global warming" *American Economic Review* 82 (1): 1-14.

Schneider S (1989) "The changing climate" *Scientific American* 216 (3): 38-47.

Schneider S and Rosenberg N (1990) "The greenhouse effect: Its causes, possible impacts and associated uncertainties" in N J Rosenberg, W E Easterling, P R Crosson and J Darmstadter (editors) *Greenhouse Warming: Abatement and Adaptation* Washington, DC: Resources for the Future.

Seneft D (1990) "Greenhouse effect may not be all bad" *Agricultural Research* 38: 20-23.

Spash C L (1993) "Economics, ethics and long-term environmental damages" *Environmental Ethics* 15 (2): 117-132.

Spash C L (1990) "Intergenerational transfers and long term environmental damages: Compensation of future generations for global climate change due to the greenhouse effect" Unpublished manuscript pp.210.

Spash C L and d'Arge R C (1989) "The greenhouse effect and intergenerational transfers" *Energy Policy* 17 (2): 88-96.

Thomas R H (1986) "Future sea level rise and its early detection by satellite remote sensing" in J G Titus (editor) Effects of Changes in Stratospheric Ozone and Global Climate, IV. US Environmental Protection Agency.

Titus J G (1989) "The cause and effects of sea level rise" in D E Abrahamson (editor) *The Challenge of Global Warming* Washington, DC: Island Press.

UNEP (1991) Montreal Protocol 1991 Assessment Report of the Technology and Economic Assessment Panel.

Whalley J and Wiggle R (1991) "The international incidence of carbon taxes" in R Dornbusch and J Poterba (editors) *Economic Policy Responses to Global Warming* Cambridge, Ma: MIT Press.

Whiteman A (1991) "A comparison of the financial and non-market costs and benefits of replanting lowland forests" Paper presented to the Scottish Environmental Economics Discussion Group.

Wuebbles D J and Edmonds J (1988) "A primer on greenhouse gases" US Department of Energy Carbon Dioxide Research Division Washington, DC: GPO.

Wuebbles D J, Grant K E, Connell P S and Penner J E (1989) "The role of atmospheric chemistry in climate change" *Journal of Air Pollution Control Association* 39 (1): 22-28.

ENDNOTES

1.   Double CO_2-equivalent is used to account for the atmospheric changes which are expected on reaching a global equilibrium of twice carbon dioxide, but which can be achieved by any mix of greenhouse gases.

2.   Cline (1992) gives an up-to-date account of economic research into the greenhouse effect.

3.   As Ingham and Ulph (1991) point out, the optimality condition is that in each time period, current value marginal control costs should be equal to the present value of marginal control benefits, where discounting takes place at the social rate of discount plus the rate at which the pollutant decays naturally.

4.   Outside of the recalculation of the Nordhaus study, more general reasons exist for going beyond the suggested 10% emissions reduction. Since the world has never experienced such rapid changes in temperature as predicted (Schneider, 1989), the uncertainty over estimates of damage costs must include the possibility of sharp discontinuities; that is, threshold effects.

5.   Ingham and Ulph's work details how industry would respond to carbon taxes, in terms of deciding whether prematurely to scrap plant which becomes inefficient to operate under a carbon tax.

6.   There are many issues (such as international policy coordination) that we have not addressed; the reader is referred to Dornbusch and Poterba (1991) for a more complete picture of greenhouse economics.

7.   A deontological philosophy sees certain features in a moral act as themselves having intrinsic value. This viewpoint contrasts with teleological systems which consider the ultimate criterion of morality in some non-moral value that results from actions. For example, lying is wrong regardless of the consequences; see Pojman (1989). Neo-classical economists operate with a teleological outlook but a considerable number of individuals may exist who hold to deontological philosophies. For example, the refusal to play and extreme bidding found in contingent valuation studies may be symptomatic of this.

14 ENVIRONMENTAL LIMITS TO CBA?

14.1 INTRODUCTION

In this last chapter, we briefly consider the case for and against the use of CBA in environmental management. The theoretical and methodological issues covered in Part I, and the empirical issues discussed in Part I, both raised many questions and require some response. In this chapter the issues raised throughout the book that seem most important are summarized and a few tentative conclusions offered. However, the final verdict must rest with the reader.

14.2 THE CASE AGAINST

What is wrong with applying CBA to environmental issues? According to critics of the method, CBA is fatally flawed (Sagoff, 1988; Kelman, 1986). In section 14.2.1 some criticisms of CBA in general are considered, whilst those particularly relevant to environmental applications are reviewed in section 14.2.2.

14.2.1 General Criticisms of CBA

Voting and the Market Place
Many criticisms of CBA have been levelled at its implications for equity. As has been stated, in neo-classical welfare economics, economic value is determined by effective demand; that is, by a willingness to pay, backed up by an ability to pay. Thus, in contingent valuation, the response that "I would pay to secure this benefit, but I cannot afford it" should not be treated as a protest bid, but as a genuine zero. Effective demand as a measure of preferences has its attractions, but one weakness is the way in which the vote in the market place is unequal.

An equal opportunity to influence resource allocation could be argued to require an equitable income distribution, since those with more resources available to them (the rich) have more votes to cast than those with fewer resources (the poor). What is certainly true and recognized by economic theory is that the outcome of any CBA is dependent on the distribution of income; changing the distribution will change effective demands. If the outcome of CBA is treated as an acceptable guide to policy, then the existing income distribution is assumed to be an acceptable basis for decision-making.

Some economists argue that, when making decisions on projects, the strength of WTP measures over political voting is that the former indicates both a ranking of alternatives and the intensity of preferences, whilst the latter can only rank preferences. That is, the political voting system is an ordinal measure while the application of CBA uses market voting which (these economists believe) is a cardinal measure. Cardinality means that an individual can decide by how much two golden eagles are preferred to two robins, for example. If WTP for the eagles was $1000 and for the robins $100 then the eagles are ten times as valuable as the robins. If WTP were an ordinal measure, all that could be said is that eagles are preferred to robins. Whilst the theoretical basis for CBA is in modern welfare economics, which assumes only ordinally measurable preferences, in fact money is commonly used as if it were a cardinal measure. Modern welfare economics has rejected the possibility of ever cardinally measuring utility and can get by without needing to do so. However, CBA assumes cardinality by adding up the money measures of utility to show how far a project is preferred at the end of the day over its alternatives, rather than merely ranking alternatives.

Even if the measurability of utility were accepted, and money were accepted to be a reasonable approximation of that measure, CBA would be unable to make objective choices. Assume that two individuals are asked to value eagles and robins; each prefers a different bird, but society can only supply one or the other. If the eagle fancier is WTP $1000 for eagles and the robin fancier is WTP only $500 for robins, we cannot conclude that robins are socially undesirable. There is no way to decide how different individuals' valuations should be weighted, even if WTP is accepted as a measure of utility. This is the debate of economic theorists concerning the comparability of utility between individuals, which cannot be decided objectively (see Just et al. (1982) for a discussion of interpersonal comparisons in terms of utils).

A democratic voting system could be seen as a preferable alternative and still able to reflect intensities via the lobbying of decision-makers (Sagoff, 1988). Yet, the political system suffers some of the same problems as market voting. For example, the fact that effective demand depends upon income distribution is the same as accepting that the system of voting determines how democracy is operated, i.e., there are many possible systems and the one chosen will affect the weight of any individual's vote in the final decision-making process. For example, proportional representation is the political hope of parties which feel disenfranchised by the current system in the UK because they can get, say, 14% of the vote and yet no seats in Parliament (e.g., the Green Party).

Gains and Losses

A related complaint against CBA is that it treats gains and losses equally, and is unconcerned about who actually gains and who actually loses. A project which yields discounted net benefits of $1000 to the rich is treated as identical to another project which yields $1000 to the poor. Yet society may well have a preference for the latter project over the former, on the grounds that it has a desirable distributional impact. This issue is discussed in detail by Gramlich (1990), who also notes that society may want to proceed with projects with negative NPVs if their distributional aspects are desirable and if they represent a more efficient way of redistributing income than the next best alternative (such as the tax system). A partial counter to this criticism has been to propose weighting schemes for CBA, which take distributional effects into account in the way suggested by the Bergson social welfare function (see Chapter 2); more commonly, however, efficiency and equity are treated as completely separate issues. However, this requires politicians or decision-makers generally actually to reveal their preferences for different social policies; i.e., they must explicitly decide upon the weights they give to unemployment versus environmental degradation, for example.

Critiques of CBA have also centred around the Kaldor-Hicks criterion. As will be recalled, this states that a resource reallocation is desirable if the gainers *could* compensate the losers and still be better off. No actual compensation need take place. Over time, it might be assumed that the government uses transfers to counter systematic redistributions following from the implementation of the Kaldor-Hicks criterion. However, if these transfers are avoided, possibly because of transactions costs, then the operation of a CBA rule may well lead to adverse distributional consequences.

In addition, the avoidance of compensation for injury can be regarded as morally objectionable. Creating harm is not equivalent to creating good. Some of the problems this raises were discussed in the intergenerational context in Chapters 8 and 13. The acceptance of moral constraints which would limit the economic system can be viewed as taking on board a rights-based philosophy. These limits to economic trade-offs are currently appearing under the guise of sustainability constraints (for a discussion see Jacobs, 1991).

Prices in the "Real" World
Market failure leads to an incorrect set of prices which inaccurately measure
marginal social costs and benefits. If these measures cannot be observed
accurately, then mistakes will be made in the allocation of resources,
resulting in efficiency losses. Thus, a correct set of shadow prices is
required to substitute for the incorrect market prices. Environmental
resources, as we have repeatedly stated, are most frequently under-priced
(including cases where they have no price due to a failure of the private
property rights system). In theory, society can derive a set of (shadow)
prices so that this criticism of CBA could be corrected. The extent to which
this mode of modelling is an acceptable abstraction from "reality" is perhaps
one dividing line in the rejection of CBA, but such abstraction is common
to all modelling.

Institutional Capture
Institutional capture was discussed in Chapter 9, where we showed that
agencies responsible for carrying out a CBA may have an incentive to mould
the analysis to produce an outcome which maximizes their utility. This may
conflict with the best outcome for society. What is more, interest groups
can lobby decision-making agencies to adopt particular values for prices,
shadow prices, the discount rate, and other aspects of the project under
appraisal. Again, a divergence can result between the outcome of the CBA
and potential Pareto improvements. More evidence on institutional capture
in CBA can be found in Green and Weitzman (1980).

14.2.2 Criticisms of Environmental Applications

Ecosystem Complexity
Ecosystem complexity makes modelling economy-ecosystem interactions
difficult, especially where damage functions are non-linear and/or stochastic;
it also challenges the notion of consumer sovereignty which is central to
much of environmental economics. We have noted the critique of Norgaard
(1989) that the individualistic, atomistic structure of neo-classical welfare
economics is at odds with the structure of ecosystems to which it is applied.
If ecosystems are so complex that individuals are poorly informed or unable
to comprehend either future or present environmental effects of economic
actions, then stated or revealed preferences are a poor guide to policy such
as on global warming. The principal alternatives to relying on consumer
valuations are either (i) to impose some scientifically and/or politically
determined constraints on economic activity (such as a minimum level of
dissolved oxygen in a river), and find the most efficient way of meeting this
constraint (cost-effectiveness analysis); or (ii) to use the closely-related Safe
Minimum Standard approach (Bishop, 1978; Ready and Bishop, 1991).
   The Safe Minimum Standard (SMS) approach involves determining the

minimum desirable level of wildlife populations, or minimum desirable areas of different habitat types. Society is interested in the minimum cost method of preserving these standards. For each standard (say the population of spotted owls in Washington State), the opportunity cost of preservation equals foregone development benefits. One can then ask politicians, bureaucrats or the general public whether these (minimum) preservation costs are too high; if the response is "yes", then development is allowed; if the response is "no", then development is rejected. For a theoretical treatment of the SMS approach, see Ready and Bishop (1991); for empirical applications, see Rollins and Bishop (1992) and Hyde (1989).

The SMS approach might be considered as one way of moving an economy towards a sustainable development path, especially if one's definition of sustainable development involves a requirement that at least part of the "natural capital stock" is non-decreasing. As was shown in Chapter 9, CBA is in general inconsistent with such a definition of sustainable development, since it explicitly allows trade-offs between consumption goods and environmental quality (Spash and Clayton, 1992). Shadow projects have been offered as a potential solution but, as noted, suffer from similar problems to CBA.

Risk, Uncertainty and Ignorance
Risk and uncertainty characterize many decisions concerning environmental management; see Chapters 11 and 13. As was stated in Chapter 1, CBA treats these two problems differently. Risk refers to situations where probabilities can be allocated to alternative future states of the world. Uncertainty refers to situations where the outcomes are known but the probability of their occurrence is unknown. This division of risk and uncertainty can be found in Keynes ([1921] 1973). CBA treats uncertainty principally through sensitivity and/or scenario analysis. Risk is calculated by using expected values which involves multiplying the outcome of a given state of the world by its probability, then summing across all probability-outcome products.

This treatment of risk valuation has been criticized for some environmental risks, especially those related to very low probability but very high cost events. An example is toxic waste disposal. Suppose that there is a plan to set up a toxic waste disposal site. There is a very small, but positive, probability that there will be a large escape of toxic matter from the site. Suppose the probability is 0.0000001 (that is, one in 10 million), but that if such a release were to occur, 50 lives would be lost. The economic value of a statistical life might be about £3 million. The expected fatality cost of the project is thus: $(0.0000001) \times (50 \times £3 \text{ million}) = £15$. This implies that the community would accept £16 to take on this risk. For such high potential cost but very low probability events (e.g., global warming or a nuclear melt-down), expected values may be poor representations of the actual costs people perceive, or the minimum compensation they would demand.

A third level of imperfect knowledge can be designated as ignorance (Faber et al., 1992). Ignorance exists when future states of the world are unknown. For example, the connection between spraying your armpit with perfume and the destruction of the ozone layer was unknown in the 1950s. Some types of ignorance may be irreducible and suggest limits to the natural sciences as well as to economics. The realization of ignorance seems particularly appropriate in the environmental context.

Where uncertainty exists about environmental impacts, there may be a case for weighting environmental costs by a factor greater than that applied to monetary benefits, as a form of risk-averse behaviour. What exactly these weights should be is, however, a currently-unanswered question (Van Pelt, 1993).

Discounting

In Chapter 8, an in-depth investigation of discounting and the discount rate was presented. Discounting is a particularly important issue for environmental management since many effects are very long-lived (such as those due to heavy metal emissions), whilst projects such as alternative energy source research and the growing of oak forests have benefits that occur far into the future. The outcome of a NPV appraisal of changes in the supply of such resources can be acutely sensitive to the choice of discount rate. Discounting of intergenerational impacts raises a number of difficult questions.

Even if discounting is accepted there is a continuing debate about what "the" discount rate should be for public sector project appraisal. Natural capital often has much lower growth rates than man-made capital and will therefore become obsolete as a form of investment if future returns to production are the sole criteria. This in turn raises the issue of whether natural capital is a substitute or complement to man-made capital.

WTP versus WTA

The WTP versus WTA compensation debate seems set to continue, with one group of researchers (Hanemann, 1991; Shogren et al., 1992) arguing that such divergences pose no threat to standard economic theory, and others (Knetsch, 1989; Knetsch and Sinden, 1984) claiming that the divergence means we need to throw out our standard conception of indifference curves. The problem is particularly worrying when linked to the issue of property rights, suggesting how different structures of property rights influence values. The justification for WTP would then depend upon the acceptance of the underlying distribution of property rights, which is an area of extreme contention in the environmental field (e.g., can land-owners do as they like with the natural resources on their property?).

Limits to Valuation Methods

All the valuation methods we have discussed above are limited in their applicability even when all the theoretical assumptions are accepted and actually hold. CVM is perhaps the most widely applicable method but works best where goods are familiar to the respondents as being traded or could realistically be regarded as such, which excludes many aspects of the environment. TCM is restricted to site specific locations and HP requires good data on a related market such as housing. HP is also limited by the availability of regionally differentiated environmental quality data (although this latter can only get better, and is already good for some resources, such as fresh water). The averting expenditure approach depends upon good substitution possibilities, between environmental goods such as water quality and private goods, which are often absent. The dose-response approach requires well-defined cause and effect models and tends to be restricted to environmental damages affecting marketed goods.

Existence Values

As research into the environment has proceeded, economists have slowly realized and incorporated a growing range of values, of which existence values are the furthest removed from standard market values. In CVM existence values are being estimated for many aspects of the environment, especially wildlife species. Boyle and Bishop (1987) report finding very large aggregate bids for extremely obscure species (e.g., the striped shiner!) and question whether a $10 million bid by the population of Wisconsin to preserve an innocuous fish could be substituted for their WTP for another equally obscure species. If this were true, then preservation of obscure species should proceed on strict cost-effectiveness grounds.

Stevens et al. (1991) have also criticized CVM estimates of existence values. Whilst in their study they produce mean preservation bids for several species (wild turkey, atlantic salmon and bald eagle) in New England, which are similar to those produced by other researchers elsewhere, they note that over half of the sample were unwilling to pay anything to preserve these species, despite the fact that over 80% said that these species were important to them. A clue to the reason for this is that 70% of respondents believed the species should be preserved irrespective of its usefulness to humans. That is, species have an inherent right to life which is independent of the consequences of their loss for human animals. This suggests non-human and human animals both have intrinsic value.

In the neo-classical utilitarian framework of economics, with human animals being the only things with intrinsic value, such findings indicate that a subset of the population has lexicographic preferences with respect to wildlife preservation. That is, they would be unwilling to exchange money for changes in species preservation. This poses awkward problems for environmental CBA, and for CVM in particular, since bids are based on just such trade-offs. Stevens et al. show that, according to the reference level of preservation, WTP will either be zero for all possible preservation levels or the same amount for all levels of population. Following a similar tack, Edwards (1992) has argued that if individuals' existence values for wildlife resources are motivated by what Kennet (1980, p.121) has called "genuine altruism" (there must be no quid pro quo), then:

> ... the theoretical basis for including maximum WTP or minimum WTAC for wildlife preservation or for resource conservation in a benefit-cost analysis is questionable.

The Context of Values

Environmental issues, along with social and educational issues, concern areas where collective or communal values are especially prominent. Thus, Sagoff (1988) has argued that the way in which individuals view decisions over environmental management differs according to the role they play: whether they act as consumers (buying petrol) or citizens (concerned over energy use). Sagoff argues that these citizen values are the most relevant to society in its decisions over environmental management. CBA reflects consumer values which people register in the market place rather than these citizen values. This leads to a preference for the political process as a means for decision-making over the environment, with lobbying reflecting both the direction and intensity of citizen preferences. This "schizophrenic split" has been noted by other writers, such as Marglin (1963).

The acceptance of the division of values into the market place and political arena still leaves unanswered the question of how these values interact. If the values are to be split in the decision-making process, there will still be an area in which CBA operates. The problem in the context of the environment is not how to exclude the environment from the market, which is impossible, but to decide upon the extent to which decisions about the environment are to be left to the market system. The values which CBA tries to assess are a limited subset of all value in society and will never be able to reflect such things as spiritual values or the intrinsic values of non-human animals. Thus, when CBA is applied to the existence of a species, the line may have been over-stepped, but how far should be the withdrawal?

14.3 THE CASE IN FAVOUR

Considering the general problems with CBA (section 14.2.1) and those particular to its application to environmental issues (section 14.2.2), some people might be prepared to throw the baby out with the bath water. In our view, CBA can be defended along two broad fronts: (i) there are positive roles that CBA can play despite the problems outlined above, and (ii) a consideration of the alternatives shows the need for CBA.

14.3.1 Positive Roles for CBA

First, CBA is a way of systematically organizing arguments about whether a project or policy should go ahead or be stopped. This is because the CBA framework distinguishes very clearly between the different aspects of a project, such as the cost stream, benefit stream and life expectancy. Thus, arguments over projects can move away from the rather black-and-white approach which a political referendum would offer (should a project go ahead or not?). This allows attention to be directed at specific aspects of a project, such as the method and cost of waste disposal for a nuclear power station, or the precise route of a new road. In this sense, CBA sets the agenda for discussion and helps reduce the likelihood of people arguing at cross-purposes.

Second, given that projects and policies consume resources, and given that these resources are scarce, society has to have some way of deciding on how to prioritize resource use. CBA does this in a very explicit way. The Kaldor-Hicks criterion selects projects in order of their efficiency (see Chapter 2). Those projects which on Kaldor-Hicks grounds reduce net benefits (losses outweigh gains) are rejected; those which produce positive net benefits, on the other hand, are ranked in order of their net present value. According to welfare economics this is equivalent to ranking them in order of their potential contribution to social welfare (so long as equal weights are assigned to all gainers and losers).

Third, the current "state of the art" of CBA means that it is possible to include environmental values in the same analysis as the development benefits that have traditionally been so measured. It might be argued that this is desirable, both on efficiency grounds and because it gives environmental effects the same weight in the decision-making process concerning possible developments (e.g., whether to drill for oil in Antarctica) as the monetary impacts of the development (such as oil revenues and exploration costs). This *could* lead to a situation where less environmental damage is inflicted than when environmental effects are excluded from the CBA.

Yet, there is no guarantee that including environmental effects in a CBA will reduce environmental damage, since such effects might have been controlled in alternative ways. For example, if the net (marketed) benefits of oil exploration in Antarctica (excluding environmental costs) are $100 million in PV terms, the environmental effects, in terms of welfare losses, might well be less than this sum. If the only way in which a decision is made is through CBA, exploration will go ahead. But if environmental effects had been excluded from the CBA, and never been estimated, then a government might take the decision that they were greater than this sum or that environmental damages should be precluded at all cost, thus imposing an environmental constraint on the CBA. However, environmental effects have often been ignored in the past and given less importance than development benefits simply because they could not be measured in the same way as new houses, barrels of oil or tonnes of timber. The early assessments of dam and forest projects are classic examples of this, and current road assessment in the UK appears equally at fault.

The inclusion of non-market environmental effects into CBA aims to achieve an improvement in the efficiency of resource allocation, which means greater welfare from less environmental degradation. If the valuation of environmental effects is thought either to under-value the environment or to violate a sustainability constraint, then environmental constraints can be explicitly placed upon the CBA process; the SMS is an example of one type of constraint. As CBA is only one input to the decision-making process and efficiency is but one goal, other constraints are likely. The distributional implications of CBA outlined in section 14.2.1 are worrying to many and could therefore require the use of distributional policy. The standard approach in CBA regards consideration of such factors as an unnecessary distraction from the main concern of assessing a project on efficiency grounds. A comfort for critics is that, in any case, CBA is very unlikely to be the sole method by which governments make decisions over resource allocation.

14.3.2 What are the Alternatives?

Critics such as Sagoff (1988) have argued that CBA should be replaced as a tool for decision making by the normal democratic process. By this, he means that citizens elect public officials to carry out their wishes concerning day-to-day decisions over resource allocations.   Interest groups are collections of like-minded citizens who get together to lobby in favour of particular alternatives.   Where large resource allocations are being considered or where a particularly controversial project is being planned, a more explicit public consultation process takes place, such as public inquiries or court actions.

However, there are flaws with this process as a way of making decisions. How do the elected bureaucrats make their day-to-day decisions? If not through CBA, then either through some other process, which may be a set-down methodology such as Environmental Impact Assessment (EIA) or through rules of thumb. Not only is there potential for self-serving action here (so that bureaucrats act selfishly rather than in the public interest), but there is a danger that individuals will lose all control over the process, except in their capability to organize as a lobby group, and in the occasional, and very indirect, way of an election every four or five years. Therefore CBA might, to a degree, be considered to preserve the democratic alternative.

Set-down methodologies include cost-effectiveness analysis (CEA), EIA and multi-criteria analysis (MCA). CEA involves the acceptance of some target, such as a minimum air quality standard or a minimum number of jobs to be created. This objective itself is not appraised, except indirectly. The cost of meeting the objective is then sought. Where alternative means of meeting it exist, the least-cost solution is of particular interest. Examples are costing alternative designs for a bridge (taking it for granted that a bridge is required), or alternative locations for an airport. If all resource inputs are shadow priced at their marginal social costs, then CEA essentially mimics half of a CBA. If market prices are used then this assumption is violated, but such analyses are often employed to discover, for example, the cost to some public agency (inclusive of transfer payments) of meeting an objective, such as job creation. The indirect light which is shed on the objective comes in terms of a cost comparison. If it is found that the minimum resource cost of the bridge is £10 million, then the question can be posed "is it worth it at that price?". The principal weakness of CEA is that only an indirect evaluation of project benefits is made. In addition, the "cost" of the project can easily include environmental costs which reintroduces all the requirements of CBA. The technique is widely used and defined in such terms as to exclude environmental impacts from "costs".

EIA is closely related to CEA in that it too considers just the cost side of a project. However, in this case only the environmental costs are relevant. A variety of methods are available to EIA analysts for measuring these impacts (see Walthern, 1988), but most share the characteristic, physical effects being identified, categorized and listed, and then scored in some way. This permits the comparison of relative environmental impacts across projects in a manner that is cross-comparable. Thus, given the decision to locate an additional airport in Scotland, EIA could identify the site with the lowest environmental impact.

The chief problem with EIA, though, is its incompatibility with other measures of a project's impact. If these are all in money terms (value of airport revenues, cost of land, cost of construction, operation costs), then environmental impacts cannot be compared as like with like. Thus, the environment is treated as separate, which may or may not improve the chances of minimizing environmental damages. The number of alternative scoring systems might also be viewed as a problem, together with the lack of a rigorous theoretical underpinning for the scoring system. Of course, those criticisms could be aimed at CBA too.

MCA involves adopting a number of criteria for project selection, which might include efficiency, equity and meeting a sustainability constraint. An advantage of MCA is that qualitative data (such as knowing whether a project's impact will be environmentally "good" or "bad") can be utilised. This may be especially important in developing countries, and in other situations where little information on environmental impacts is available. CBA can be used to address the efficiency criterion within MCA. Van Pelt (1993), which is a powerful plea for the use of MCA in project appraisal, notes that the approach has recently been recommended by both the World Bank and the United Nations. For further details on MCA, and an example of its use, see Van Pelt.

One version of MCA is known as goal programming. Goal programming assumes that public agencies have a number of objectives, some of which may be in conflict with one other. For example, a regional authority may wish to minimize environmental disruption, cut local unemployment and increase regional incomes. Goal programming involves setting targets for each objective, then minimizing the sum of deviations of realized levels for each variable for which there is a target from this target level. Weights may be placed on each variable to reflect the relative importance placed on each by the agency. This minimization occurs subject to a set of constraints, which principally reflect resource demands and therefore conflicts between simultaneous maximization/minimization of all objectives. However, data requirements are large, whilst the setting of targets may be problematic. For an application to fisheries policy and an introduction to the goal programming literature, see Sandeford (1986).

Many other methods exist for taking decisions: an entire academic discipline is directed towards their description and analysis (decision analysis). The confines of this book prevent a complete account. However, the few alternatives considered serve to make our point: that none of the alternatives to CBA is problem-free, whilst many are less comprehensive. In principle, CBA is able to say a great deal about the effects of a resource reallocation. It provides a guideline to efficiency in resource use and, by identifying gainers and losers, makes a statement about distributional effects. Also, the time pattern of gains and losses is explicitly considered. If one is unhappy about parts of the CBA process, such as the valuation of the environment or discounting, then as Swartzman et al. (1982) have suggested, these elements of the method can be ignored: environmental benefits and costs can be listed, and benefit and cost flows presented undiscounted. What will then emerge is not a full-blown CBA result, but may be a useful way of presenting information about the effects of a project.

14.4 CONCLUSIONS

Our principal view on CBA is that it is a very useful method of presenting information in a systematic way about the effects of a project which changes the environment. As we have said above and on occasion repeated, CBA is very unlikely to be employed as the sole means of reaching a decision, and we recommend this be so. However, CBA is too useful a decision tool to be totally discarded. Many improvements can, and will, no doubt be made to the various component parts of CBA, though many problems will remain. So long as the analyst, the interpreter, the end-user and the general population (!) bear these problems and limitations in mind, and so long as CBA is subject to public inspection and peer group review (to minimize the risk of institutional capture), then in our view CBA provides a useful input to managing our environment.

REFERENCES

Bishop R C (1978) "Endangered species and uncertainty: the economics of a safe minimum standard" *American Journal of Agricultural Economics* February.

Boyle K and Bishop R (1987) "Valuing wildlife in benefit-cost analysis: a case study involving endangered species" *Water Resources Research* 23: 943-50.

Edwards S (1992) "Rethinking existence values" *Land Economics* 68 (1): 120-122.

Faber M, Manstetten R and Proops J L R (1992) "Humankind and the Environment: An Anatomy of Surprise and Ignorance" *Environmental Values* 1 (3): 217-242.

Gramlich E M (1990) *A Guide to Benefit-Cost Analysis* London: Prentice-Hall.

Green M and Weitzman N (1980) "Cost, benefit and class" *Working Papers for a New Society* 7 (3): 39-51.

Hanemann W M (1991) "Willingness to pay and willingness to accept: how much can they differ?" *American Economic Review* June: 635-647.

Hyde W (1989) "Marginal costs of managing endangered species: the case of the red cockaded woodpecker" *Journal of Agricultural Economics Research* 41 (2): 12-19.

International Institute for Applied Systems Analysis (1990) *Options* September Laxenburg, Austria: IIASA.

Jacobs M (1991) *The Green Economy* London: Pluto Press.

Just R E, Hueth D L and Schmitz A (1982) *Applied Welfare Economics and Public Policy* London: Prentice-Hall International.

Kelman S (1986) "Cost-benefit analysis an ethical critique" in D Van De Veer and C Pierce (editors) *People, Penguins, and Plastic Trees: Basic Issues in Environmental Ethics* Belmont, Ca: Wadsworth.

Kennet D (1980) "Altruism and economic behaviour: developments in the theory of public and private redistribution" *American Journal of Economics and Sociology* 39: 183-198.

Keynes J M [1921] (1973) *A Treatise on Probability* London: Macmillan.

Knetsch J (1989) "The endowment effect and evidence of non-reversible indifference curves" *American Economic Review* 79 (5): 1277-1284.

Knetsch J and Sinden J (1984) "Willingness to pay and compensation demanded: experimental evidence of an unexpected disparity in measures of value" *Quarterly Journal of Economics* 99: 507-521.

Marglin S (1963) "The social rate of discount and the optimal level of investment" *Quarterly Journal of Economics* 77: 95-111.

Norgaard R (1989) "The Case for Methodological Pluralism" *Ecological Economics* 1: 37-58.

Ready R and Bishop R (1991) "Endangered species and the safe minimum standard" *American Journal of Agricultural Economics* May: 309-312.

Rollins K and Bishop R (1992) "Net social costs of preserving biological diversity" in Forestry and the Environment: Economic perspectives. Forestry Canada, Edmonton, Alberta.

Sagoff M (1988) *The Economy of the Earth* Cambridge: Cambridge University Press.

Sandeford F (1986) "An analysis of multi-objective decision-making for the Scottish inshore fishery" *Journal of Agricultural Economics* 37: 207-220.

Shogren J, Shinn S, Hayes D and Kliebenstein J (1992) "Experimental evidence on the divergence between measures of value" mimeo Economics Department, Iowa State University.

Spash C L and Clayton A (1992) "Strategies for the maintenance of natural capital" Conference paper to Second Meeting of International Society for Ecological Economics, Stockholm, Sweden, August.

Stevens T H, Echeverria J, Glass R, Hager T and More T (1991) "Measuring the existence value of wildlife: what do CVM estimates really show?" *Land Economics* 67 (4): 1991.

Swartzman D, Liroff R and Croke K (1982) *Cost Benefit Analysis and Environmental Regulations* Washington DC: Conservation Foundation.

Walthern P (editor) (1988) *Environmental Impact Assessment* London: Unwin and Hyman.

Index